A Garden by the Sea

A BOOK LABORATORY® BOOK

First published in the United States of America in 2005 by
Rizzoli International Publications, Inc.
300 Park Avenue South
New York, NY 10010
www.rizzoliusa.com

© 2005 Leila Hadley

Designed and produced by
The Book Laboratory® Inc
Bolinas, California

Project editors:
Manuela Dunn and Kimberley Roosenburg

Design and Art Direction:
Victoria Pohlmann
New York

2005 2006 2007 2008 2009 / 10 9 8 7 6 5 4 3 2 1

Printed in China

ISBN: 0-8478-2651-1

Library of Congress Catalog Control Number: 2004093655

A Garden by the Sea

A Practical Guide and Journal

by Leila Hadley

RIZZOLI
NEW YORK

Contents

I care about . . . the mix of greenery and
color, the scents of flowers, line, texture,
proportions, the contrast and balance of the
landscape and seascape.

Introduction

All my life I've known gardens, grown gardens. I was given my first garden when I was six years old. I watched the gardener as he carefully double-dug a rectangular plot in the apple orchard at our place in Westbury, Long Island. Over the fresh-smelling earth my English governess fitted a black sheet of weed-preventing, cardboardlike material incised with designs into which I sifted seeds from labeled packets.

For weeks, forever it seemed, I waited for the seeds to sprout. When the seedlings blossomed into a riotous motley of cleome, ageratums, nasturtiums, marigolds, zinnias, snapdragons, coreopsis, and cosmos, the gardener, governess and I agreed it was all a terrible mistake.

My mother was dismayed. "It looks like the smell of a dead mole," she said. Our garden would have been infinitely nicer, she informed us, had we planted a carpet of clove-scented cottage pinks, or cleome and white cosmos, or columbines in different colors, or a mix of white phlox, a few blue or purple spires of delphiniums, and some pink poppies. "Not red poppies, of course. They only look right with white daisies and those deep blue bachelors' buttons in the vegetable garden." I could see what she meant. I understood what she meant. Restraint. The wisdom of choosing flowers in harmonious, complementary, or contrasting colors, shapes, and forms, with some pleasing

scent. I thought of pinks, roses, lilies of the valley, lavender, and mint. I imagined having a garden of my own someday where I could have each of these as a star attraction in a special planting of its own.

I had a garden in South Africa, where the times of the year are topsy-turvy: May is midautumn and July is winter. I had a garden in Aiken, South Carolina, with a magnolia tree and a wall blanketed in fragrant scarlet rambler roses. I had a garden in Jamaica, in the West Indies, where I could push a caladium leaf into the moist, rich black earth and the next week see it rooted. I coaxed blue Himalayan poppies to grow in a Bucks County garden in Pennsylvania and gentled the architecture of a California veranda with honeysuckle, passionflower, and clematis vines twining around its posts. I grew a jungle of blue morning glories in terracotta pots on a New York apartment's trellised balcony that was no larger than a bath mat. I still get a frisson when I remember them. My Greek housekeeper declared the blue thicket of morning glories so exquisite that it was "better than the marriage bed."

But it was not until 1990, when my new husband Hank, whom I had known for fifty years, presented me with a cliff-top house and five acres of beachfront property on Fishers Island, that I had ever gardened by the sea.

I felt like Browning's "Last Duchess," who smiled at everything she saw and whose looks went everywhere. The Atlantic to the south; Fishers Island Sound and the Connecticut shoreline to the north; Long Island Sound and Orient Point to the west; Watch Hill, Rhode Island, and Block Island Sound to the east. On either side, beaches of tawny sand with stretches of terminal glacial moraine and granite boulders garlanded with windrows of seaweed and mussel shells. Views of dandelioned lawns and sun-dazzled sea, pine trees above clumps of billowing, pillowing blue hydrangeas, hostas with leaves the size of a baby elephant's ears. Bliss.

The naysayers chirped as loudly as summer crickets. I was told that the roses I envisioned would be impossible. Rabbits would eat them and the wind—which not uncommonly can reach a velocity of sixty miles an hour or more—would not only shred them but also fell them as casually as one might snap one's fingers. I was warned about the dampness of fog, the heat at noon, the burning effects of windswept salt spray. I was told that the soil was mostly too rocky, too sandy, too alkaline from accumulated salt, too acidic from the natural mulch of pine needles, too *everything* to cope with unless we were planning to have a sizable gardening staff, which we were not.

I was told not to try to cultivate the overgrown areas on the property as I would get poison ivy, be blistered by poison oak, and be bloodied by the thorns of wild blackberries and raspberries, wild roses, and other local brambles. I was told that nothing would ever grow along the concrete-and-boulder seawall beneath the house foundation, nor bloom along parts of the south-facing rocky bluffs. If, by some miracle, anything did take root, I was assured it would only last until hurricane tides scoured everything but rock away.

I thought a seaside garden should look and be simple, easy, harmonious with sea and sky, serene, tranquil. Simplicity should be key, I thought, both in the way our place would look and in the way this look would be accomplished. It hadn't occurred to me that this might not always be as simple nor as easy a project as I imagined.

From the start, I was determined that the property would be organic, environmentally friendly for visiting children, plants, our Scottish caretaker's dog, birds, bees, butterflies, bats, and beneficial insects. Everything was to be nontoxic, healthy, no herbicides, no pesticides, no chemical sprays. Away went the poisonous rat pellets and powders and ant traps I found in the cellar, garage, laundry room, and kitchen. Away went the outdoor electrical insect zappers. Ferried across the Long Island Sound from

Lycoris squamigera on the eastern point, castle-side; our south-facing bluff.

New London came sealable food and garbage and birdseed containers, bird feeders, suet cages, Audubon-approved nesting boxes, birdhouses from Duncraft, birdbaths. Three years ago, we invested in Mosquito Magnets, mosquito trappers par excellence.

Last year we invested in a four-tiered fountain with a battery-operated pump, which meant that we didn't have to dig up anything to install it nor worry about draining water pipes in cold weather.

Ever since Hank and I were married, we have cleared, pruned, weeded, staked, planted, planted, planted, replanted, mulched, divided, cut back, fertilized, and amended the soil, sedulously deadheaded,[1] experimented, mowed the grass.

"We" comprises my husband, myself, and a succession of part-time gardeners and hired hands who came and went until the advent of José Antonio Rios, the married father of two teenage daughters and a son. José gets along well with me and we work well together. He has an affinity for growing healthy plants from seeds, bulbs, and

Flowering crab (*Malus*), one of many fruit trees at Brillig.

cuttings. He is attentive to the requirements of plants and their appearance and nurture. Quick to do what I need done, orderly, thoughtful, observant, cheerful, intelligent, organized, patient and good humored, José can also weed, prune, and make a border of beach stones with the eye of an artist.

Like one's tastes in books and clothing, art, and household decor, gardens are great signifiers. I care about the colors of leaves and flowers, the way the plants look, the mix of greenery and color, the scents of flowers, line, texture, proportions, the contrast and balance of the landscape and seascape.

I want everything to be well maintained, for plants to be healthy, for the house and land to be clean and uncluttered. I have a compulsive need to snip off withered flowers, yellow or damaged leaves, and I am forever deadheading not only for the sake of appearance but also to encourage new growth and reblooming. I try to keep the beaches on both sides of our property litter free, cleared of six-pack plastic tops, tangled fish lines, hooked lures, the remains of lobster traps and their garish buoys, plastic bottles, beer cans tossed from fishing boats, and other detritus that mar the natural beauty of the beach and that often endangers fish, horseshoe crabs, shorebirds, and the bare feet of swimmers.

Hank named our Fishers Island house "Brillig." He is fond of reciting Lewis Carroll's *Jabberwocky*: "Twas Brillig, and the slithy toves did gyre and gimble in the wabe; All mimsy were the borogoves, and the mome raths outgrabe." I like that feeling of play about the house and garden and seashore. A house by the sea should be able to accommodate sandy feet, wet bathing suits, children's bucketfuls of seashells, collections of horseshoe crabs, starfish laid out to dry on driftwood, and feathers of pheasants, gulls, and crows to arrange in a beanpot.

~ ~ ~ ~

I love our quiet, secluded beach. I'm fascinated by the waves rolling inshore, drawing back, rushing forward bearing seaweed, shells, gravel, bones of birds and fish, treasures to be found or to be carried off by the sea to reappear, perhaps, another day or in another place. Quickened by the hushing sibilance of the water, the throaty cobble-cobble-cobble sound of the backwash, beckoned by curiosities posited on the sand, I never tire of questing, discovering, meditating, imagining. The pleasure of a beach I have to myself is comparable only to the pleasure I have in my own garden where there is also an ancient sense of myth and worship from long ago. I think that people who love beaches almost always love gardens.

To plant seeds or bulbs or cuttings and to watch them grow, evolve, flower, their colors constantly changing, to see flowers bloom and die and bloom again in time; to watch a pollinating honeybee tumbling in the heart of a scarlet poppy; to listen to bees as they buzz and hum ecstatically around clumps of Hidcote lavender; to walk along the cutting garden's paths with a catbird hopping companionably parallel among the rosebushes and holly-hocks; to see branches of buddleia quivering with black and yellow swallowtails while monarchs swirl in low surveillance flights above a swathe of hemerocallis; to

breathe the scent of a fragrant spill of dianthus, brugmansia, roses, or Casablanca lilies; to stroke a child's arm with the silvery fuzz of a leaf of stachys, a tomentose lamb's ear, as I look at the blue of a cornflower, delphinium, or Johnson's blue geranium blend with the blues of sky and sea, that's all I need to sense the flow of nature, the rhythm of the seasons, the ephemeral beauty of life and the wonder and joy of being alive, alive—oh in a simple, peaceful, serene, and tranquil pocket of the world.

Although Brillig is an all-year-round house, our garden is primarily a May-to-October one that peaks in midsummer. No garden can be at its best all of the time. The garden is affected by constantly changing light and weather. The

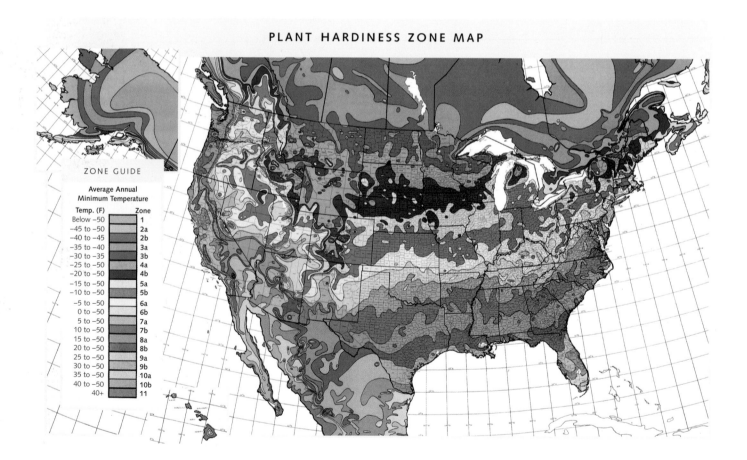

PLANT HARDINESS ZONE MAP

ZONE GUIDE

Average Annual Minimum Temperature

Temp. (F)	Zone
Below −50	1
−45 to −50	2a
−40 to −45	2b
−35 to −40	3a
−30 to −35	3b
−25 to −50	4a
−20 to −50	4b
−15 to −50	5a
−10 to −50	5b
−5 to −50	6a
0 to −50	6b
5 to −50	7a
10 to −50	7b
15 to −50	8a
20 to −50	8b
25 to −50	9a
30 to −50	9b
35 to −50	10a
40 to −50	10b
40+	11

translucent quality of the seaside light seems to have a freshness that isn't found in an inland garden. Colors change from the time a plant pokes up from the earth to when it is in bud, to when it is flowering, and on through its demise, but always there is that inescapable context of greenery.

The eastern tip of Fishers Island, with Brillig its penultimate house, is two weeks behind the western end of the island, and about a month behind other areas classified as Zone 7. We are between Zones 7 (0 to +10°F) and 6 (0 to −10°F).[2]

We made a point of planting trees and shrubs that not only do well by the sea, but also are protective cover and food sources for birds, butterflies, and flower-pollinating bees.

Year by year, the garden changes and evolves. We plant new trees to replace those uprooted by storms. We move plants. We encourage plants that are tolerant of sea spray: hydrangeas, potted hibiscus, yucca, daylilies (hemerocallis), Asiatic lilies, Oriental lilies, lavender, laurel, pyrecantha, crab apple trees, *Lycoris squamigera*, rosa rugosa, holly, Roses of Sharon, among others. We transplant. We try plants in different locations. We get rid of plants that don't do particularly well—off to the compost with them! We add. We subtract.

The wonder and subtle beauty of a garden is a gift made all the more lovely by the sea, whether hidden by fog, storm-lashed when the rain pours down like gravel, or sun-washed and sparkling as gulls and oystercatchers lazily rise from the beach. I wanted at Brillig what I have wanted everywhere else: a serene and tranquil retreat, a muse, a mentor, a place where an unknown hidden scent can startle you into wondering, dreaming, remembering. As I smell the roses and the scented-leaf pelargoniums, I think that is exactly what I have.

How to Structure Your Garden

Here is the space for your garden. You look at it, you walk around it, and then what? How do you want your garden to be? How do you want your garden to look?

There are many sound, good, proven ideas in garden design. As everyone must know by now, the garden is an extension of your house and can be divided into "rooms," each with a different atmosphere, an idea first developed in the early part of the twentieth century by Gertrude Jekyll, a famous author and horticulturalist and a friend of my Scottish grandmother. Miss Jekyll also developed the idea of the one-color garden, although it was made famous by Vita Sackville-West when she created her dramatic white garden at Sissinghurst in the 1930s. Color control, using cool pastel colors and hot bright colors like reds and yellows, was another of Jekyll's widely copied ideas. Naturalizing bulbs and informal drifts of daffodils, now mainstays in garden design, were developed by contemporaries of Miss Jekyll at the turn of the twentieth century.

Although we cling to the familiar, garden design is an ongoing creative process that involves time, thought, and conscious intent, giving substance and form to our hopes, needs, desires, and emotions. Garden design isn't about what other people have done but what's right for your site, what's right for **you**.

Gardens are as personal as the clothes you wear, the music you enjoy, the books you read, the paintings you like. To create a garden, **your** garden, get a notebook, or a folder, or something to put your writings in and a pen, a pencil, or your computer to write with. Start by listing what's important to you about the way you want your garden to be.

What will the **function** of your garden be? Entertaining? A child's play area? A private haven for meditation and a quiet refuge? A place to relax, read, or just bliss out? A setting for a swimming pool, tennis court, putting green, badminton court, or a pier, dock, beach for water sports and sailing?

What is your **personal style**? Is your idea of a dream garden soothing and serene? Elegant? Laid back and informal? Formal and organized, perhaps with boxwood parterres, a knot garden, patterned brick paving? Would a focal point be a fountain or various traditional or modern pieces of sculpture? Would you like your garden to impart a sense of cheerful happiness or mystery? Do you prefer simple drifts of hydrangeas? Do you dream of a white garden or a linear *allée* of fruit trees? Do you like old-fashioned flowers and plants? Do you see in your mind's eye lots of swings, slides, rings, a jungle gym, and maybe a

Birdfood and flowers in the vista.

the feathery fronds of flower tamarisk, plants are meant to be touched, caressed like rose petals held against your cheeks. Do you like the feel of pebbles, sand, sun-warmed stone, or springy grass beneath your bare feet? Is the thought of walking slowly on the beach sand in the early morning appealing? Or stepping in sandals on thyme-covered steps that release their spicy fragrance as you walk over them? Leaves can feel glossy, soft, silky, fuzzy, prickly. Remember that hardscaping materials in your garden for sculpture and for seating also have texture, such as marble, granite, wrought iron, wood, fieldstone. What are your preferences about these?

Do you dream of a moonlit garden of brugmansia, lilies, stock, nicotiana, moon flowers, and others that only release their scent in the evening? Or do you prefer rose gardens redolent with tea roses and old-fashioned rambler roses? Do you crave a border of clove-scented dianthus? Or a bed of Casablanca lilies so fragrant that a breeze carries their scent to you before you can see them?

And **sound**? Do you want a quiet garden, or do you enjoy the sound of a gently splashing fountain, a murmuring stream, the flow of a waterfall, birdsong, rustling leaves, children laughing, people playing tennis?

If the sense of **taste** is important to you, what do you want your garden to provide? Raspberries, strawberries, white peaches, pears, apples, grapes, or sun-warmed tomatoes and fresh peas in a pod?

How will you **view** your garden? From a deck, through windows, from a balcony? Will you see your garden all at once, or will you see small "rooms" as you walk around, move about? Will you see distant parts that hide or reveal themselves as you approach them on curving or straight paths? Seeing your garden at ground level or from a rooftop captain's walk can totally change your garden's perspective.

And **form**? Plants can be clustered together, spaced apart. Plants can be round, billowing, fountainlike, upright, spreading, short, tall, columnar, pointed like

tree house for your children or grandchildren? Do you like armillaries and gazing globes? Would you like a pergola to sit beneath? What has special meaning to you that you can convey in your garden?

Do you like complementary and harmonious or contrasting **colors**, or just one color for a bed of flowers? Do you prefer soft blues, lavenders, whites, pinks, or intense splashes or bright oranges, reds, yellows? Do you prefer a little **contrast**—soothing—or a lot of contrast—stimulating? Do you feel overwhelmed with a sense of beauty when you see a rose garden with the same flower presented in many colors, from creamy ivory to brilliant scarlet? In the winter, do you like seeing flashes of berries among bare branches?

What sensory effects are important to you? What sort of textures do you like to **touch**, look at, walk on? From the velvety, silvery leaves of lamb's ears (*Stachys lanata*) to spears, fluffy, geometric, spiral, triangular, or two-dimensional like vines on a wall or an espaliered tree. What appeals to you the most?

What **categories** of plants are you interested in? Do you dream of an herb garden or a vegetable garden as perfect as a French *potager*, or a vegetable garden casually laid out and interspersed with marigolds and nasturtiums? Do your thoughts run to orchards, an arbor of many kinds of grapes, a few pear trees, an espaliered peach tree, a bramble patch of raspberries, or tropical plants that you can bring out during the summer and overwinter inside? Would you like a rock garden with interesting heathers

and alpine plants or other flowers? Or would you be more interested in having a water garden, a small pool or several small pools, or perhaps even a long rectangular reflecting pool with goldfish or koi swimming in it?

And **motion**? How will you make your way around your garden? Will you move along curving, meandering paths in one area and along straight, direct paths elsewhere? Do you prefer paths of wood chips, paths of paving stones, or brick walks? Perhaps you have a ravine or a stream that needs a bridge. What sort of bridge do you envision? Water running through a streambed, birds flying through the trees, butterflies flittering about a

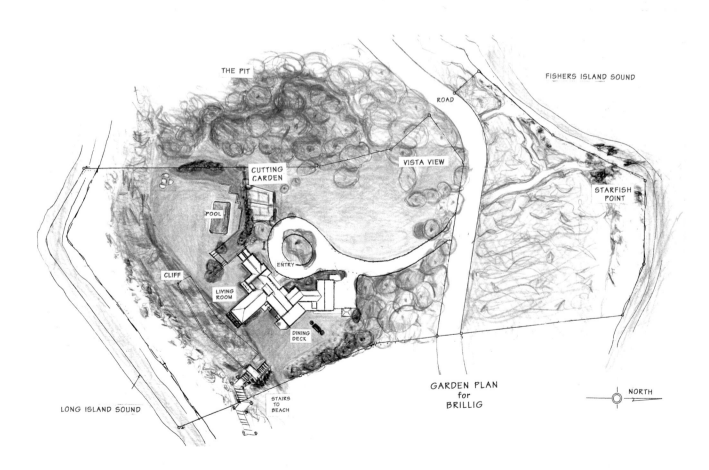

butterfly bush, a waterfall, a fountain, and trees, flowers, grasses swaying in the wind, shifting patterns of light and shade give life to a garden.

What about **hardscaping**? What are your favorite elements? Steps and stairs? Would you like a gazebo? An archway? A single bold piece of sculpture? A sundial? A trellised, covered bench? Statues? Urns for flower containers? Would you like a religious shrine? A hammock? A grown-up swing in the shade? Benches encircling trees? What about boundaries for your garden, for gardens should, I think, be defined by boundaries, fences, walls, hedges, a windbreak of massive trees, a hedgerow of shrubs or evergreens, mixing in roses, perhaps, but something, whatever you decide, that will define the boundaries of your garden, leaving the center open, with a bit of lawn, a tapis vert, to allow your eyes to rest.

I made a notebook like this when I first came to Brillig. Brillig wasn't a completely blank slate. There were things there that had to be fixed as soon as possible, such as ugly concrete walls in the swimming pool area that we covered with lattice and grew clematis on. There were clotted tangles of taxus and poison ivy beneath two clusters of pine trees, dark thickets that blocked light, air, and views. These had to be pruned and thinned and dug up. Two small yews had been planted in front of a copse of trees, destroying a clean line for no reason, marking no pathway, just plonked there; they had to be dug up and replanted somewhere else. Then there was the "bunker" of concrete and boulders, the seawall fronting the south side of the bluff, preventing erosion and the action of a hurricane's high tide in scooping out the house's supporting foundations of natural rocks and earth. How could that be disguised? How could that be covered with green and growing plants? I was told no way, nothing would ever grow there. But, of course, that wasn't true. A few holes drilled in the concrete to poke in honeysuckle, porcelain berry (*Ampelopsis*); some chopped up, washed seaweed added to topsoil and compost; regular watering, additional soil and compost shoveled on year after year until the entire stretch along the south-facing bluffs was covered.

The western side of the bluff parallel to the swimming pool area was partly terraced and planted with white rosa rugosa. Had I not needed an upright planting to hedge the south side of the swimming pool area, I might have covered the bluff with creeping phlox or rambler roses.

There are often site problems like these in a garden, bluffs or banks that have to be terraced or planted to prevent erosion. Hilltop sites are prone to wind and drought. Hillside gardens are likely to be thin-soiled, but well drained. If you have a garden slope, hillside, or bluff as we have that faces south, know that this is the sunniest side, and in summer, the hottest, a good place for tomentose, heat- and drought-tolerant plants like artemisias, sedums, rosa rugosas. A north-facing slope is cooler in summer, colder in winter, less sunny. East-facing slopes mainly receive the morning sun. West-facing slopes mainly receive the afternoon sun.

It's important to understand your site. Go slowly, take your time to study how much sun each area gets. How and what you can grow successfully depends on your site con-

ditions, and the soil conditions that should be tested in a soil laboratory. The wooden palisade of our cutting garden creates a microclimate, because the garden is protected from winds, and our swimming pool area is another microclimate as it is sheltered by a bank of hydrangeas on both its northern and its western side as well as by the house on its eastern side.

The topography of some sites may be billiard-table flat. In that case, you may want to create contoured planting mounds, or construct a berm, or carefully place groups of trees or rounded rocks to improve the structural elements of your garden. For this sort of extensive work, I would recommend consulting with a licensed landscape architect who is a member of the American Society of Landscape Architects.

I think the main thing with a garden is to start small. First to test your soil (See "Compost"). Amend your soil. Start a compost heap. Confine your planting the first year to a group of shrubs, or a vine-covered arbor, or a modest bed of herbs, lettuce, and some lavender bushes. Lavender,

by the way, is a wonderful soil improver. When there were areas I wasn't sure about, I opted to plant them with creeping juniper so that later, when I could plan more, I could put in Siberian iris and other irises in a weed-free area.

Before you really start to do anything, you have to live with what you have and carefully watch patterns of sun, shade, wind, rain. Pay particular attention to **what types of plants do well and where they do well.**

~ ~ ~ ~

Make small plans. Whether you design your own garden or get a professional to help, planning is time extremely well spent. Then, live with the plan in your head for a while. You may have other ideas, and you'll be glad you didn't just jump in and follow what you first had planned.

With all the notes you made, you can tailor and carpenter your garden to fit your particular needs and integrate the look and character of your house with that of your garden.

You have to take your time to get rid of what you don't want and to think about what it is you do want. There are things I knew I definitely wanted. I wanted hydrangeas, blush pink roses, and white Siberian irises and lavender-blue irises on the western side of the house; and on the eastern side, masses of daylilies (*Hemerocallis*). After friends gave us a few dozen daffodils and I planted them, I knew I wanted more. I planted a few roses the first year to see how they would do. I did the same with different kinds of iris.

What did well, I got more of. What didn't do well, what was too much trouble to just get to the point of surviving, I didn't bother with.

Preparation is all-important. When you are planting trees, take a lot of trouble to prepare the hole. I was told it was a good thing to add half a dozen potatoes in the hole to feed a tree along with compost and rotted down leaf mulch. The trees we planted that way all seem to be doing well.

It's important to have places to sit and read and look and have a drink of lemonade or iced tea on a hot summer day, as well as a place to sit and think and look and write, perhaps, on a cooler day in autumn.

I am still thinking about a gazebo, if I would really like one, and, if so, where exactly would I like to see it standing.

One of the first things I did after I came to Brillig was to work out with a wonderful young helper where we could put nature paths in the wooded area from the vista garden up to the south-facing ridge, and in the brambly, overgrown area of Starfish Point facing north. We walked the property to figure out the lay of the land, to see where there were particularly good views, and to find out where it was comfortable to walk.

Once that was settled, we just hacked through the brush to clear pathways that we lined with wood chips.

Remember that plants may look small when you buy them, but they don't stay that way. They change and grow. Proper spacing will save you the effort of thinning or moving your plants later on.

The hardest job for me was to plant for four-season interest. In general, plants that take center stage each season, individually varied though they may be, are those found in the subsequent chapters of the book.

At the front entrance driveway circle, our four-tiered fountain with a battery-operated pump and stepping stone rocks is an attraction from spring through autumn for multitudes of birds.

I have been enchanted by the way our
daffodils have flowered this year, flowered,
danced, scented the air.

Chapter 1

Heralds of Spring: Tulips and Daffodils

I'd bought a patch of wild ground.
In March it surprised me. Suddenly I saw what I owned.
A cauldron of daffodils, boiling gently.

A gilding of the Deeds—treasure trove!
Daffodils just came. And kept coming—

"Blown foam," I wrote, "Vessels of light!"
They raced under every gust
On the earth-surge. "Their six-bladed screws
Churning the greeny-yellows
Out of the hard, over-wintered Chlorophyl."...

...I thought they were a windfall. I picked them. I sold them.[1]

In April, the daffodils come out in a burst, masses of them, naturalizing in clusters on the upper stretch of the bluff that rises steeply from the beach facing the Atlantic, and among the trees and bushes of the northern roadside bank. Streaming southward toward Brillig, our weather-beaten, cedar-shingled house on the bluff, the daffodils, like a waving river of flowers along the western edge of the driveway, look as though they had just been painted. Their clean, shining brightness, the scent of young leaves and damp spring earth, everything glowing and blowing, hint at the bliss of May and the hope and magic of summer ahead.

Years before William Wordsworth, wandering lonely as a cloud along the shores of Ullswater, immortalized "a crowd, a host of golden daffodils...fluttering and dancing in the breeze," William Shakespeare wrote in *The Winter's Tale* [2] of "daffodils that come before the swallow dares and take the winds of March with beauty..."

April is the time of poetry and pilgrimages. I remember the Prologue of Chaucer's *Canterbury Tales* that opens with the words, "When April with his showers sweet with fruit..." that I first heard read in Middle English when I was a Four, a junior, at St. Timothy's, a boarding school in Maryland. It sounded sweet, dream like, like candy for the mind, and when I read the sonnet in updated English, I kept it also pinned to my mind's bulletin board so that I could always have it on hand when April came around again, when Zephyr inspired with his sweet breath the tender shoots and buds, and April sired the flowers, and people long to go on pilgrimages to distant shrines. My shrine is here in the garden.

I am mesmerized by the sight of daffodils at their April peak. I remember Daphne Du Maurier writing in *Rebecca* about the daffodils at Manderley. I find the book in our library, turn a few pages, and meet within minutes: "The daffodils were in bloom, stirring in the evening breeze, golden heads cupped upon lean stalks, and however many you might pick, there would be no thinning of the ranks, they were massed like an army shoulder to shoulder."

I don't want to pick daffodils. I'd rather see them growing outside. I've seen them starring the turf beneath the oaks of Windsor Castle. I've seen them gleaming like pale golden lamps on the island of Mainau in Lake Constance in southern Germany where tulips and daffodils swirl in serried drifts around a baroque eighteenth-century castle.

On a Bucks County farm where I once lived in Erwinna, Pennsylvania, I discovered a galaxy of naturalized ruffled daffodils with satiny saffron-yellow petals growing nearby in woods that were going to be bulldozed for agricultural acreage the next day. It was a weekend—Sunday. I was alone, without day workers. With a trowel, I managed to dig up hundreds of daffodils and trundle load after load in a wheelbarrow back to the farm.

There had been many April showers. The alluvial soil was soft and moist. I decided not to even think about troweling holes, but simply to take a broomstick, plunge it into the ground, pop in a flowering bulb, leaves, stem, flower and all, fill up the hole with scraped-in dirt firmly patted in and hope for the best. I planted the daffodils as a border along both sides of the driveway, along woodland paths, circling the weep line, or branches' edge, of a pair of hundred-year-old maples, and bordering stone walls at our entrance gateway in a bed planted with daylilies as well as Asiatic and Oriental lilies. Where I planted the daffodils was ideal. Daffodils are best planted in fields, along woodland paths, circling the weep line of trees, bordering driveways, fences, hedges, and stone or brick walls. Landscapers recommend interplanting daffodils with daylilies to mask their withering, to spare one the sight of their sallow dishevelment until the first of July, or at least six weeks after they have stopped flowering, when their leaves and stems can be cut back or mowed over. The nutrients daffodils store during their dying-back period feed the bulbs for next spring's flowering. It's essential to let all bulb foliage and stems mature and fade to yellow before you mow them over or cut them down. I've forced myself to bear in mind that four months of fresh air and sunlight this year are needed to assure robust bulbs next year. I wanted daffodils bordering the western edge of the driveway at Brillig. I didn't want to interplant them with daylilies bordering the driveway. Hostas or ferns wouldn't do all that well in the sun, and I didn't want hostas and ferns bordering the driveway. For my sins of stubbornness, my husband, Hank, and I are stuck in May and June with a driveway bordered on one side with mounds of yellowing leaves. Well-meaning neatnik friends have suggested bending the leaves back and securing them in tidy knobs or braiding the leaves. I thank them for their advice: I tell them, even when I know they don't care, that this practice leads to far fewer and punier flowers the following year. I'm learning to put up with and overlook necessary uncomeliness along the western edge of the driveway for the sake of the spring glory I am confronted with in April and May. I tell my ostrich self that by June there will be so much else to look at that no one will notice how the driveway looks.

To get back to the Pennsylvania daffodils I planted in good places, but with appalling crudity. What happened to them? They flourished and continued to naturalize. Zone-hardy daffodils are tough. For both practical as well as aesthetic reasons, they are probably the most universally grown and beloved of all spring-flowering bulbs. In my own experience, they are pest and disease free. They are about as rat, mouse, mole, vole and deer proof as any plant can be. They tolerate summer moisture better than most bulbs. With their eclectic intensity of color, their breathtaking vividness, their practicality, their hardiness, few people know or care that daffodils are toxic, mildly poisonous. The mucilaginous sap of daffodils contains sharp crystals of calcium oxalate, an irritant that keeps animals from eating the plant.

Daffodils, narcissi, and jonquils are members of the Amaryllis (*Amaryllidaceae*) family. Also in this family are the Tuberose (*Polianthes*); Amaryllis (*Hippeastrum equestre*); *Lycoris Squamigera*, sometimes called Naked Ladies or Surprise Lilies; Snowdrops (*Galanthus*); *Agave*, often referred to as Century Plant; *Nerines*, or Guernsey Lilies. The flowers of the Amaryllis family are similar to those of the Lily family. A noticeable difference is the position of the ovary. In Lilies, the ovary is enclosed and hidden by six petal-like parts. In members of the Amaryllis family, it is a conspicuous bulge that extends beneath the petals. The strappy leaves of the two families look very much alike. Lilies have scaly bulbs. Amaryllis family members have solid bulbs.

Daffodils, narcissi, and jonquils belong to the genus *Narcissus*, and all share Narcissus as a botanical name. All daffodils are narcissi, but not all narcissi are daffodils, a botanical distinction that has to do with the length of the flower trumpet, technically termed the corona, and the six flat petals that compose the perianth. There are about 50 species and more than 300 cultivars of narcissi, daffodils, and jonquils, which have a dozen classifications:

Trumpet cultivars with solitary flowers, flowering early in the season, planting distance 3–6 inches;

Large-cupped cultivars with solitary flowers, flowering usually in mid-season, planting distance 6 inches;

Small-cupped cultivars with solitary flowers, mid- and late-season flowering, planting distance 6 inches;

Double cultivars with one or more flowers, some sweetly scented, usually flowering mid- and late-season, planting distance 6 inches;

Triandrus cultivars, each stem producing 2 to 6 nodding flowers, mid- and late-season flowering, planting distance 2–3 inches;

Cyclamineus cultivars with solitary flowers, early and mid-season flowering, planting distance 3 inches;

Jonquilla cultivars with each stem producing 1 to 5 scented flowers, mid- and late-season flowering, planting distance 3 inches;

Tazetta cultivars producing up to 20 small flowers on a stem, or larger-flowered cultivars bearing 3 to 4 flowers a stem, usually scented, flowering late autumn and early winter in warm areas such as southern California and the Gulf of Texas area, planting distance 3 inches;

Poeticus cultivars with fragrant, usually solitary flowers, flowering mid- and late-season, planting distance 6 inches;

Wild species including wild daffodils and their wild hybrids such as the little hoop-petticoat daffodil, autumn-to-spring flowering in varying climates, planting distance 2–3 inches for smaller bulbs, or 6 inches for larger bulbs;

Miscellaneous cultivars includes daffodils not in other divisions, planting distance 2–3 inches for small bulbs, or 6 inches for larger bulbs.

Daffodil blossoms range from yellow and white and apricot to a demure pink, and some even have scarlet trimmings. They are borne on stems from four to twenty inches, or more. Jonquils have one to five blossoms on a stem and a trumpet that is half as long as their petals. Daffodils generally produce only one flower on a stem. Narcissi come in single-, double-, and multi-flowered varieties.

Some twenty years ago, the Planting Fields Arboretum near Oyster Bay, Long Island, which originally was a family place that belonged to Green Vale schoolmates of mine when I was a child, listed varieties of daffodils that consistently produced a lavish, healthy abundance of flowers. Among them are those in the table on page 19.

Our driveway daffodils at Brillig began with a present of some four dozen bulbs from friends. I then sent for The Works, advertised as daffodils for naturalizing, from White Flower Farm, Litchfield (See "Sources and Advice: Where to buy plants, seeds, garden furniture, pots and urns, both resin and clay, etc."). This mix is made up of 100 top-size bulbs of no less that thirty daffodil varieties, Trumpets, Large Cups, Small Cups, Poeticus, Split-Coronas, Jonquilla hybrids, Triandrus, Cyclamineus, many fragrant, some with frilled cups, a congenial range of sizes. After sending annually for more sets of The Works for

Springtime daffodils flowing like a river along our driveway.

several years, a trickle of daffodils became a broad stream and now it's a wonderful waving naturalizing river to which I've added quite a few dozen heirloom species bulbs mentioned in the preceding list. I've sent friends in Virginia and Texas The Works, Southern Style, which includes Tazettas as well. I love White Flower Farm. Their catalogue is great. Their flowers and plants are exceptional, and their prices are reasonable.

Whether you want to buy a daffodil bulb in Boston or Baluchistan, any flower nursery will recognize what you want by its botanical name *Narcissus*. Each and every flower and plant has only one botanical name by which it is known worldwide. The Paper White narcissus bulbs we're all familiar with, the forced bulbs that bear strongly scented glistening white flowers from winter to early spring, are *Narcissus papyraceus*, also referred to as Paper White Grandiflorus (Paper-white narcissus), a Tazetta daffodil cultivar. The name narcissus comes to us from the Greek myth about the handsome youth of that name who was so captivated by his reflection in a pool that, leaning over to embrace his own image, he fell, was drowned, and transformed by the gods to a flower with a mesmeric scent.

Jonquil comes from the Spanish *junco* (rush), referring to its rushlike leaves. Daffodil came by its name through

DAFFODIL VARIETIES

Variety	Color	Height
Arctic Gold	Yellow	18"
Binkie	Yellow and white	11"
Carlton	Yellow, two-tone	18"–20"

One the world's best-selling bulbs with a vanilla fragrance, early April to midseason flowering, available from White Flower Farm as of 2003

Dove Wings	Yellow with yellow	8"
February Gold	Bright two-tone yellow	10"
Hawera	Creamy yellow	6"–8"

Abundantly flowering, with several creamy, yellow-belled flowers a stem, 4–9 stems a bulb, flowers having the swept-back petals and delicate cup of a Triandrus group, late-season April–May flowering, available from White Flower Farm as of 2003

Hoop Petticoat	Bright yellow	6"
Ice Follies	Ivory and lemon yellow	16"–18"

Lightly scented with frilly cups, a vigorous, bountiful early midseason April bloomer, available from White Flower Farm as of 2003

Jack Snipe	White and lemon yellow	8"–10"

A Cyclamineus variety which spreads freely, white petaled with clear lemon yellow cups, tolerant of shade, damp soil, southern heat, flowering midseason April, available from White Flower Farm as of 2003

Mrs. R.O. Backhouse	White and pink	18"

This white petaled daffodil was the first bred in England in 1923 with a pink trumpet. Well known in England, it is pronounced as it is spelled, author and horticulturalist Lady Mary Keen assures me, and not as my prim-and-proper mother—who associated backhouse with an outhouse—bowdlerized the pronunciation "backhoosie."

Spellbinder	Yellow and white	20"
Tête-à-Tête	Yellow	6"–8"

Buttercup yellow petals with a corona the color of country-cultivated farm egg yolks, this little daffodil produces multiple blooms, early-season April bloomer, available from White Flower Farm as of 2003.

Thalia	White	14"

A Triandrus daffodil, snow-white and fragrant, with 2–3 blossoms on a stem, flowering late midseason in April–May, available from White Flower Farm as of 2003.

the age-old tendency to spurn the familiar. The British preferred the imported white asphodel and affadil, or poet's narcissus, because they both produced many white flowers, to their native species of daffodil (*Narcissus pseudonarcissus*) that yielded only a single yellow flower that was regarded as a false narcissus—hence its botanical name—and commonly called a bastard affadil, an Old English word meaning "early comer" (the daffodil then, as now, was for many the symbol for springtime). Over the years, the pronunciation of "bastard affadil" eroded, and most of the "bastard" crumbled away, leaving only the final d. By the time Queen Elizabeth I reigned, the bastard affadil had become daffadil, sometimes called daff-a-down dilly, daffodilly, and the Lent lily.

In Good Queen Bess's and Shakespeare's time, daffodils were yellow, golden, ivory, white, or had saffron or deep orange trumpets or cups. From the beginning of the twentieth century, hybridizers have been working on apricot, peach, pink, and red shades and tints in bicolored daffodils. A leader in this field was the late American hybridizer Grant E. Mitsch of Mitsch Novelty Daffodils (See "Sources and Advice: Where to buy plants, seeds, garden furniture, pots and urns, both resin and clay, etc.").

Mitsch was responsible for a daffodil with white petals and a deep pink cup called "Accent," winner in 1987 of the American Daffodil Society's Wister Award. He introduced a multitude of pink cyclamineus, jonquil, split-corona, and triandrus hybrids. You can see them on the Mitsch website. If there is more that you'd like to know and see of daffodils, log on to the American Daffodil Society website (See "Sources and Advice: Where to buy plants, seeds, garden furniture, pots and urns, both resin and clay, etc.").

I am poring over the Mitsch catalogue and wondering whether white and pink daffodils might look well somewhere in the vista garden or in the cutting garden where the apple tree is flowering with pale blush pink blossoms. Which bulbs I shall choose, how many bulbs I shall order, and where José and I shall plant them is something, like Scarlett O'Hara, I shall have to think about later. I've heard about a jonquil narcissus with white petals and an apricot cup called "Divertimento" that has an exquisite scent that sets my heart dancing like—what else—a daffodil.

It delights me that botanists and biologists worry about why daffodils dance in the wind and tulips don't. S.A. Etnier and Steven Vogel have written an article entitled "Reorientation of Daffodil (*Narcissus: Amaryllidaceae*) Flowers in Wind: Drag Reduction and Torsional Flexibility."[3] Daffodils, they said, have a propensity for "dancing" in the wind—but tulips don't. Why the difference? "According to biologists at Duke University, the fact that daffodil flowers are asymmetrically oriented (that is, they point in a particular direction), while tulip flowers are symmetrical, is key to the contrast. Regardless of wind direction, tulips present essentially the same shape and thus are subject to about the same force due to wind pressure. But a wind's force on a 'forward'-facing daffodil flower is considerably greater than that on a 'backward'-facing one. In high winds, daffodils reorient to the 'backward' position, with their trumpets pointed downward, so as to lessen the chance of structural damage. In gusty winds, the periodic reorientation results in the 'dance' of the daffodils. The biologists also discovered that the non-circular form of daffodil stems helps them to accomplish their pirouettes."[4]

Here's how to plant daffodil bulbs adapted to your local climate so that they will naturalize (reproduce themselves and bloom year after year in a virtually fail-proof way): If, after a few years, some form thick clumps of foliage but steadily produce fewer flowers, it may be due to overcrowding. If that happens, simply dig the bulbs up after the leaves have withered, separate the bulbs, and replant, giving the bulbs more space.

First of all, bear in mind that the glorious springtime fling of daffodils will become a sloppy mess of dying, yellowing leaves for at least six weeks before you can mow them down or cut them back. At the end of our daffodil cycle at Brillig, the grass along the western edge of the driveway grows about knee-high above the tangled mess of withered daffodil leaves, a sight welcomed only by our resident pheasants, ducks, and ground-feeding birds. Other gardeners on the island plant later-flowering bulbs such as day lilies (hemerocallis), or astilbe or irises or *something* to conceal the unsightliness, while others, like me, just avert their eyes and look elsewhere for a month and a half.

With this cautionary advice in mind, choose the site or sites for your daffodil-bulb planting. Daffodils love sun. The soil should be well-drained, moderately fertile and in an area that gets sun—preferably morning sun—at least half the day. The **time for planting** is early autumn. September is ideal, even August; October at the latest. Daffodils need a long period of dormancy in order to bloom in April and May the following year.

In choosing bulbs, pick **colors** that complement each other. Two-tone yellows of different kinds look better than white-with-pink daffodils combined with deep yellow daffodils. White with pink daffodils look fine mixed with all-white daffodils. For **height**, mix tall and short-growing bulbs for visual impact. By combining early

and late varieties of bulbs, you can **extend the flowering** for several weeks. **How many** bulbs will you need? Think wheelbarrowsful. At least fifty. A hundred is better. (White Flower Farm solves all your problems with The Works.) To give you an idea, if you want to have a 4'-square bed of daffodils, you'll need fifty bulbs. If you measure the ground you want to cover for a border (figure on planting bulbs 6" apart, or 4" apart for a more closely-spaced, lush look) you'll have the number of bulbs you need for one row. Rather than rows, I plant bulbs for each unit in a diamond shape with one in the center, 6" apart. Odd numbers look more natural than even. Plant bulbs in clumps of three, five, seven or more in drifts, or in randomly spaced clusters, much as they appear growing wild in nature.

Since daffodils are one of the earliest blooming of bulbs, you can plant them under deciduous trees, where they can grow and bloom before the trees leaf out. Obviously, don't plant bulbs right up against a tree trunk, but plant them in a circle close to the weep line or drip

line (the fringe of the tree's canopy branches), avoiding the tree's roots above and below the ground. You can scatter bulbs on the ground and then just plant them where they have landed, or plant them in bewitching blankets, or borders and margins—the thicker the better—along walls, paths and fences. Don't plant daffodil bulbs on the north side of trees, as they won't do as well with a minimum of sun. They won't thrive at all under evergreens or in full shade. Some wind protection is always a good idea

as the flowers will last longer and look lovelier with less weather-frayed petals.

Everyone has different requirements, different time and money budgets, different amounts of space to allot to a host of golden, white, apricot, peach, pink, or combinations thereof of daffodils. Just know that the rewards of your efforts will pay off for decades. Plant bulbs in the right spot, let them naturalize and spread into ever-winding pools of beauty for years to come, and rejoice.

Tulips flowering among daffodils on the roadbank hillock below the vista area.

But first, here you are with bare ground and sacks of bulbs. The land should be cultivated. Holes for the bulbs should be dug.

José, a loyal aficionado of Jerry Baker and his Grandma Putt and their just-folks, easy to understand advice and wacko-sounding tonics that are based on admirable healthy organic ingredients good for your garden (See "Sources and Advice: Composting in the Kitchen and Outdoors"), prepares 100 sq. ft. of soil by working in 10 lbs. of Epsom salts, just under the top layer of earth. Jerry Baker then suggests adding bone meal, but this commercial animal by-product is processed differently than it used to be, and the new process removes many of the nutrients valuable for bulbs. I prefer using organic bulb food stocked by our local hardware store. Remember, no horse or cow manure because they tend to rot bulbs if they come in contact with them. Since bulbs grow roots from their bases, use a spoonful of a mix of 10 lb. of compost and 1 lb. of Epsom salts to drop into the bottom of each bulb-planting hole.

Make digging easier by softening hard or dry soil with a good water-soaking the day before planting. Before you begin planting, loosen the soil so that it's easier to add the mixture of compost, blood meal, and Epsom salts.

José tells me that Jerry Baker suggests mixing up a pre-planting beauty bath for bulbs. An hour or two before we are ready to plant our daffodil bulbs, we drop them as they are—never, ever, ever peeling off their papery, onionlike skins—into 2 gallons of warm water into which we have stirred 2 teaspoons of Johnson's baby shampoo or other baby shampoo, 1 teaspoon of Listerine antiseptic mouthwash, and 1 teaspoon of Lipton's instant tea granules.

The specific garden tool called a bulb planter is one that José shuns. He says it takes too much time and is a nuisance to use. A Cape Cod weeder/planter, a sharp-tipped tool, works well, as does a very narrow trowel. I've been told that the best bulb planter is called the red bulb planter, invented by Brent and Becky Heath, a modified pine-tree planter that works well in unprepared soil, around tree roots, in groundcovers (See "Sources and Advice: Where to buy plants, seeds, garden furniture, pots and urns, both resin and clay, etc."). An Ames True Temper versatile utility shovel, available at most home-improvement stores, is also recommended. The shovel is light and compact and works in tight, hard-to-maneuver spaces. Remember, I also used a broomstick to make the holes in moist, soft soil, so digging holes isn't all that arduous. Just remember to pop in a little bulb snack food.

How deep should the holes be for daffodil bulbs? Plant about 6" from the soil level to the bottom of the planting holes. Some people tell you to plant daffodil bulbs from one and a half to five times their own depth, but those were directions I couldn't cope with. Someone else told me to plant daffodil bulbs a depth of twice their height that came to about 6". For containers, I know that 6" deep beneath the soil is ideal for daffodils. Then at a depth of 2–3", you can plant little grape hyacinths (*Muscari*)—as you can outdoors in a thinly wooded copse of birch trees or mountain ash/rowan trees for lovely looking lemon and gold and bluish-purple clusters. Still other people will tell you to follow the "three times" planting rule, a rule I grew up hearing my mother and her gardening help talk about. You plant bulbs at a depth three times the height of the bulb (a 2"-tall bulb goes in to the ground 6" deep, good for most daffodils) and space them apart the same amount. Where winters are severe, you should make sure that there is at least 3" of soil covering the daffodil bulb. Plant larger bulbs deeper, smaller ones less so. Plant deeper in sandy soils, less so in heavy claylike soil, both of which soils should be amended with compost or a variety of other organic matter such as leaf mold or humus or peat moss, or with other amendments to adjust the soil's pH (See "Sources and Advice: Composting in the Kitchen and Outdoors"). Plant deeper in the North, less deep in the South. Planting deeper helps protect bulbs against the cold, enhances their longevity. You plant deeper (say about 8" for daffodil bulbs) to slow the rate of the prolif-eration of offsets (little bulbs that grow at the base of the mother bulb). Planting shallower for faster proliferation of offsets means you get more, but smaller flowers.

The faster the bulbs increase, the more flowers you also have to dig up and move around. It's all right to err on the side of shallowly planting daffodil bulbs and *Lycoris squamigera*, daylilies, lilies, and more that I can't think of at the moment, because they have contractile roots that serve to relocate the bulb to its ideal depth. This is *not* true for tulips. This feature is what allows seedling bulbs to end up magically at the right depth.

You can space bulbs three times their width apart, or estimate anywhere from three to ten bulbs per square foot. Spacing bulbs 6" to 8" apart for larger bulbs, and 4" to 5" apart for smaller bulbs, will give them a bit more room to increase over the long run in a naturalized setting.

Plant bulbs with the pointy side of the bulb facing up. If you can't tell which is the rooting end and which is the sprouting end, just plant the bulb on its side. It will figure out which way is up.

After you have planted the bulbs, use fertilizer (analy-sis 5[parts nitrogen]–10[parts phosphorus]–20[parts potassium]) developed specifically for daffodils and other members of the Amaryllis family that like extra potassium in their diet. Scatter the granules on top of the ground in the autumn after planting your bulbs. Then again, in the spring, apply a light dressing (¼ cup per sq. ft.) as new growth begins to push through the earth. This special Daffodil Fertilizer comes in a 10 lb. bag to cover 200 sq. ft., or a 25 lb. bag to cover 500 sq. ft., from White Flower Farm. To order, call 1-800-503-9624. You can also use this daffodil fertilizer for tulips. José always adds extra compost to this fertilizer. I'm told that a hearty sprinkling of Epsom salts or triple super phosphate enhances the colors of daffodil and tulip bulbs if added to the top dressing of fer-tilizer and compost. I don't notice all that much difference whether I do this or forget to. **Be sure, though, to thor-oughly water the area of newly planted bulbs.**

If daffodil clumps lose vigor and produce fewer flow-ers, or don't multiply as readily as they have in the past, this problem is usually due to overcrowding. Just dig the bulbs up when the leaves are withered and replant to give the daffodils more space.

After your daffodils have flowered and begin to wither, you can deadhead them, cutting off spent flowers to pre-vent seed formation except, perhaps, for some special flower you would like to have reseed. From seed, it takes a daffodil about seven years to flower. Planting daffodil bulbs is infinitely quicker and more satisfying. Remember, after the daffodils have flowered to leave the leaves, flaccid and tatty though they may be, to lap up sun and air for at least six weeks in order to power up for the following year.

I have been enchanted by the way our daffodils have flowered this year, flowered, danced, scented the air.

Tulips

Silky tulip goblets flare along the roadside banks before you can see or get to our driveway, and once you enter the driveway, you can see a sweep of global scarlet tulips joyfully flowing into the grape arbor garden, a surprising, yet pleasing blazon of springtime.

Daffodils, those marvelous flowers, naturalize, are abhorred by deer and all other destructive furry creatures because of their toxic calcium oxalic crystals. Tulips, on the other hand, regarded by the ancient Persians as aphrodisiacal confections when their stamens and ovaries were sautéed in almond oil, are also considered delicacies to feast on by deer, rabbits, mice, moles, voles, and squirrels. Tulips don't naturalize. They perennialize. Some last only for a year or two, coming back with smaller and fewer flowers, petering out, disappearing. Others, such as Darwin Hybrids, Fosteriana, Greigii, Kaufmanniana, and some Perennials will last reliably for quite a few years, not the decades and decades that daffodils do, but for at least five, six, seven years.

TULIP VARIETIES

Darwin Hybrid Group (Zones 3–8)

Single flowers to 3 inches across, height 20–30 Inches, flowering midseason in May. Shades of pink, orange, red, yellow, often flushed, flamed or margined with a different color, and often contrasting bases. Tall, strong, long lasting, reliable. T. 'Pink Impression,' T. 'Red Impression,' T. 'Apricot Impression,' T. 'Dawnglow,' pale apricot; T. 'Golden Parade,' pale buttercup yellow; T. 'Golden Appledoorn,' golden yellow flowers, 14–18 inches; are suggestions

T. fosteriana and hybrids mainly derived from it (Zones 3–8)

Single, bowl-shaped flowers to 5 inches across, height 8–26 inches, flowering early April to midseason, in May. White to yellow or dark red, sometimes margined or flamed in another color. T. 'Orange Emperor,' carrot-orange flowers with yellow bases and lighter interiors, flowering in April, height 10–14 inches; T. 'Purissima,' pure white flowers in early or midseason, height 10–12 inches; T. 'Sweetheart,' ivory-white flowers with flames of lemon-yellow, deep yellow interiors with ivory-white margins, midseason flowering, height 10–14 inches; T. 'Candela,' produces large, pure yellow flowers in April, height 10–12 inches. All happy selections.

Greigii Group (Zones 3–8)

Comprised of T. greigii and hybrids mainly derived from it, this group has single, bowl-shaped flowers to 5 inches across, height 6–12 inches; broad, spreading, richly mottled, usually wavy-margined gray-green leaves; yellow to red flowers sometimes margined or flamed in a different color, and with contrasting bases. Usually early April if midseason May flowering. T. 'Plaisir,' a true pleasure, with carmine-red flowers margined in sulphur yellow, vermilion interior with sulphur-yellow margins, height 8–10 inches; bluish maroon leaves, an incandescent tulip, early- and midseason flowering; T. 'Sweet Lady,' peach-pink flowers with yellow-tinged greenish bronze bases, dark bluish maroon leaves, flowering April-May, height 8–12 inches. T. 'Dreamboat,' red-tinged, amber-yellow flowers with petals the color of peach sorbet, midseason blooms and dark bluish maroon leaves. Many more picks form the Greigii Group. Maroon foliage may be a challenge or a good match with plants you have.

Kaufmanniana Water-Lily Tulip (Zones 3–8)

T. Kaufmanniana and hybrids mainly derived from it. Single bowl-shaped flowers 1¼–5 inches across are often multicolored, frequently with distinctively colored bases. Early April or midseason flowering in May; height 6–10 inches. Their gray-green leaves are long, lance-shaped. T. 'Ancilla,' a tulip that looks like a water lily, its gentle pink flowers, flushed rose red, with red inner and outer basal rings, revealing a white interior with a golden center, blooming in early April, height 6–8 inches. The impression you get of a pink, white, yellow flower with green leaves is winsome. One of the earliest tulips to flower, T. 'Ancilla' is ideal for rock gardens.

Early-blooming tulips tend to be short-stemmed to protect them from the strong early-April winds. The later tulips, which appear after the daffodils, are taller, showier.

Tulips are Hank's most favorite flowers. Many men enjoy, like, and appreciate tulips. They usually pronounce them "two-lips," and I think the reason men like tulips so much is because they remind them of kissing.

José and I go through pretty much the same procedure planting tulip bulbs as we do daffodil bulbs, the same preplanting watering, the same preparation of the soil with compost, organic bulb fertilizer, blood meal, Epsom salts. Tulips like soil rich in humus, light in texture, well-drained, six hours or more of sun. Because tulips don't have contractile roots, we have to be sure not to plant them shallowly. We dig holes 10" deep to accommodate all but little short-stemmed tulips for which we dig holes 8" deep. We add humus and mothballs in the planting holes and lavishly sprinkle the holes and the tulip bulbs, after their beauty bath, with cayenne pepper, chili powder, dry mustard, and cheap stinky-winky talcum powder that make tulip bulbs less appetizing to mice, raccoons, rabbits, squirrels, and deer. We also sprinkle mothballs over and around tulip beds. We water and fertilize with the White Flower Farm's Daffodil Fertilizer after planting and fertilize again in the spring when tulip shoots push through the earth.

As a child, when I used to spend winters in Aiken, South Carolina, our tulip bulbs were kept some eight to ten weeks in the icebox, kept dry with a mix of sand and silicon, before they were planted in November, after Thanksgiving, when we would arrive. Tulips need a jolt of cold weather in order to bloom well. Without cold weather, or its icebox/refrigerator facsimile, tulips come up almost as squatty as crocuses. This is not a problem at Brillig. Our winters are cold. The tulips we have on the road bank and those leading into the grape arbor are thriving.

Successful tulips at Brillig include the slim, neat, elegant lady tulip, *Tulipa clusiana*, named by Charles de Lecluse, or, as he preferred the Latinized version of his name, Carolus Clusius. White with red stripes, a foot tall,

appearing in April, this lady tulip reminded Vita Sackville-West when she wrote her book *Some Flowers*, of "a regiment of little red and white soldiers…a Lilliputian army deployed at its spring maneuvers." Less like a lady, more like "a slim little officer dressed in a parti-colored uniform of the Renaissance." I planted some near a gray boulder dolphining up from the lawn near the vista area. Violets had reseeded themselves along the large boulder in such a way that they remained out of the lawnmower's reach. The group of *Tulipa clusiana* and wild violets with glossy heart-shaped leaves delighted me, just as Vita Sackville-West was delighted with another grouping around a "solitary huge boulder, a cushion of silence pressed against it, a few mauve violas blowing lightly a foot away, a dab of pink thrift, some blue lances of Gentiana verna, and there it is, complete…Just three or four square yards of minute perfection round that you could put a frame, detaching them from the sunny immensity and leaving them just as self-contained, self-sufficient." She wrote what I felt. What a treat to read her book, *Some Flowers*. [5]

I like what are known as Lily-Flowered tulips. Their six-pointed petals curling back on themselves are correctly called tepals and give these flowers their resemblance to lilies and stars borne on tall stems. T. 'China Pink' has soft pink, 3"-long sumptuous flowers on 16"–18" stems and is noted for its resistance to disease. I grew some in the cutting garden where they succumbed early on to attacks from rats and rabbits. The elegant flame-colored T. 'Ballerina,' another May bloomer, had a sweet, light scent, and petals/tepals that curved back sulphur yellow revealing fiery red insides. I grew those in the cutting garden also. I planted the 'Ballerina' tulips a year after Hank and I were married. After they had diminished and disappeared, to my amazement, a 'Ballerina' shot up a few years ago in the cutting garden's peony bed—a tulip reseeding itself. Without contractile roots, how did the bulb locate its proper depth? A horticulturist friend explained that a tulip seed, after being exposed to the cold winter temperature it needs to satisfy its dormancy requirements, germinates. In the spring, the seed leaf actively begins to grow. The seedling produces a hollow, underground stemlike apparatus called a "dropper." This "dropper" grows downward, dropping down eventually to produce a bulb at its tip, an inch or more beneath the surface. In four to seven years, new droppers yield bulbs deeper and deeper until the magic moment arrives and the tulip grows and flowers.

Once tulips have flowered and their blossoms spent, they should be deadheaded as seed production weakens the flower; unless one wants to save the seed. The 'Ballerina' that took all that time to spring up from a seed returned to flower for a year or two. I tried Tulipa 'Tarda,' a 6"-tall, white-and-yellow, star-shaped Lily-Flowered tulip by the forsythia bushes where it looked and smelled rather sweet, but somewhat strangely, like burned sugar. Caramel? I went away one weekend and when I came back, the 'Tarda' tulips were gone. Rabbits had eaten them. Until I could solve the rabbit problem, I gave up on tulips; that is, on planting more tulips.

Rather than plant tulips, I read about them. Researching their history, I became fascinated by them.

Where did tulips originate? Surprise—not Holland. The hardy single-colored scarlet, yellow, or white botanicals, which comprise the 120 or so wild species of the genus *Tulipa*, come from Asia Minor and the Mediterranean regions. They extend west into Spain and east into China's Tien Shan mountains, and into Japan. Horticultural consultant and garden writer Scott D. Appell says they have "an outstandingly wide geography," and that "there is a word for 'tulip' in practically every language in the world."[6]

The name "tulip" comes from the Latin *tulipa,* a Latinized corruption of the Arabic word for turban, *dulband,* signifying the shape of the flower. Because the Turkish word for tulip, *lale,* contains the same letters used in Arabic script to write Allah, the tulip was venerated by the Turks as a sacred flower symbolic of perfection and eternity, the most holy of flowers, a talisman of protection believed to be the only flower accompanying the Ottoman Turks as they swept westward from Asia into Europe. Tulips entered Europe in the sixteenth century from the court of the Turkish sultan Suleiman the Magnificent, and quickly rose to the status of royal favorites in English and Dutch gardens.

Tulips belong to the *Liliaceae,* or Lily family, which includes hostas, hyacinths, daylilies, and crocuses, as well as asparagus, onions, garlic, and chives. Many other bulbs and flowers are toxic, but tulip bulbs are edible. In the late sixteenth century, Carolus Clusius, a Flemish botanist who did more than anyone to popularize the tulip and describe, catalog, and understand the flower, sampled some tulip bulbs that had been preserved in sugar as sweetmeats, and declared them far tastier than orchids. Outside of Persia, tulip bulbs never caught on as delicacies, but they were consumed in quantities by the Nazi-threatened Dutch during the hungry winter they suffered at the end of World War II.

By the seventeenth century, the largest concentration of tulip enthusiasts could be found in the Netherlands. The Dutch merchant class and their backers were enormously better off than most of their contemporaries in England, France, or the Empire, and their riches fueled the acquisition of luxuries of all kinds, from magnificent houses to paintings to rare tulips, making possible the munificence of the Golden Age enjoyed in the Dutch Republic between 1600 and 1670. At this time, the most popular tulips were streaked red or pink on white petals, purple or lilac on white, or red, purple, or brown on yellow. The patterns, the feather and flame shapes and borders excited gardeners. To understand the tulip craze that followed, one has to understand how different tulip cultivars were from every other flower known to horticulturalists in the seventeenth century. Brilliantly defined, the tulips' colors were more intense than those of ordinary plants: red became incandescent scarlet; plum became a velvety shade of almost-black. A unicolored tulip one year that bloomed the next with an eye-catching array of colors, patterns, or stripes was said to be "broken" (broken away from its former image). "Broken" tulips, streaked with strong colors, were also referred to as Rembrandt tulips, as Rembrandt van Rijn and other artists were fond of painting them. The most highly prized were the "broken" varieties that displayed their contrasting colors in slender stripes that ran along the center of the edges of their petals, or in colored feathering as delicate as a dragonfly's gossamer wings. Because these superb varieties were scarce, they were coveted, expensive, and increasingly lucrative to grow. Choice bulbs served as currency when financiers speculated on tulip futures, and rare bulbs were traded for grand houses, large estates, and veritable fortunes, as bulb prices soared astronomically. The feverish boom in tulip trading, the hysterical obsession described as Tulipomania, lasted from 1634 until the crash in 1637 when the government forbade further speculation. By then, the Dutch had become so skilled in growing and hybridizing tulips that they offset domestic catastrophe by developing an export business that has enjoyed dominance in the international trade since 1650.

The irony of the tulip mania was that the most coveted tulips, the most elaborately or delicately colored, whose contrasting streaks and flares of pigment made each bloom a living canvas, were infected with a virus apparently unique to tulips. This virus caused the astonishing intensity and the variations in colors and patterns that collectors craved, yet at the same time weakened the bulb, cutting short the life of the tulip. The mystery of "breaking" remained unsolved until well into the twentieth century when the John Innes Horticultural Institution in London identified the aphid-carried disease, termed the mosaic virus, and celebrated its demise, the florists' equivalent of eliminating smallpox. The famed "broken" varieties of tulips and their successors, doomed to flourish for only a short time, have mostly died out. Only the

Rembrandt varieties available today are suspected of still harboring the mosaic virus, and it is advisable for reasons of health as well as for appearance and style to keep these bulbs away from larger hybrids. Today, flared and flamed tulips are produced by painstaking crossbreeding. The flower lover of Clusius's day had only a handful of species to enjoy, but now close to 6,000 different tulips have been bred, catalogued, and described. Among them are magnificent, large Darwin hybrids with a satin sheen, derived from crosses between *T. fosteriana* and *T. greigii* and the Darwin tulips; the lily-flowered tulips flowering in the late spring with long, pointed, graceful petals, or, properly, tepals; the late spring *Viridiflora* tulips, whose white petals are flushed with emerald green.

Many of the finest species and the ancestors of some of the most recent hybrids come from Russian Turkestan. They include *eichleri*, *fosteriana*, *greigii*, and *kaufmanniana*. Almost all of these cultivars originate from areas that have cold winters without letup, short springs with plenty of moisture from snow melt, and long, hot, dry summers during which the bulbs are dormant. Because rainy spells can rot dormant bulbs, many gardeners go to the trouble of lifting bulbs in summer and replanting them in autumn. Tulips require plenty of water in the springtime when they are storing food for next year's blooming, and in the autumn for root making. Some gardeners treat tulips as annuals, planting them in the autumn, pulling them up and composting them the following spring after the tulips have flowered. The season for tulips begins in March with the early-flowering species and is followed by the large cultivars that make a splendid display in April and May, especially if you underplant them with clear or royal blue forget-me-nots (*Myosotis*) or with blue grape hyacinths (*Muscari armeniacum*). If you love tulips, you'll find your own way to plant and cultivate them. Author Drew Riddle underplants his emerging tulips with leaf lettuce, not only a good companion to tulips, but also a source of fresh spring salad. This appeals to me, and I would like to have a few special tulips to gaze upon in our cutting garden's lettuce patch, such as archival, heirloom, and antique varieties recommended by Scott D. Appell in *Tulips*. Mr. Appell, a splendid lecturer and writer, mentions that the archival

Single Early 'Keizerskroon,' which dates back to 1750 in Holland, is available commercially to the home gardener; also the Single Early 'La Tulipe Noire,' the first "black" tulip, an heirloom introduced in 1891 (named in honor of Alexandre Dumas' romantic novella of the same title); and antique introductions, including the fragrant orange-golden Single Early 'Generaal de Wet,' selected in 1904.

To pore through the richness and variety of the colorings of tulips, some the color of fire, fruits, tethered tropical birds and exotic butterflies, "the lipsticks of the garden," Amos Pettingill, of White Flower Farm, calls them—I recommend the coffee-table-size picture book *Tulips*.[7] *Tulipomania*, by Mike Dash [8], offers a mesmeric account of the coveted tulip and the extraordinary passions it aroused. Local garden centers offer a good choice of hardy daffodil and tulip bulbs. Many bulbs are imported from Holland, where strict government controls mean only high-quality bulbs can be sold. For a greater variety of choices and for rare, unusual, and heirloom bulbs your grandparents probably had in their garden, these generalist bulb dealers are the top specialists in hybridizing and selling *narcissus* and tulips and have many cultivars from which to choose.

Chapter 2

Irises:
Those Reliable Bearded, Dutch, Siberian, and Japanese Beauties

May, the merry month. Bergen Evans, a lexicographer and philologist, told me that merry means to shorten time. "As Shakespeare wrote in 'As You Like It,'" he explained. "'Time travels in divers places with divers persons. I'll tell you who Time ambles withal, who Time trots withal, who Time gallops withal, and who he stands still withal.'" He went on to explain that the word *merry* was also associated with the word *thumb* because, in medieval times, men used to cut off their thumbs in order to cut short the time they spent soldiering.

I remember Bergen with love and gratitude as I look at beautiful bare spare trees flown through by cardinals and blue jays and goldfinches who perch on the feeder by the forsythia. I think of May as green-thumbed and galloping, the season of growth in everything.

"Growth in everything—

Flesh and fleece, fur and feather,
Grass and greenworld all together;
......
And bird and blossom well
In sod or sheath or shell..."

So wrote Gerard Manley Hopkins, a Jesuit, in *The May Magnificat*.[1] He also wrote: "May is Mary's month and I Muse at that and wonder why..." He was teasing, of course. He knew why. The Queen of Heaven has many names. She is Artemis, Astarte, Cybele, Diana. May, the month of summer's return, is her season. She presides over the May Day dances, and over the lighting of the Beltane fires. She is the May Queen or May-lady, the Lady of the Trees.

The walled garden, typical of a medieval garden where animals and intruders had to be kept out, is a metaphor for the Virgin herself, who is often shown in paintings enclosed in a garden. Flowers associated with the Virgin Mary[2] are intertwined with ancient lore and Roman and Greek myths. The Romans had scores of

Japanese *ensata* irises outside the cutting garden.

*I favor irises for their long-lasting vertical
blue-green leaves that continue to define
areas long after flowers have vanished.*

minor deities associated with gardening. My Latin teacher at Green Vale School, Mr. Green, used to remind us that despite their warlike behavior, the Romans considered themselves an essentially agrarian people. As a toast to Mr. Green (his real name, I cross my heart and swear to you) is a list of a dozen Roman gardening deities:

Insitor	God of seed sowing
Lactanus	God of crop vitality and growth
Libera	Goddess of vine cultivation
Mellonia	Goddess of beekeeping
Messor	God of mowing
Patelana	Goddess who protects young shoots
Promitor	God of fruition and the coming-readiness of crops
Puta	Goddess of pruning
Sarritor	God of hoeing and weeding
Segetia	Goddess of sprouting seeds
Seia	Goddess who protects stored seeds and seeds in the ground
Sterculius	God of manure

In mythology, a nymph resided in every tree. The laurel was sacred to Apollo in honor of Daphne who was transformed into a laurel to escape his advances. The anemone, poppy, and violet were sacred to Venus, the dianthus to Jove; the asphodel, crocus, and lily to Juno.

Early Christian missionaries adopted many customs and rites as well as symbols of other religions that were compatible with their own faith. Plants and flowers sacred to Venus, her Scandinavian counterpart, Freya, or her Teutonic doppelgänger, Frigga, became associated with Mary, as were plants and flowers formerly associated with Diana and Juno and the Teutonic Bertha and Hulda. The month of May, originally sacred to Flora, Roman goddess of flowers and spring, easily became May, the month of Mary.

Everything is greening and thriving in the freshness of this May day, though I feel as though I were floating in ice cubes. I used to be surprised to read classic descriptions of May Day when the weather seems always to have been warm, almost summery; then someone explained that the first of May fell two weeks later according to the Old Calendar, which perhaps is why in England the hawthorn, which was so dominant in the English landscape in May that it was called May, is often not in full voluptuous bloom until early June, although our early-flowering hawthorn is already whitening, its snowy candor breathtaking. An ancient magical tree, the hawthorn is associated with erotic love. On May Eve, Beltane night, you could revel in the forest and bring back hawthorn branches to hang over the door for protection, but hawthorn is considered so hallowed by witches, fairies, and spirits that you never thought of bringing it inside the house; "never even twitched a muscle to think of such a thing," my Scottish cousins told me when I was a young girl.

May is the great tree-month. Our honey-locusts are the latest to come into leaf. Along the driveway across from the great river of daffodils flowing toward our house and curving toward the cutting garden on our house's west, the willows are feathering into foliage.

There are birds everywhere. After our dead tree on which we hung bird feeders was uprooted by a storm, Austin, our caretaker, built a bird-feeder platform outside the dining deck. It's a simple construction made from a telephone pole sunk in concrete 4' below the earth, with a round wooden platform secured on top to which two birdseed feeders and a suet dispenser have been attached. Austin refills the feeders every day, and from sunrise at 5:45 a.m., fish crows, goldfinches, purple finches, white-throated sparrows, brown-headed cowbirds, starlings, mourning doves, boat-tailed grackles, a hairy woodpecker are eager to get at the suet; red-winged blackbirds, a catbird, a black-backed herring gull ferociously peck at the suet; one mature mockingbird and two juvenile mock-

Hawthorn bearing white blossoms for Easter time.

ingbirds, a pair of our resident mallards beak up fallen seeds. There may have been other birds, but that's the list I've noticed.

I've glimpsed a rufous-sided towhee scratching up grubs in the astilbe bed by the gateway path leading to the downstairs guestroom; a robin enjoying a bath in the small round birdbath on the ground in front of the fountain; cardinals and bluejays visiting the feeders on the west side of the house facing the swimming pool, and—great excitement—a migratory oriole enjoying half of a fresh orange as well as some grape jelly in a shallow bowl I've put out in the bird feeder at the end of the iris bed in front of the downstairs guest room. Cardinals and catbirds have also winged in for this treat. The bluejays prefer peanut butter, crumbled nuts, and raisins.

I go into the garden to check out the irises that will be at their peak in a few weeks. Instead of tulips, which I don't think go all that well with everything else at Brillig or don't seem to belong by the seaside as other plants and flowers do, I've gone in for irises at Brillig, irises in beds beneath the living room windows on the western side of the house, irises in a bed with Siberian irises in front of the downstairs guestroom facing the shallow end of the swimming pool, and irises also in a bed of Siberian irises facing the deep end of the swimming pool, both beds also on the western side of the house. In front of the cutting garden, on the north side, I have a border of irises and more irises in the vista area. I favor irises for their long-lasting vertical blue-green leaves that continue to define areas long after flowers have vanished. Tulips aren't as accommodating.

They bloom for a few weeks, and then they and their leaves are withered. You're supposed to leave those floppy leaves alone to soak up nutrients for bulbs to flower healthily the following year. Irises, I felt, were a far better choice than tulips for Brillig. In spite of the inconvenience of their withering, I had to have masses of daffodils. I also wanted masses of irises. With tulips, I felt that a small annual showing was all I could cope with, just enough to be a delight but not burdensome.

Our bearded irises with their basal fans of green-gray leaves are budding, and the beardless irises or *Iris sibirica*, Siberian irises, are already in bud, the white ones, white with yellow haft marks, 'Fourfold White,' 'Wisley White,' and 'Anniversary'; and the small clump of deep purple ones I was given and don't know the name of, which I've planted off to the side, close to a pine tree and a bank of hydrangea.

Siberian and other irises outside the steps leading to the pool.

The wild iris, the flag iris, which looks much like the Siberian iris, is said to have saved the life of the sixth-century Frankish king Clovis, who was trapped by the Goths at a bend in the Rhine River. He saw wild irises growing where he knew the water would be shallow enough for him to cross the river and escape, which he did. He then succeeded in conquering much of France held under the Christian banner. In gratitude, Clovis adopted the iris as his emblem, and it became the heraldic symbol for the kings of France. Irises embroidered on the banner of Louis VII during the Second French Crusade in the mid-twelfth century were called *fleur de Louis*, then *fleur-de-lis*, or *fleur-de-lys*, or *fleur-de-Luce*. The last spelling, connoting a flower of light, was adopted as my husband Henry (Hank) Luce's family flower. The iris, *fleur-de-lis*, though it was called, or a flag lily in my grandmother's day, is definitely not a lily of the genus *Lilium*, but a flower belonging to the Iridaceae family, with some 300 species and over 25,000 named cultivars.

Irises are sometimes called the "poor man's orchid." Their leaves are equitant, one astride the next higher one, "like a horseback rider," in Latin. The ovary is beneath the flower, as in flowers belonging to the Amaryllis family.

The flower is named for Iris, the messenger of the gods, as well as the rainbow linking earth with other worlds. The "iris" is also what we call the part of the eye that gives it its color and into which we look for recognition, perhaps glimpsing an expression that also is a kind of bridge between the known and the unknown. With its trinity of petal "falls," the flower was especially dedicated to the Virgin Mary as a symbol of her celestial queenship.

Irises are among the oldest known plants. The Egyptian pharaoh Thutmose III adorned his gardens with irises. The Romans carved iris motifs on their tombs. In Knossos, the Cretan palace of King Minos, there is a wall painting of a young boy in a field of irises in bloom. White irises, the color of mourning in the Near, Middle and Far East, are sometimes planted on Muslim graves. In imperial

Japan, irises were not on the approved list of garden flowers, a ban ingenious gardeners circumvented by planting irises on the roofs of their houses. That's why *Iris tectorum*, a species native to the Far East, is often referred to as roof iris.

Irises, hardy from Zones 4 to 9, are broadly classified as bearded or beardless, rhizomatous, or bulbous, and classified again according to their height as dwarf, intermediate, and tall. All irises have complex flowers composed of three large down-turning outer petals called falls, and three inner up-turning petals called standards. The falls sometimes are crested with a raised central ridge. The "beard" of the iris is the furze of hair filaments that emerges from the throat, the part of the falls closest to the center of the flower.

The stamens and pistil are hidden beneath the topknot of the three standards. Look inside the topknot and you'll see that the pistil divides into three straplike stigmas, under which are hidden their own pollen-covered anthers, which the stigmas try to avoid. On the throat of each lower petal is a velvet beard. The beard leads to the honey at its base. A bee, its back covered with pollen from the last flower visited, lights on the beard and pushes it way beneath the stigma strap. The stigma takes as much pollen as it can, and then springs up to avoid any of its own pollen, with which the bee will be newly loaded as it backs out. Because of this complex maneuver between bee and iris, irises never come true from seed and have almost endless color combinations, hundreds of tints, and mixtures of blue, lavender, purple, a violet so dark it looks black, pink, red, beige, white, orange, yellow, with an ornamental choice of ruffles, beards, and luscious dark and pastel falls.

Blooming in midspring, in Zones 3 to 9, miniature dwarf bearded irises are less than 10" tall, with 1½" to 2½" flowers. Standard dwarf irises grow 10" to 15" tall with 1½" to 2½" blossoms that flower a week later than the miniature variety. Intermediate and border varieties of iris

A tall bearded iris (*Iris germanica*).

include plants 15" to 28" tall with 2" to 4" flowers. Intermediates bloom in midspring, borders in late spring to early summer. Among the tall bearded irises, *Iris germanica* is a catchall category for the many hybrids that have *I. germanica* as an antecedent. Tall and striking with a slight fragrance, they grow upward of 28", are generally about 36" in height, with flowers to 8" across in late spring to summer. Less known, but of great value, are reblooming, or remontant, bearded iris, which come in many flower sizes and heights. They blossom in spring and blossom again anytime from midsummer to autumn.

The beardless iris group comprises *Iris sibirica*, or Siberian iris, one of the most trouble-free species, the flowers 2" wide on stems to 4' tall in late spring, hardy in Zones 4 to 9; *Iris cristata*, the crested iris, native of the woodlands of the southeastern United States, considered the best of the small irises, with yellow or white crested

Japanese irises and honeysuckle fronting the cutting garden's palisade fence.

ridges blazoning its blue flowers on 6" to 9" stems early to midspring, hardy in Zones 6 to 9; *Iris pseudocoros*, commonly known as yellow flag, considered in many areas as an invasive, is a waterside plant with sunny flowers radiant in any boggy, marshy, wet place where it flourishes and naturalizes as long as it receives full sun; and *Iris tectorum* or root iris, with lilac or white-crested flowers up to 6" wide.

Then there is one of my favorites, Japanese iris, *Iris ensata*, sometimes listed as *Iris kaempferi*, the largest-flowered of all the irises, with beardless blooms of many colors up to 10" across that blossom from early summer to midsummer on stems that can grow up to 4'. The rhizomatous group of irises refer to not only bearded irises with tuberous rhizomes (a rhizome is a thick, fleshy, elongated

root), but also to beardless irises with lots of small roots, growing points, and buds, characteristic of the Japanese, Siberian, roof, crested, and Louisiana varieties.

The bulbous iris group, Zones 5 to 9, comprises *Iris hollandica* or Dutch iris; *Iris bucharica* or Bokara iris; English, *reticulata*, and other types. Dutch irises, some of which are scented, naturalize early, rapidly forming large clumps. Both Dutch and Bokara irises make excellent cut flowers that can last up to two weeks. With bulbs set 4" deep, bulbous irises do best in well-drained, sandy soil. Flowering in spring or summer, they are heavy feeders, quickly depleting the soil of nutrients. They require lifting while dormant, every two to three years, and replanting in a new location. They are propagated by the removal and replanting of the qualities of small offsets that form alongside mature bulbs in autumn. *Iris reticulata*, known to open its buds above snow, begins to leaf and bud in March or April, and does best in rich, well-drained, slightly alkaline soil. If planted too shallowly, bulbous dwarf irises, blooming a few weeks later, produce many non-flowering bulblets. Any fertile, well-drained garden soil, other than heavy clay, is good for all bulbous irises. With the exception of *Iris cristata*, which prefers an acid, humusy soil (weed free, if you want the iris to naturalize), and light shade, all irises do best in full sun.

For the cultivation of bearded irises, add superphosphate and gypsum to fertile garden soil when planting. Soil should be easy to crumble. If soil is heavy, lighten it with sand or with wood ashes. Animal manure should **not** be used on bearded irises. Cow and horse manure tend to rot bulbs. To fertilize bearded iris, mix superphosphate and wood ashes together with a commercial fertilizer low in nitrogen and high in phosphorous for strong root development. ("With a first number lower than the other two numbers, and a second number higher than the first and third," I used to tell beginning garden helpers). To prevent overcrowding and to assure good bloom, tall bearded irises require dividing every couple of years. Plant rhizomes level with the surface of soil in well-drained, sunny beds. Tops should be visible. In very light, sandy soil, or in extremely hot climates, the rhizomes can be covered an inch or so; but in average or heavy soils, they should be left with their tops exposed and not covered with soil or mulch, in order to avoid rot. Although their main planting time is in June or July, after they flower, bearded irises can also be planted in the spring and autumn. Bearded irises are easy to grow, but they cannot tolerate wet feet, so you have to be sure that the soil is well drained. Although bearded irises prefer full sun, they will bloom if they get sun for at least half the day, preferably the morning sun. When planting rhizomes, be sure that the top of the rhizome is visible. Newly set plants need moisture to help their root systems become established; deep watering at long intervals is better than more frequent shallow waterings. Once established, bearded irises normally don't need to be watered except in arid areas. You can control iris borers with neem extract or beneficial nematodes, plus a thorough garden clean-up in autumn. You can control aphids with insecticidal soap or just plain dish-washing liquid-soap solution. **Problems:** Planting too deeply and overwatering can lead to fungal diseases, leaf spot and iris borers (*Macronoctua onusta*), the leading cause of iris death.

Cultivation of Siberian, Japanese, and other bearded irises? Most important is full sun. The yellow flag, *Iris pseudocorus*, and Louisiana irises require constant moisture. If they like the spot where they are planted, they will naturalize and can turn a beastly bog into a prospect of beauty. Siberian irises are tolerant of alkaline soil, but they prefer soil that is somewhat acid. They are heavy feeders and require plenty of fertilizer, rich compost, well-rotted manure, and plenty of

moisture. In contrast to some of their other family members, Siberian irises are untroubled by diseases and pests. When they become crowded, flower production falls off and flowers become noticeably smaller, so divide them in late summer or autumn. The roots can become so dense that this operation may require a lot of exertion with a garden fork to separate them. For Japanese irises, a moist but not waterlogged soil is ideal. When planting, incorporate plenty of leaf mold, peat moss, and rich compost in the soil for best results. Japanese irises require acid soil. **Never** apply lime, wood ashes, or bone meal to Japanese irises. In autumn, mulch Japanese irises with peat moss and leaves. In May or early June, apply a commercial fertilizer formulated for acid-loving plants. Japanese irises should be planted in early spring, before growth starts, or in late August or early September, after the blooming season. Crowns should be set about 2" below the surface. When dividing Japanese irises, which you should do when flowers become smaller and plants overcrowded, cut the leaves

White Siberian irises edging the steps leading to the swimming pool.

Yucca facing north across Fishers Island Sound.

halfway back, chop the rootstock in pieces that have three or four growths on each of them. Save only the young, vigorous portions, and do this work in the cool of autumn, in the shade, to keep the roots from drying out. I mist the rootstock lightly, lightly, and handle it with gentleness. Needless to say, plants, like children, appreciate and respond to being treated with tender, loving care.

The strappy leaves of *Lycoris squamigera* flourish and retreat into an unsightly disheveled state at the same time as the daffodils fade and wither. The beautiful Oriental pink poppies with their coal-black centers crumple into forlorn desuetude after they have reigned in beauty and splendor. Not so our Siberian, bearded, and Japanese irises. After their white, lavender-blue, and deep purple blossoms have faded, their upright basal fans of pale sword-shaped

leaves and the narrow, arching, bright green, grasslike foliage of the Siberian irises remain and provide texture, structure, and definitive borders until heavy frosts nip them ruinously. The Siberian, bearded, and Japanese irises we have are stalwart in the face of winds, salt spray, fog, and summer drought. Although they have a reputation of not liking to be disturbed, moved, or replanted after having been divided, our irises have come through all these events in good humor. None of them has ever suffered a disease or been plagued with insects. All of them have proffered welcome cutting flowers that are long lasting. Rabbits don't bother them, and they are only occasionally eaten by deer (See "Sources and Advice: Where to buy plants, seeds, garden furniture, pots and urns, both resin and clay, etc."). The American Iris Society has divisions devoted to each of the major types of iris and can be reached through the American Horticultural Society. ("See Sources and Advice: Where to buy plants, seeds, garden furniture, pots and urns, both resin and clay, etc.")

Yucca Plant

When it is young and new, the sword-leaved yucca looks like iris from a distance. Up close, its clumps of pointed leaves could be agave or aloe. A plant native to the American Southwest, yucca was used by American Indians as food as well as for medicinal benefits. The roots of yucca have a saponin content that has a soaping action. Often used to prevent erosion, yucca can be grown in sandy and alkaline soil. It grows wild by the roadside here and there on Fishers Island, is drought tolerant, loves the sun, tolerates a morning shower from our underground-based sprinkler system, endures winds, rain, cold, hurricanes, salt spray, fog. It requires almost no maintenance, and its gray-green leaves seem to be immune to all diseases and insect attacks.

In early July, yucca erupts in a cascade of ivory-white bell-shaped flowers, which look like giant lilies of the valley, and are even more dramatic and impressive when staked. Yucca stays in full bloom for about two weeks, a glorious fortnight, during which time it attracts small white butterflies, orange and black monarchs, yellow swallowtails, and black swallowtails.

Like most flowers that flourish in the wild, yucca doesn't do well when brought inside. Standing some 4' tall in a ceramic urn, or in a pair of galvanized iron containers weighted inside with stones, the flowering stalks look magnificent for an evening, then drop dozens of flowers. The next day, the stalks of yucca look mingy and moth-eaten.

We have a small grove of yucca on the right hand side of the driveway as you drive in, as well as five plants for sentinels along the path up from the beach by the railway-tie steps. We have a few more clumps of yucca on the left side of the driveway in the arbor area, and also close to the gateway of our neighbors, the Hanleys, who live in "the castle."

If you dig up yucca from the roadside, or buy plants at the nursery and replant them, yucca takes about a year to settle in, get acclimated, and then flower the following season. I like yucca for its texture and structure, and am wild about it when it is in full, magnificent creamy-white flowering.

I love white flowers. From mid-May until mid-June, our garden is dazzling with pristine, omnipresent white. March and April are rich in the yellows and gold of daffodils, the blues of *Scilla sibirica* and grape hyacinths, the scarlet of tulips. But May, like a bride is robed in sparkling white. There are sweeps of Siberian irises, white with their sunny yellow hafts. The hawthorns are foaming with white. The apple trees are blossoming with pale, pinkish white flowers. There are white rhododendron and white azaleas in the woodsy area we have called the Pit, ever since Hurricane Bob in 1991 blew down all the sumacs and other trees that comprised the little forest next to the vista area. We replanted, put in a nature path, and now the Pit is well wooded, planted also with azaleas, rhododendrons, angelica, buddleia.

The Cousa dogwood, the Asian dogwood, *Cornus Cousa*, is in shiny snowy bloom. Our large mock orange will soon be blooming with single white flowers that have an unimaginably sweet scent, a scent that used to intoxicate me as a child, and still does. "If I were a cat," I once said, "I'd roll around in mock orange instead of catnip." I remember saying that as a child, and I say it again to myself and smile.

Everything is so incredibly beautiful in May, green and fresh and lush with all the dazzling white around and about, a veritable tide of white. There are white peonies among pale silvery pink ones.

To my joy, the lilies of the valley are beginning to flower. Their proper name is *Convallaria majalis*, a name I

Siberian irises, pink poppies, and potted petunias by the steps leading to the swimming pool.

don't like to call them. To me, they will always be lilies of the valley. Snowy white bells with a delicate haunting scent, they bloom on 4" to 8" stems rising from furled fresh-as-spring green leaves. They have rhizomatous roots you can plant in early spring or autumn in rich, humusy, somewhat acidic soil in the light shade of trees or shrubs. If they like the spot they're in, lilies of the valley are an idyllic ground cover, spreading evenly, thickening at a steady pace over time. Wonderful. Hardy in Zones 2 to 7, they are easily cultivated. In midautumn or very early spring—around March is good—bury the fleshy potato-like roots, or rhizomes, so that the pointed tips or pips are near the surface in well-drained, humusy, somewhat acidic soil (the pH should be about 5.0 to 6.0); in light or dappled shade of trees or shrubs. Occasionally, you'll see a round, smooth red berry growing from a stem, a seed that is as poisonous as are the roots and the flowers of this beautiful and fragrant plant. I grew up seeing white-flowered lilies of the valley, and have now been exposed to the pink hybrids that I don't think can compare to the white-flowered lilies of the valley. I don't even think the scent of the pink variety is as enchanting. However, that's a matter of choice. What both varieties *do* share are their furled leaves that remain green and lovely after the flowers have faded. I'm all for flowers with long-lasting foliage.

The garden isn't really monochromatic. I'm overly aware, perhaps, of its springtime, May-time freshness, the tender greenery, the whiteness here and there and *there* and *there.*

Chapter 3

Hydrangeas

June. I wake at dawn to see the horizon opening the door to day. I slip my feet into sheepskin-lined moccasins, pull on a terrycloth wrapper, slide open the door of the upstairs balcony, and step outside into the misty air. The terra-cotta pots, in which the hibiscuses have been planted, have been weeded. The hibiscus leaves look fresh and green. The hibiscus buds are so plump I know they will flower soon.

Purple finches are at eye level on the branches of a pair of honey locusts growing in the driveway island, where the three hawthorns are frothing with white flowers. Austin will turn on the four-tiered fountain between the hawthorns and the honey locusts when he comes back from the village with the morning papers. We turn the fountain off at night, unless we want to sit outside on the white benches circling the honey locust tree trunks, talking, while we listen also to the fountain's sustained sostenuto. If we leave the fountain turned on unattended, a chance breeze may blow away the splashing water, the basins may run almost dry, and the fountain pump may burn out and the fountain go on the fritz, on the blink, or on the kibosh, in the terms of my father's vocabulary. This is parlance familiar to Harvard's Class of 1914, phrases I trot out for the pleasure of remembering my father, as mechanically disaffected as I am. Thank heavens for Austin, who knows how everything works and how to keep everything in good working order.

The fountain, from the time it was first set in place, is mystifying. Only black birds are attracted to it: starlings, boat-tailed grackles, brown-headed cowbirds, rusty blackbirds, blackbirds, red-winged blackbirds, grackles. I've asked Austin to fill all four basins with small beach rocks so that the birds can enjoy drinking and bathing in water no more than 2" deep. Any water over 2" deep, and the birds just perch on the rims of the basins.

Robins, catbirds, blue jays, mourning doves, cardinals, mockingbirds, sparrows, wood thrushes, and finches all spurn the fountain, whether it's splashing or still. They prefer smaller birdbaths on the ground or on pedestals or set on the low stone wall in front of the downstairs guest bedroom. Of course, the boat-tailed grackle (16.5"), the common grackles (11" to 13.5") and the crow (17.5") are bigger, but a robin (9" to 11"), a catbird (9"), a blue jay (11" to 12.5"), a mockingbird (9" to 11"), a cardinal (7.5" to 9"), a mourning dove (12") are all the same size or larger than the starling (7.5" to 8.5"), the red-winged blackbird (7" to 9.5"), the brown-headed cowbird (7"), the rusty blackbird (9").

If it isn't the size, what is the deterrent? Is the architecture of the fountain of less appeal than simpler, smaller, round shapes? Or is it the black birds' icterid familial

Their flowers look like airy puffs of dozens of small blue cup-shaped florets, yet are so heavy that they can bow down the stems that carry them.

clanship? Nanny used to say, "Birds of a feather flock together." But why so clubby that no other bird ever joins them? Whatever the original deterrent, the all-black icterid fountain club of 2003 accepted all who arrived for drinking or bathing in 2004, including nine mallard drakes and a female duck, given to swimming in the fountain's bottom tier for a few turns before she jumps out and makes her way to the ring of corn around the driveway's fountained island. Conspicuous at various bird feeders, catbirds, blue jays, goldfinches, wood thrushes, sparrows, the icterid clan of blackbirds, cowbirds, red-winged blackbirds, rusty blackbirds, starlings and crows also drink at the fountain as do robins, with some exceptions, they are enthusiastic and frequent bathers. I have yet to see a cardinal, blue jay, or mourning dove taking a bath.

Hummingbirds sip nectar from many flowers and enjoy light showers from garden sprinklers. Barn swallows and tree swallows visit neither bird feeders nor the fountain or other birdbaths. Jinking across the swimming pool, they dip their wings in the water and often rest on the living room roof in the wetness of the air conditioners' condensation that drains from a second-story gutter.

There are daisies growing on the bluff in an area between a lush strand of white rosa rugosa and the drifts of white and blue *Scilla sibirica*, white daffodils, tufts of strappy *Lycoris squamigera* foliage, all of which have passed their peak.

I see along both sides of the steps leading from the top of the bluff to the beach that the 'Stella de Oro' *hemerocallis* bearing bright yellow, sturdy, reblooming or remontant flowers are blooming on their lovely slender scapes. There are other daylilies or *hemerocallis* planted among them, and the walkway is already vibrant with color.

There are the beginnings of the muted deep reds, oranges, apricots, yellows in different hues of *hemerocallis* or daylilies in the castle-side garden as well as the urns of nasturtium seedlings, and the portable grove of brugmansia lined up along the brick path that connects the garage courtyard with the daylily bed—a great sweep of *hemerocallis*—and the walkways to the bench and the dining deck area. On the east wall of the house, the stand of hydrangeas is the fullest, the deepest blue of any we have. These hydrangeas get the early morning sun. They are partly shaded. Their soil is rich and acid. A pair of our resident mallards are resting by the hydrangeas beneath the dining deck. I make a note to myself to put out a bowl of popcorn as a treat for them tomorrow. Our pheasants are territorial. Our wild resident ducks go about together in twosomes, foursomes, sometimes eight or nine ducks and drakes together White ducks eat cracked corn circling the driveway's fountained island, they preen, often tweaking off their white breast feathers. Airborne or on the grass, these white duck-breast feathers are instantly beaked up in the nesting season by finches and sparrows who fly away with them clenched in their bills.

Among the lavenders and light blues of irises beneath my bedroom and balcony, pink poppies are flowering. Their shining black centers could be black-sequined bodices of pink crushed silk tutus left to air by elfin ballerinas, a wardrobe from the classic film *Fantasia*.

between the reproductive organs of flowers and people. Linnaeus explained that the "calyx is the bedchamber, the filaments the spermatic vessels, the anthers the testes, the pollen the sperm, the stigma the vulva, the style the vagina,"[1] (which caused a clergyman to protest that "Linnaean botany is enough to shock female modesty."[2] Both Carl Linnaeus and Bergen Evans were wordsmiths and had genius in their capacities for making complicated things simple. What I couldn't understand or didn't want to know or see years ago, I now hear in Francis Thomson's voice. In the purity of the early morning's cool Apollonian

Bachelor's buttons in the cutting garden.

The early morning is absolutely ravishing. Still in my terrycloth wrapper and sheepskin moccasins, I go downstairs and out into the cutting garden. All the flowers are delicate pinks, whites, blues in June outside the westside cutting garden, but inside the cutting garden, the scarlet poppies are hot as Francis Thomson's "swinkéd gypsies" in his poem *The Poppy*, "lethargies with fierce bliss," "drowsed in sleep savageries," each poppy breathing through its "yawn of fire."

Long ago, I was embarrassed, startled, when Bergen Evans told me that flowers are the sexual organs of plants. He told me that Carl Linnaeus, (1707–1778) the Swedish pastor who introduced a new way of classifying plants, had been the first, he believed, to cite the analogies

light the scarlet poppies have the surreal look of Dionysian erotica.

White daisies, red poppies, blue cornflowers. The spring straw hats of my childhood often had Della Robbia wreaths of these familiar cornfield flowers. Blue cornflowers, called bachelor's buttons because men so often used blue cornflowers for their boutonnières, are flowering with clear, happy brightness beneath the rosebushes in the cutting garden, masses of blue cornflowers, blue bachelor's buttons, crisp, fresh. As long as they are sedulously deadheaded, they will last all summer.

I agree with Page Dickey who advocates in her book relating garden to house, *Inside Out*,[3] that gardens extend from houses like outdoor rooms, rooms outlined by walls, fences, trellises, or hedges that screen one part of the garden from another, providing elements of surprise. The Moguls were masters of this magical element of surprise, and so was Gertrude Jekyll, who gave my grandmother one of her paintings, mixed flowers in pastel colors, in a craqueline container. My grandmother used to quote Miss Jekyll—"Her name rhymes with 'treacle,' Dear, not 'heckle,'"—that "What is hidden in a garden and what's revealed should be like yin and yang, a harmonious balance."

For simplicity, unity, and ease of maintenance, I like masses of similar plantings. Hydrangeas fill the bill. A dramatic revelation when they begin to flower in June, visually connected to the house, their large, fresh, glossy leaves also conceal pathways and the palisaded fence of the cutting garden as well as edging the beds of creeping juniper that flank two sides of our swimming pool.

Our 'Nikko Blue' *macrophylla* hydrangeas, the so-called common greenhouse or French variety, big-leaf mop-heads, also known as hortensias, native to eastern Asia, form mounded deciduous shrubs, 4' to 5' tall. Their flowers, described by the nursery they came from as "global inflorescences," look like airy puffs of dozens of small blue cup-shaped florets, yet are so heavy that they can bow down the stems that carry them. The *Hydrangea macrophylla* leaves, large as the name macrophylla implies, bright green, are deeply veined and make a design like a stick tree with swirling uplifted branches. The leaves look deceptively thick and leathery. They feel light and somewhat rough as they touch my bare arms as if children's chapped fingers were stroking me.

Until recently, hydrangeas belonged to the *Saxifragaceae* family, along with shrubby kin such as gooseberries, currants, mock oranges, as well as feathery astilbe and delicate coral bells. Horticulturalists have now shifted them to the *Hydrangeaceae* family, which includes 17 genera of shrubs, woody vines, and small trees. The garden hydrangea, originally named *Hortensia* by Philibert Commerson, a botanist who sailed with Louis Antoine de Bougainville on his circumnavigation of the world, was renamed in 1830 to become *Hydrangea macrophylla* (large leaved). The name "Hydrangea", given by Carl Linnaeus, comes from the Greek *hydro* (water) and *aggeion* (vessel). Some people believe that the name may refer to a lacecap hydrangea's saucer shape, or a *macrophylla* hydrangea's requirement for lots of water for the maintenance of its lush growth. Diana Wells, a scholar of horticulture and author of *100 Flowers and How They Got Their Names*,[4] a delightfully readable book, claims that a large hydrangea can lap up 10 to 12 gallons of water a day in hot weather. I'm sure that's true. When hydrangeas suffer from a lack of water, they droop pathetically, their flowers wilt, their branches take on the pallor of death as their leaves furl like *tuiles* to show only their pale undersides. Thirsty mop-head hydrangeas set up such visual clamor that I rush like the wind for a hose to give them the water they crave. Their plea to assuage their thirst is as demanding and as irresistible as that of a baby at midnight. From seeming near death, they recover with dramatic haste, often looking totally spectacular within a few hours, once more imperturbable and dewy, mirroring the bluest of skies among their lovely large leaves.

One of the amazing things about big-leaf hydrangeas is that some selections are able to bloom in a range of hues between blue and pink, depending on the soil pH. The concentration of free (unbonded) aluminum ions in the soil is the key to this anomaly. The availability of aluminum ions is related to the degree of acidity or alkalinity of the soil. More acid soil (pH 5.5 to 6) produces bluer flowers, and less acid, or alkaline, to neutral soil (pH 6 to 7) induces pinker flowers. We heap on the aluminum sulphate (1 pound for each square yard of ground area) and water weekly, using 1 level teaspoon of aluminum sulphate for each gallon of water to keep the soil acid and the 'Nikko Blue' *macrophylla* hydrangeas as intensely blue as possible. Aluminum sulphate, harmless to birds and animals, is a deterrent to snails and slugs. For pink hydrangeas—

'Rosea' is a good variety—you cultivate by applying wood ashes, about ½ to 1 pound around each plant, which also provides the nutritional benefits of potash.

Some mop-head hydrangeas remain adamantly blue or pink. Some blue hydrangeas turn a marvelous deep purple-blue. Some white hydrangeas blossom with pale-pink and lavender flowers along with their white ones. When I used to see a pink hydrangea among my 'Nikko Blue' ones, I'd ask the nearest garden helper to dig it up and replant it in the rich, acidic humus of the Pit, in the vista area. By the following year, the plant would be in blue flower and would be readmitted to the all-blue hydrangea hedgerow and kept blue by regular administrations of aluminum sulphate. But sometimes, when 'Nikko Blue' hydrangeas were ordered, a pink hydrangea would be included by mistake. So many pink hydrangeas accumulated that I had to find a place for them. Relegated to hedging a bank of white rosa rugosas just before our drive-

way entrance on the lawn-side of our property, with a large grouping of yuccas on their eastern boundary, and a buddleia and a tiny bed of dianthus on their western boundary, the pink mop-head hydrangeas are growing slowly and have ceased to bother me, now that they are grouped en masse. When any among them turn purple or bluish, I relocate them among the blues. We have a pair of white *macrophylla* hydrangeas in our vista garden, a 'Blue Wave' lacecap hydrangea on the eastern side of our entrance driveway, and a quintet of 'Blue Wave' lacecap hydrangeas hedging the south-facing palisade fence of the garage courtyard. Lacecaps have flatter, less mounded corymbs than mop-heads. They feature a central core of tiny fertile flowers ringed by rows of larger sterile flowers. Both the lacecaps and the mop-heads do best in well-drained, rich, humusy soil, partly shaded by background trees. Pines are ideal as the fallen pine needles help create the rich acid soil beloved by mop-heads that also helps

Lacecap hydrangeas by the garage courtyard.

Tree hydrangeas (*Hydrangea paniculata 'Grandiflora'*) by the downstairs guest bedroom.

them to keep the intensity of their blueness. Both lacecaps and mop-heads are cold hardy in Zones 6 to 9, and heat tolerant in AHS Zones 9 to 2.

We have a climbing hydrangea (*Hydrangea petiolaris*), cold hardy in Zones 4 to 9, heat tolerant in AHS Zones 9 to 1. By means of aerial roots, the climbing hydrangea, a decidous vine, scaled the brick wall behind the library fireplace and has now clambered over to adjoining shingle walls on either side of the brick wall. Happily, climbing hydrangeas harm neither brick nor shingled walls. As it established a strong system of roots, our climbing hydrangea was characteristically slow in growing for four years. But then, a scraggly 15" tall, yard-wide wannabe-hedge one year was transformed the fifth year by luxuriant growth and the production of lacy, white flat-topped flower clusters, looking like a mix of lacecaps and snowflakes, forming a white-flowering thick green banner that I am hoping will grow to its maximum height of 60' or more, carrying on up over the walls on to the roof and

maybe even to the roof's west-end chimney. In summer it flaunts its panicles of white flowers, and looks as well, if not better than English ivy, when its flowers vanish. In winter, after its leaves drop, the twists and tangles of its reddish brown exfoliating bark look attractive against the brick and weathered shingled walls. It does best in semi-shade, in rich, moist soil.

Growing nearby is a *Hydrangea paniculata 'Grandiflora,'* a panicled hydrangea, a treelike hydrangea some call a Peegee hydrangea. Native to China and Japan, our *paniculata 'Grandiflora'*—Peegee is too pejorative a name, I think, for this pleasant tree—bears large white flower clusters in inverted pyramidal panicles in late summer that change to pink, then bronze, lasting well into autumn—a small tree, 10' to 20' tall. Hardy in Zones 3 to 8, heat tolerant in AHS Zones 8 to 1, it prefers a neutral, slightly sweet, alkaline soil, with a pH of 6 or higher. It flowers on new wood or the current season's growth.

We tried an oak-leaf hydrangea (*Hydrangea quercifolia*), hardy Zones 5 to 9, heat tolerant in AHS Zones 9 to 1, some years ago. Its flower buds, like those of the macrophylla variety, form in the autumn. Owing to its unprotected eastern exposure, its buds were injured during a severe winter because we neglected to wrap the plant in burlap or straw and didn't mulch the soil heavily enough around it. Our other hydrangeas, mulched lavishly with leaves during the winter and sheltered more from the east winds, have generally survived the winters unscathed.

Hydrangeas, all varieties, are known to grow particularly well by the sea. They are tolerant of salt spray, fog, and winds. Although they do well in the sun, blue-flowered plants keep their color longer if they have the comfort of light shade. As I've mentioned before, pine trees are ideal companions for the blessing of their acid-rich pine needles. Some hydrangea species, such as *Hydrangea paniculata 'Grandiflora,'* bloom on new wood, and these plants can be pruned and shaped in early spring. **Not** so with the macrophylla variety. For lacecap and mop-head varieties, shape plants after flowering. With these, the buds originate near the tips of the canes formed the preceding year, and these plants should be pruned **immediately** after they flower, or not at all. Otherwise, one can unwittingly snip off the buds and get only a few flowers, if any, the following year. Allowing faded blossoms to cling through the winter helps protect next year's buds. I don't like the look of faded corymbs. I deadhead the withered flowers in August and September. To remove old flowers in the preceding autumn is less risky. I've had "helpers" who snipped off

dead flowers and the new buds as well in the spring. You can prune *paniculata 'Grandiflora'* hydrangeas in early spring before new leaves emerge. For both types, you can remove dead wood at any time during the year.

To keep mop-head hydrangea blossoms, pick partially dried, papery flower heads just before frost. Stand stems upright in a container, or hang blooms upside down until completely dried. Some people like to spray-paint the flowers silver, white or gold for decoration, and others like to leave them as they are for dried-flower arrangements.

Hydrangeas along the northern side of the pool.

. . . a sparkle of color as pleasingly bright as the sea diamonded by the morning sun.

Chapter 4

Geraniums and Pelargoniums

Our living room and my choice of plants for its tables and balcony have been a learning experience. Separated visually from the front hall by the "ship room," where Hank has a large model of a French channel boat with a red hull mounted on a table easily seen from the front door, the living room reaches all the way to the edge of the south-facing bluff. Its side walls are windowed. At the far end of the living room, sliding doors open on to a railinged balcony, which is cantilevered above the bluff. The furniture is upholstered in a plumbago-flowered cream-and-blue chintz that complements the changing blues of the ocean beyond and the sky above and doesn't distract from the views of the landscape on either side. In front of one of the sofas is my shell table, filled almost to the brim with nautilus shells, tritons, tridacnas, conchs, murexes, sand dollars, sea urchins, cockles, and seashells of every shape and size that I have collected on my travels and lugged back with me in baskets, tin trunks, and duffel bags.

The shell table has style. Simple yet sumptuous, it enhances the simplicity and airiness of the living room with its space flown over by a life-size wooden sculpture of a gull suspended from a high ceiling beam. Layered and mounded in the table, the shells blend together, ivory and pinky beige; touches of brown, green, yellow, black, rusty red, and lavender are hardly noticeable at first glance and

don't provide the accent of color or adornment—something simple but decorative—the living room requires. I tried blues—hydrangeas, delphiniums, platycodons. I tried other flowers. I tried picking up on the red of the model channel boat's hull with red roses from the cutting garden. Neither always available nor particularly reliable, the roses weren't really right. They were the wrong shape and texture—too soft, the wrong red, too dark. Flame-red hibiscuses in pots were perfect when they were in flower, but I never could be sure when they would flower.

What to do when neither roses nor hibiscuses were flowering? Going against everything I thought I believed, I poked some red silk fake geraniums (pelargoniums) I'd found at the island's Our Lady of Grace Church's weekly rummage sale into pots of hibiscus and hoped no one would notice anything except agreeable flecks of the same intense vermilion we see every night as the sun drops beneath the horizon across Fishers Island Sound.

Other than roses, I'd always thought I didn't like red flowers, certainly not red geraniums (pelargoniums). Contrary to what I'd thought, there obviously is a place and a setting for all sorts of flowers. In the living room, looking out to sea, the blues of the sea, sky, sofas, and chairs refine the reds of the flowers, transforming the garish to a sparkle of color as pleasingly bright as the sea diamonded by the morning sun. It was an easy step from fake pelargoniums to real ones.

I massed them in terra-cotta pots with terra-cotta-colored plastic saucers on side tables, plonked them in a Hawaiian cachepot, given to Hank by his stepmother Clare Boothe Luce, that was made from a gourd the size of a pumpkin posited in the center of a large square table spread with magazines, massed them in terra-cotta pots on the balcony with the same size pots behind them filled with flame-red hibiscus for the hummingbirds and boats passing by to enjoy, and also planted tall flame-red hibiscus standards in urns on the patio off the ship room where they can be seen from the living room.

This geranium(s) pelargonium(s) business is to reassure you, and myself—and to honor the memory of my grandmother who cared deeply about correct nomenclature—that I have finally come to know the true genus for what I have mistakenly called geraniums most of my life. My grandmother would say to my cousins, "Kids are not children. They are baby goats. Please try to speak correctly." To me she would say, "It's not cotton easter, my precious. It's co-to-ne-as-ter. Remember that every vowel in botanical Latin makes a new syllable. And you're right, darling, it *is* CLEM- a- tis, not cle- MAT- is as some people say. But better a mispronounced name than an incorrect common one. Miss Jekyll said that people who sell flowers often refer to certain bulbs as belonging to the genus Amaryllis when they should know they belong to the genus Hippeastrum. Remember to look things up, darling."

I have abided by her advice, which is how I've discovered that the name "geranium" was actually in use long

before the flowers that we call geraniums were known in the West. The wild or garden geranium, the cranesbill, was named by Dioscorides, author and physician to Anthony and Cleopatra. The term derived from the Greek *geranos* (a crane), suggestive of its long, beaklike seedpod that looks like the bill of a crane.

The flowers we colloquially call geraniums actually belong to the genus *Pelargonium* in the botanical family *Geraniaceae*. As plants have been widely hybridized, crossed, and recrossed, their ancestry is bedimmed. Their bloom time is summer until frost, hardiness USDA Zone 10, height 12" to 20", spread 12" to 20", colors white, pink, red, peach, lavender, and patterned with these colors. They need sun, moist and well-draining soil. Their legacy of botanical misunderstanding began when Meinheer Jan Commelin, director of the Hortus Botanicus in Amsterdam, came upon a plant growing on the Cape of Good Hope, which he called a geranium and which he introduced to Europe in the early 1600s. In 1772, Francis Masson, an English botanist, sent hundreds of species of this South African plant back to the director of Kew Gardens, Sir Joseph Banks, calling them "geraniums," as had Commelin. By 1787, when Charles Louis l'Héritier de Brutelle, a French botanist, published *Geraniologia*, South African geraniums were so mani-

fold that he invented another genus for them that he called Pelargonium, or "stork's bill," from the Greek *pelargos* (a stork), with reference again to the shape of the plant's seedpod. He divided the geranium family (Geraniaceae) into three: the cranesbills, both wild and cultivated, which kept the name Geranium; the rock-plant Erodiums (from the Greek *erodios*, a heron); and the Pelargoniums, which are the South African "geraniums." However, by the time the proper nomenclature got sorted out, the name "geranium" was firmly attached to the hundreds of

Potted scented geraniums (pelargoniums) and large potted hibiscus outside our guest bedroom patio.

flowers that are offspring of species that originated in South Africa, and which most people (other than horticulturists, and those who prefer not to misspeak) continue to call geraniums. (I, until recently, was among them.)

Now that I hope all this is clear, I will write about geraniums when I mean the original, true geranium or cranesbill that comprises a large family of hardy plants that flourish in a sunny place and in well-drained ordinary garden soil. Easily propagated by seed, their pods have a clever trick of throwing seeds far and wide, so that they also naturalize with no difficulty. They are perennials, which means that they can be left in the ground to bloom, die back, and bloom again, year after year.

Pelargoniums, on the other hand, are annuals. If you want them to winter over, you have to bring them inside before the first frost. Otherwise, they shrivel to yellow, turn black and die with no possibility of resurrection after the frost hits them. Pelargoniums are the ones you see in window boxes all over the world. All pelargoniums have a scent, some intensely aromatic, some pungent, others with a strong, sweet fragrance.

It took more than a century before pelargoniums made their way to North America. By the late 1800s, there were more than 150 varieties described in catalogs, treasured for their use as flavorings in jams, jellies, confections, and beverages, and as fragrances in potpourris, sachets, colognes, and soaps.

The red pelargoniums on the living room balcony are the ordinary sort you can buy in the supermarket. Since they turned out to be such a success, I got dozens of white pelargoniums to put with lobelia in urns by the front entrance beneath a cluster of apricot-colored hibiscus. Other white pelargoniums I mixed with ivy and white petunias and used in square planters flanking the outside steps to the dining deck on the south side of the house. The common white and red pelargoniums have been an unexpected yet ideal choice, both indoors and out. They withstand wind and salt spray. They are hardy, easy to grow, don't attract aphids or other pests, produce lots of leaves and bloom continuously from May to November. In the dozen years I've had them, I've never yet seen a seedpod from which their genus name derived. However, they are simple to propagate by cuttings taken in autumn and spring. There are innumerable hybrids, cultivars, and species, and dozens of fancy-leafed ones with markings, colors, shades, and shadings from which to choose, but for where I have placed them, all I feel like having are simple white ones, simple flame-red ones, and some peach-colored ones.

We overwinter our indoor and outdoor pelargoniums in the living room that, emptied of furniture, becomes a cool (60°F) storage area or make-do greenhouse. With windows on two walls and a French door on the south-

Johnson's blue geraniums (pelargoniums) in the vista.

facing wall, there is adequate light and sun for plants to go dormant or keep their leaves or flower as the jasmine and some of the amaryllises do, so all works out well. In the vista garden I thought I would try an Iberian cranesbill called *Geranium cinereum* var. *subcaulescens ibericum,* 'Johnson's Blue.' A perennial, I thought I'd have no trouble having it grow like a thicket among Oriental lilies and white irises. However, the north wind crushed our 'Johnson's Blue' geraniums, demolished them to the point that perennials became annuals after one season. Now that I have planted a backdrop of white phlox, more Asiatic and Oriental lilies, more irises, I think we have a better windscreen for them and shall try again to grow them. From the vista garden, across the road, the vista is Starfish Point, an area overgrown with rosa rugosa, ampelopsis (porcelain vine), and brambles.

In the Geraniaceae family, scented-leaf pelargoniums were a good choice for two areas: the downstairs guest room's patio and the brick patio off the "shiproom" where two standards of flame-red hibiscus are planted in urns. The plant forms, growing from 1' to 4', and the leaf shapes, are variable. Hardy only in USDA Zones 10 and 11, scented pelargoniums are tender perennials to be over-wintered indoors, or treated as annuals. Some can grow 7' tall, but most top out at 1' to 2'. The flowers that bloom in June and July are sparse and small, each about the size of a snap fastener on an old-fashioned baby's dress, and appear as flecks of white, pink, rose or lavender among leaves that may be crisp, smooth or velvety. Their scent is a mild version of the surrounding leaves. It's the underside of the leaf that releases the embedded fragrance of long-lasting oils for which each pelargonium is known and named. The full scent is given off when the leaves are gently stroked, rubbed, or brushed against. There are more than fifty types of pelargoniums with a rose scent, of which the most popular is rose geranium. The best known is *Pelargonium graveolens,* rose geranium, sweetly scented, with gray-green crenate leaves and rose-pink flowers with a dark-purple spot in the middle of the upper petal, introduced into England in the eighteenth century from South Africa. Its sweet rose fragrance is an addition to any fragrant potpourri as well as kitchen use for rose-flavored cake and apple jelly. From the eighteenth century, it was a good cook's knowledge that when a jar of apple jelly was filled, the delicious fillip of a leaf of *Pelargonium graveolens* was an enchanting finishing touch. *Pelargonium capitatum*, 'Attar of Roses,' is another top choice among the rose-scented geraniums. Its three-lobed light-green leaves are soft and furry, its flowers bright pink. *Pelargonium graveolens*, 'Lady Plymouth,' is slow growing but develops into a shrublike plant with leaves suitable to perfume your bath or scent your pillowcase. *Pelargonium graveolens*, 'Gray Lady Plymouth,' has creamy bordered, silvery-green leaves, which possess the warm rose scent of old-fashioned rose geranium. As it may revert to all sage green, clip out any errant shoots. It's good in potpourris and bouquets of cut flowers. *Pelargonium crispum* 'minor,' the finger bowl pelargonium, has a tart lemony scent, tiny crinkled leaves and pinky-mauve flowers. Introduced from South Africa to England in 1774, its pungent leaves were floated in Victorian times in crystal finger bowls to cleanse and scent the fingers, a practice still observed to this day. The leaves are splendid for bouquets and cooking. *Pelargonium crispum*, 'French Lace,' has lemon-scented variegated (green and white) leaves. *Pelargonium crispum*, 'Prince Rupert,' has a robust lemon fragrance, vigorous growth and pale lavender flowers. *Pelargonium odoratissimum*, introduced from South Africa to England in 1724, applescented, is deliciously fragrant with velvety, ruffled glaucous leaves, white flowers, trailing stems. *Pelargonium quercifolium*, oak-leafed geranium, is a rangy, shrubby plant. Its spicy, peppery scented leaves excel as garnishes for salads, fish and meats. *Pelargonium tomentosum*, peppermint geranium or woolly pelargonium, has large-lobed, velvety light green leaves that smell like peppermint candy canes, and purple-veined white flowers. *Pelargonium denticulatum*, 'Filicifolium,'

The common pelargonium, colloquially called a geranium.

is a fern-leaf type with a refreshing pine scent. *Pelargonium x fragrans*, 'Nutmeg,' has a particularly captivating fragrance. The wavy leaves are small and grayish green. It is a creeper or, if in a container, a trailer, ideal for indoor flower arrangements. I'm not one for hanging baskets of flowers, but if I were, I'd put in a few *Pelargonium x fragrans*, a late eighteenth-century hybrid that originated in Germany's Berlin Botanic Garden. Its graceful stalks are tipped with clusters of white flowers. Other scented geraniums smell like eucalyptus, cinnamon, ginger, chocolate peppermint, apricots, strawberries, oranges, limes, coconut, even citronella. One of the types that is not for eating, Skeleton Rose, a Pelargonium cultivar also called 'Dr. Livingston,' contains almost 100 times as much citronella as an over-the-counter citronella insect repellent. The scent is lemony rose; the flowers are pale lavender speckled with purple.

Scented pelargoniums, or scented geraniums as some nurseries persist in calling them, make great houseplants. Just brush your hand lightly across them as you walk by—

Potted geraniums (pelargoniums) flower in abundance, indoors and outdoors, from spring through autumn at Brillig.

instant aromatherapy! They rarely produce the long pointed seedpods that evoked their genus nomenclature, but like my common red and white pelargoniums, my ones with scented leaves are easily grown from cuttings. An annual or tender perennial in Zones 9 to 11, they are great candidates for growing in containers. They prosper in sunny locations in evenly moist soil. When older leaves turn yellow or autumn-leaf red, I nip them off—daily, for that matter. Pelargoniums really do well if you take the time and effort to groom them as often as possible. Their delicious scents make this hands-on aromatherapy relaxing, pleasing.

To care for pelargoniums, you should grow them in a good soil-based or soilless potting mixture with a soil pH adjusted between 6.0 and 7.0, with some added organic matter, such as well-rotted cow or horse manure or compost. At planting, add some all-purpose dry fertilizer. Fertilize containers every two to four weeks during spring and summer with a balanced fertilizer. Most organic fertilizers are good. José likes to use fish emulsion. You deadhead by cutting not only the flower but the entire flower stalk back to the main stem. Never let the container become dry as dust, bone dry. In hot, dry weather, you may have to water them twice a day.

Pelargoniums grow best with at least some direct sun. Our living room pelargoniums, our pelargoniums growing between the downstairs guest room patio's pink hibiscus and the stonewall behind the bed of Siberian iris on the bank of creeping juniper, and our pelargoniums by the shaded front steps, one in full sun, one in partial-light shade, and our pelargoniums in pots by the sliding door leading from the downstairs guest room on to its roofed-over open patio lined with hibiscus all do well. The potted pelargoniums by the downstairs guestroom door only get the slanted rays of the late-afternoon sun, and yet they are healthy, leaves green, peach-colored flowers a lovely color. All our pelargoniums in containers seem to be extraordinarily adaptable, adjusting to fog, wind, and salt spray with robust imperturbability.

I'm aware of all sorts of fancy-leafed pelargoniums with chartreuse, bronze, gold, and patterned leaves, cultivars with blooms like small tulips, rosebuds, and carnations, dwarf and trailing cultivars, pelargoniums with flowers that have strappy petals and the white flowers of 'Arctic Star' that have petals that look like a mix of dogwood and lilies, and some with leaves easy to mistake for coleus, others with veining in their leaves caused by a microorganism that gave them the name of 'Crocodile.' I'm more interested in acquiring new scents or another old favorite, such as 'True Rose,' 'Rose-Scented Geranium,' *P. graveolens*, advertised in Logee's Greenhouses catalog as a cherished vintage rose, which traveled across the country with the pioneers. "It remains a favorite ideal for potpourri and rose cake." How can anyone resist that? (Full sun, grows to 12" to 18" in container, minimum temperature 35°F, requires cool night temperatures below 60°F to bloom, blooms in spring and summer.)

Many friends and visitors ask for a cutting of a scented pelargonium, and I'm always happy to cut a piece, wrap the stem with a wet paper towel, and enclose it in a Ziploc plastic bag for them to take away, knowing that propagating pelargoniums is wonderfully easy.

All you do is take stem cuttings any time you feel like doing so. Each piece should be about 2" to 4" long, with a node, or leaf joint, at the bottom. Take off the lower leaves and any flower stalks, and poke the cuttings an inch deep into a pot of potting mix, perlite, a mixture of one part sand and one part peat moss, or a mixture of one part peat moss and one part perlite. Whatever medium you choose, press it firmly into a container. A plastic pot 5" in diameter can hold five cuttings. Use a wider pot to hold more cuttings. You don't even have to use a rooting hormone. Just keep the mix moist but not soggy, and keep the cuttings in an airy sunlit area but out of direct sunlight, hot sunlight. Within two or three weeks, the stem cuttings will have rooted and you'll see new growths on the stems. You can then pot up the cuttings individually. For each cutting, half-fill a clean 4" pot with fresh potting mix. Carefully dig up each rooted cutting with an old kitchen fork and place it in the pot. Gently press additional potting mix around the roots, water the pots and place them in a bright area out of direct sun for a few days to let the plants recuperate. Then move them to a sunny windowsill. When more leaves appear, begin a monthly feeding program with liquid houseplant fertilizer at **half the recommended** strength. When the plants have grown about 5" tall, pinch out the tips to encourage the growth of side shoots. Be sure to keep the potting medium moist when you move the pots outside and accustom the cuttings gradually to direct sun for a week or so.

If you overwinter pelargoniums as we do, water them when the soil feels almost dry. (Pelargoniums will rot if overwatered.) They may look rather leggy by spring. Wait until warm spring weather, cut back the plant severely, repot, and fertilize. You can use the cuttings to start new plants. José lets some of the cuttings develop roots in old glass honey and jelly jars filled with water, and then plants them directly in pots, ensuring us a generous annual supply to keep or give away.

Chapter 5

Pinks

The way Hank works a room at cocktail parties, chatting with everyone he knows, exchanging remembrances, catching up on what's going on at the moment, is the way I walk about the garden in the early morning in June.

A cock pheasant with a sweeping tail is up as early as I am, guarding and guiding his harem of four hen pheasants who are timid and easily spooked until they have baby chicks to guard and guide, which they won't have until July or later. That is, if they can keep eggs and chicks safe from feral cats and raccoons. At the moment, the cock pheasant proceeds across the lawn edged by the driveway in a continuous, even, flowing legato gait. The hen pheasants twitch and flitter as they follow. Happily, no red-tailed hawks, which can pounce on a hen pheasant and carry her off, just like that, are anywhere to be seen.

I am conscious of breathing, of feeling alive, of meditating, dreaming, planning, enjoying looking at the bluff where there is an artful carelessness about the way cultivated plants, like the white rosa rugosa, merge with invasive *Ampelopsis* (porcelain berry) a vigorous grower that is ideal to shore up the bluff and cover the cement and rock foundation beneath Brillig that people used to call "a bunker," now a jungly mass of ampelopsis and wild honeysuckle, with a few mulleins spiring up along the edges.

Three female mallards and nine baby ducklings are swimming close to the beach.

In the containers on the inner dining deck for the kitchen herb garden, there is a gentian-blue flower blooming in a pot of borage. Borage is a plant said to have antidepressive virtues, a cordial plant "to expel pensiveness and melancholy." As a sprig was often infused in wine for medicinal purposes, perhaps the wine increased its "cordial" effect.

Borage is the same bright blue as bugle weed, or bugloss, which grows seemingly everywhere in part-shade, its flowers a favorite of Hank, and pleasing to me as well as when I see it growing beneath evergreen or elsewhere. It is an attractive, although rather tall, ground cover that is also said to possess antimelancholic virtues. Bugle weed is a vulnerary herb, guaranteed to cure any wound with an infusion made from boiling its leaves, or even with just an application of its leaves themselves, uncooked.

Our pink and flame-red tulips are still blooming. In the Pit white azaleas are still in bloom, along with a small pink azalea we were given by a friend. The white flowers of the shiny-leaved rhododendrons in the same area have peaked and are now somewhat droopy and limp. Azaleas and rhododendrons were recommended to me when I first

I loved pinks in my childhood, and
my heart still lifts when I see their fringed
petals and smell the delicious clove-
vanilla spiciness of their scent.

came to Brillig as plants that did well by the sea, which they do, with few or no maintenance problems. They thrive in gentle sun or light-dappled shade, in wind-protected, well-drained, moist, humus rich, acidic soil, and are hardy in Zones 5 to 8. Ours are planted in a wind-protected area, and we mulch them in the winter. In the wild, woody area where they are growing, we have a birch tree; five buddleias in different colors, Black Knight, a deep purple; others that are light mauve, white, lavender, which we just let grow, pruning them only when they become gawky and graceless. In this overgrown coppice we also have marsh mallows, naturalized *Angelica archangelica* and *Angelica gigas*, as well as sumac, wild cherry, and shad, or serviceberry (*amelanchier*). There's a nature path, but its an area we let grow wild, more or less, cutting down a strangler vine, or doing a bit of weeding, but not much more than that.

Springtime rhododendrons along the vista's nature path.

One weed I instinctively uproot and get rid of is Woody Nightshade, *Solanum dulcamara*, a trailing, raggedy-looking plant with red berries and small purple flowers, commonly found in bushes, hedges, and brambles. Our garden helpers used to insist that it was called Deadly Nightshade. Not so. Deadly Nightshade, *Atropa belladonna*, has broad oval leaves, large, purply-brown foxglovelike flowers, and is rather rare. The berries of both Woody Nightshade and the Deadly Nightshade are poisonous, as are their stems and leaves. Black Nightshade, with white flowers and black berries, is more poisonous than Woody Nightshade, but by no means as powerfully and lethally toxic as the real Deadly Nightshade. The family of Nightshades, *Solanaceae*, includes the toma-to (*Lycopersicon esculentum*) and the potato (*Solanum tubero-sum*), the Jerusalem cherry (*Solanum psuedo-capsicum*), and the Chinese lantern plant (*Physalis alkekengi*). Potato seeds are poisonous, and the element of poison that lurks in the Nightshade family also develops in the green of sunburned potato tubers. Among the cousins of this large family are petunias, jasmine, tobacco, *Nicotiana alata*, *Datura fastuosa alba*, *Nierembergia*.

The hostas in the garage court-yard and along three of the cutting garden's palisade fence walls are lush and green. White and purple violets are flowering in the vista area and in the little driveway garden in front of the downstairs guest room. They are not Parma violets, but they have a delicious scent. Every time I see the violets in the vista garden I am enamored of them as a beautiful, ornamental ground cover. Their large, glossy, deep-green, heart-shaped leaves are charming, with or without flowers. And our violets self-sow with abandon. Before mowing the grass, José instructs his helpers to dig up the violet seedlings and replant them. The cost of violas, as they are listed in catalogs, can be as much as $10 a plant, and here we lucky ones are, with dozens of new seedlings, seemingly every other week. Easy to grow, abundant, extravagantly self-sowing, healthy violets—I find it difficult to think of them and pansies as violas—are a thoroughly satisfying success at Brillig. They like light shade and humus-rich soil, slightly acidic. Nearby, both pink and white bleeding hearts (*dicentra*) are doing well, newly in flower. Columbines are budding. Most elegant of all American wildflowers, an imported native of England, columbines are classical beauties unrivaled, I think, in their delicacy, their colors, like wine called white though yellow combined with lavender, or purple, or blue, or coral, or carmine. The common columbine name and the botanical name, *Aquilegia*, refer to the shape of their flowers, suggesting in one case, the form of a dove, and in the other, the talon spurs of an eagle. Columbines like humus-rich soil, no fertilizer; they self-sow a little, and are frequented by hummingbirds when they flower. Irises are budding and flowering. I tell them how beautiful they are. Exquisite. Exquisite. Exquisite. The wisteria in a container by the downstairs guest room is blossoming, as are the small, young, new ceanothus bushes beneath the south-facing downstairs guest room windows. Silvery pink peonies are flowering in the cutting garden, and I pick an armful of sumptuous white peonies for the dining room table centerpiece, a four-legged wooden bowl Hank and I brought back from a vacation in Fiji. The white rosa rugosa is in bloom, as is the large mock-orange bush (*Philadelphus coronarius*) in the garden. The new young *Philadelphus coronarius* plants in a bed along the driveway

Springtime violets are a wonderful ground cover.

look scraggly but are budding with a few fragrant flowers. They grow best in full sun, in well-drained soil. I've been told not to fertilize them if I want them to flower. Hardy in Zones 3 to 7, enticingly fragrant, *Philadelphus coronarius* can grow to 9' tall. Only the bush in the garden has done well. The other plants we have tried have been slow to grow. The new ones we put in last year have taken hold in the bed where we have planted them, but they look skimpy. I think our hot and occasionally humid summers exhaust them. Perhaps the hybrid, 'Buckley's Quill,' with double flowers, growing to 6', hardy in Zones 5 to 8, would do better. I shall try it next year. Our low-growing *Potentilla* (cinquefoil) hedge, growing about 2' tall and wide, a tough native plant, tolerating poor, dry soil, bordering the east side of the Pit area, is in flower. Said to do best with full sun, light shade, moderately fertile, sandy, well-drained soil, our shrubby *Potentilla fruticosa* with five-petalled white flowers just over an inch diameter and gray-green foliage, hardy in Zones 3 to 7, AHS 7 to 1, does all right, but isn't all that wonderful. Perhaps the *Potentilla* and the *Philadelphus coronarius* would perform better in colder areas. I like to give plants a chance to adjust, acclimatize, but I like them to do well, not just struggle.

~ ~ ~

Our three hawthorn trees are in frothy white flower in the driveway island next to the fountain. They are beginning to carpet the driveway with their petals. The pink poppies are flowering along the far side of the wall in front of the downstairs guestroom, along with the early-blooming lavender-blue iris. The Japanese ensata irises won't be in flower until July. Honeysuckle that has no scent and that was in place when I arrived at Brillig, is flowering in the cutting garden. An attractive coral color, its lack of perfume distresses me because I love the smell of honeysuckle, but happily it attracts hummingbirds with its nectar.

I wander down to the vista garden where I have a minuscule garden of pinks close by a buddleia bush and a hedge of pink hydrangeas that flow behind a large yucca

Many varieties of sweet- and spicy-scented pinks (dianthus).

bed and above white rosa rugosa bordering the island road. I loved pinks in my childhood, and my heart still lifts when I see their fringed petals and smell the delicious clove-vanilla spiciness of their scent.

Pinks (*Dianthus plumarius*), with blue-green foliage and a clove scent, feathered pinks, antique border pinks, old-fashioned grass pinks, star pinks, pheasant's eye pinks, cottage pinks, garden pinks, snow pinks, maiden pinks, cheddar pinks, call them what you will, are ancient flowers that belong to the *Caryophyllaceae* family and to the same genus as Sweet Williams (*Dianthus barbatus*) and carnations (*Dianthus caryophyllus*), once known as gillyflowers.

The Greek botanist Theophrastus, who first classified plants according to their form and structure, called them Dianthus, from the Greek dios (divine) and anthos (flower), an allusion to their heavenly fragrance and color.

In her book *100 Flowers and How They Got Their Names*, Diana Wells explains that pink was not a specific color until after the eighteenth century, and that this term almost certainly came from the name of the flowers and not the other way around. In the eighteenth century, flowers might be described as pale red, light red, rose, blush, flesh-colored—never pink. Peggy Cornett Newcomb, Director of the Thomas Jefferson Center for Historic Plants, loud pedals this fact in her 1998 article "Pinks, Gillyflowers, and Carnations, the Exalted Flowers," in *Twin Leaf*, the Center's annual catalog.

Pinks may have derived their name from *pinksten* or *pfingsten*, the German name for flowers that blossomed during the season of the Christian feast day at Pentecost or Whitsuntide. Diana Wells believes that pinks came by their name from the Middle English *poinken*, which originally meant to "pierce holes in" leather or cloth, and then acquired the meaning of decorating the edges—as we do with pinking shears—like the jagged edges of dianthus petals.

Pinks, which are generally white, pink, or varying shades of rose, pale pink, to crimson have five flat-fringed, notched-edged to deeply-cut petals, sometimes with a darker eye zone, flaring out of a deep sacklike calyx.

Annuals, biennials, perennials, and subshrubs, growing from about 10" to 12" tall in blossom, they clump and mat in evergreen, silvery blue-green mounds. They hail mostly from northern temperate regions of Europe and Asia. They have slender stems that bear narrow leaves that are opposite each other at little swollen bulbous joints. Mat-forming, with mounds of silvery, bluish green clumps of foliage, pinks are appealing for edgings and ground covers.

Pinks do well on Fishers Island. They grow best in well-drained, well-aerated neutral or slightly alkaline soil in full sun. Although hardy in USDA Zones 4 to 9, not all are very heat tolerant, nor do they easily survive other than mild winters. I fertilize them with a commercial organic liquid fertilizer with low nitrogen such as a 5-10-5 mix. If you deadhead pinks regularly, they will bloom from June through late summer. *Dianthus plumarius* and its fragrant and

long-lived hybrids form natural cushions that should be sheared immediately after blooming. Using a sharp pair of hedge shears, remove the old flower stems and at least one third of the foliage. Don't prune in winter; to keep your tuffets of pinks looking neat, cut them back in early spring.

Cheddar pinks (*Dianthus gratianopolitanus*) are named for the Cheddar George in Somerset, England, where there is an ancestral enclave of these low-growing perennials (4" to 6" tall) with strongly scented five-petalled rose pink flowers that bloom all summer, if regularly deadheaded. Once established, cheddar pinks are drought and heat tolerant. 'Bath's Pink,' named in 1983 for Jane Bath, from Rehoboth, Georgia, a small town east of Atlanta, is a cultivar of *Dianthus gratianopolitanus*, with fragrant clove-scented light-pink flowers, compact gray-green foliage that remains evergreen, which seems far more sturdy and hardy than most pinks, even in what the Brooklyn Botanic Garden describes as "rather brutal conditions."

You can grow pinks from seeds. Sow seeds, barely covered, in moist, well-drained, soilless potting mix. Bottom heat will speed up germination, which takes about one to four weeks. Move seeds to a cool locale once they have sprouted. Under a grow light in the cellar is a good place. When seedlings have developed true leaves, they can be transplanted to peat pots for convenience.

To ensure that your species pinks come true to type, propagate them by cuttings or division. Most species of pinks, expert Rand B. Lee says, are short-lived perennials that need to be divided every two or three years. Division, he informs gardeners, can be done in early spring or autumn. Cut clumps into pieces about 3" or 4" in diameter, being sure that each piece has a healthy root system and new shoots on stem buds. Rand Lee says you should take

Clove-scented pinks in the vista.

cuttings in the cool of the day from vigorous plants in active growth—ideally, right after flowering. Cuttings should be made just below the swollen stem nodes of non-flowering shoots. Remove the lower leaves and poke cuttings into moistened vermiculite. Keep the humidity high around cuttings by covering the containers they are in with a tent of Saran wrap or plastic. Bottom heat will encourage rooting that may take as long as three months.

When I was hospitalized in 1992 for a broken femur, tibia, fibula, damaged kneecap, and ankle in my left leg, Milbry Polk gave me a planter filled with deep-red Sweet Williams that I transplanted in a sunny spot near the arbor archway in what is now the vista's white garden. Phillip Bauman, M.D., Milbry's husband, and one of New York's most highly acclaimed orthopedic surgeons, promised me 80 percent recovery of my left leg. A few years later, I had 100 percent recovery. Like this miraculous recovery, the Sweet Williams Milbry gave me exceeded all my expectations. Sweet Williams (*Dianthus barbatus*), a hardy biennial, was a flower I expected to be short-lived. Instead, it created a little self-seeding patch for itself and has flowered and flourished for over a dozen years (See "Sources and Advice: Where to buy plants, seeds, garden furniture, pots and urns, both resin and clay, etc.").

For a remarkable selection of seven scented and unscented pinks—Bridal Veil, Essex Witch, Fair Folly, Gloriosa, Inchmery, Lady Granville and Mrs. Sinkins at $5.50 per plant, contact the Thomas Jefferson Center for Historic Plants (See "Sources and Advice: Where to buy plants, seeds, garden furniture, pots and urns, both resin and clay, etc.").

For those gardeners who truly delight as I do in the decorative and charming qualities of perennial pinks, Sweet Williams, and carnations, I can recommend unconditionally a quarterly journal, *The Gilliflower Times*, published by the American Dianthus Society (See "Sources and Advice: Where to buy plants, seeds, garden furniture, pots and urns, both resin and clay, etc.").

You can see the mallows if you are in the
vista area or are walking along the nature
path and come upon them as a sort of
secret garden.

Chapter 6

Marsh Mallows:
The Innocent Botanicals

The marsh mallow flowers in mid- to late summer with a clear pink freshness.

The sudden keen vision of marsh mallows fringing the shore of the eastern golf course, or westering along the island's dispersion of ponds, evokes a frisson, a hint of the magic and mystery, the rapture and reverence that has affected our sense of nature since our most ancient days.

Native to Europe, a perennial herbaceous flowering herb that has traveled the world except for the Arctic zones, the marsh mallow (*Althaea officinalis*, Malva species) belongs to the Malvaceae, or mallow family.

Like hollyhocks, formerly *Althaea*, rosea, now *Alcea rosea*, or holy-hock—hoc is Old English for mallow— brought to England from the Holy Land by the Crusaders, marsh mallows are related to the genera *Abutilon*, *Lavatera*, and *Hibiscus*, including the woody shrubs of the latter, such as *Hibiscus syriacus* 'Diana,' (Rose of Sharon), and herbaceous perennials, such as *Hibiscus moscheutos* (swamp rose mallow), cultivated for its white and pink blossoms that can grow to the size of Frisbees. Parenthetically, although the white form of marsh mallow, like other mallows, comes true from seed, if pink mallows are planted close by, pink-flowered plants eventually will predominate.

A cottage-garden flower and valuable medicinal plant, the marsh mallow grows in marshes and meadows border- ing the seacoast in eastern North America. Hardy from Zones 5 to 9, the plant adapts well to ordinary, well- watered, humusy soil, in full sun or partial shade.

Each luminous pink flower, about 3" across, is a sym- metrical round of five heart-shaped petals, with the club-like pistil characteristic of the mallow tribe protrud- ing from the middle of the blossom and grown about with stamens to form a sturdy peg. If you hold this peg between thumb and forefinger, an inverted blossom can be trans- formed into a dancer twirling in a ballerina's tutu, or an old-fashioned hoopskirt, a flower doll that most children seem born knowing how to make.

The marsh mallow grows to 4' on an often-branched staminal column that glistens with all but invisible hairs, the way children's bodies glint in the sun on a beach in summer. On pliant stems, the broad alternating leaves, soft as old silk, tender green above, palest of gray beneath, rounded at their base, with three tapering pointed lobes, are crenulate, their margins minutely, irregularly notched and scalloped in barely perceptible yet per- durable variations.

Among the 116 genera of the mallow tribe that com- prise some 1,500 species, the marsh mallow is kin with okra, or gumbo, brought from Africa in the days of slave trading; cotton; and velvet-leaf (*Cissampelos pareira*), a crop

August blooming fresh pink marsh mallows.

therapeutic qualities—a gummy sap present in their roots, leaves, stems, seeds, and flowers—are heralded in the Latin names for their species type, Malva, and family classification, *Malvaceae*, which means mucilaginous, sticky, and, by association, of value for these honeylike properties. The common name, mallow, comes from the Greek *malakos* (soft, soothing). The generic name of the marsh mallow, considered the top source for tisanes and therapies in the entire clan, is *Althaea officinalis*, mentioned above, which derives from the Greek for "that which heals," and the Latin term *officinalis* (from the [apothecary's] storeroom), a designation for medicinal plants.

For more than 2,000 years, all parts of the marsh mallow, especially its roots, readily available today at most health food and herbal stores, have been regarded as a panacea and prophylactic. Mothers continue to buy roots as pacifiers for teething children. According to first-century Roman naturalist Pliny the Elder, "Whosoever shall take a spoonful of the mallows, shall that day be free of all diseases that may come to him."

Notwithstanding this classic hyperbole, the root of the marsh mallow is "high in minerals, especially an easily usable form of calcium," avers "Wildman" Steve Brill, who offers a number of therapeutic uses for the marsh mallow in his book, *Identifying and Harvesting Edible and Medicinal Plants in Wild (and Not so Wild) Places*.[1]

Our marsh mallows are planted in a woody hollow, tracked through by a nature path that meanders from the vista garden up to the south-facing ridge that belongs to our neighbors. The marsh mallows are grouped on one side of the path, in our wildwood, greenwood coppice, around a birch tree among Kousa dogwoods, a willow tree, and plantings of white rhododendrons and azaleas, wild angelica, *Angelica gigas*, white, lavender, purple, and deep purple, 'Black Knight,' *Buddleia davidii*. You can only see the mallows if you are in the vista area or are walking along the nature path and came upon them as a sort of secret garden.

cultivated in China for its tough fibrous stems once used as backing material for nearly all Chinese rugs.

As much a confection as a plant, whether white puffs stuck on wands for convivial toasting until charred and oozing over a campfire or billowing sweet stickiness as a sauce or topping, the marshmallow as candy is compressed into one word that traditionally retains its eighteenth-century British pronunciation, rhyming not with fallow, but with fellow.

Originally, marshmallows were made by peeling the plant's large white roots and boiling the inner parts with sugarcane and water. Spoonfuls of this glutinous liquid were cooled on a flat surface to create the sweetmeats now mostly prepared with gelatin, corn syrup, and egg white.

All parts of the marsh mallow are edible. Its flowers are an attractive garnish, and a handful or more, mashed, boiled, and strained can be added to chilled fruit soups and desserts. Young, small marsh mallow leaves may be substituted for spinach in vegetable pies and quiches— one-quart of fresh mallow leaves equals one cup of cooked mallow greens.

Herbalists call the mallow family "innocents" because they contain nothing harmful to body or mind. Their

Marsh mallows really look best when they grow around the ponds and marshes of Fishers Island. Where I've got them, along the nature path, they seem somewhat cramped for space. Nevertheless, I wanted to have marsh mallows, and this habitat was the only area on our property where I thought there was a place for them, where the soil was rich and humusy, where there was protection from the wind, and where it was well watered. Elsewhere on the island, marsh mallow branches get broken by the wind and the plants don't grow as tall and full as ours do in their protected enclave. Wherever they are growing, looking at marsh mallows evokes in me a sense of melting *tendresse*.

In June, the marsh mallows are leafing in the green wood, the open, overgrown coppice, but they won't be in flower until late July, early August. I like to look at them as they are growing, all tender green leaves, hidden away in the Pit. The nature path leads from the overgrown coppice into the wildwood, dark wood, with its living roof. Woods and forests are symbolic of the unconscious, the mind's necessary wilderness, and I like to wander along the nature path, looking at the tender green promises of the innocent mallows, that beautiful, clear pinkness that is to come, and to watch the silky wings of yellow swallowtails and the velvety dark wings of black swallowtails as these butterflies and others perch like flying sailboats among the lavender and white deep-purple buddleia bushes.

I wander back across the lawn toward the house, and look in on the cutting garden. June is the month of roses, and half of the garden is filled with them. Total ecstasy. Without even opening the gate I can smell their combined scent, and then, of course, have to run in and stand or bend before each one, inhaling great draughts of the sweetness of damask, musk, tea rose, antique rose, and the spicy scents of vanilla, ginger, cinnamon; and subtly fruity perfumes of peach and apple and berries; and citruslike whiffs of tangerine, lemon, and orange. I believe that

inserting garlic cloves under the earth around the stalks of roses increases the strength of roses' fragrance. Some gardener in my childhood told me that and I have carried the thought and practice with me since then. My American-Scottish grandmother had an American uncle, the plant breeder Luther Burbank, whom she idolized and quoted as having said: "Flowers always make people better, happier, and more helpful; they are sunshine, food, and medicine to the soul." Absolutely true. But also true, a garden is never finished. A garden is always in a state of becoming different, changed, and that process itself is fascinating.

Are the bleeding hearts (*dicentra*) flowering in mid-June? Yes. I have two 'King of Hearts,' with blue-green leaves, and rosy-pink, heart-shaped flowers that bloom nonstop all summer. Growing up to about 14" tall and wide in rich, humusy soil, in part shade, they are cold hardy in USDA Zones 3 to 8, and heat tolerant in AHS Zones 10 to 1. Their leaves are like the leaves of ferns,

Mallows by the vista's nature path.

their profuse, long-blooming flowers are poetic, romantic, like heart-shaped lockets strung across slender stems with twin spurs that dangle and then lift up when white petals appear to fall from the center of the heart. As a child, when this happened, I would turn the blossom upside down to see a white lady with arms akimbo wearing a full-skirted pink dress. The plant's botanic name, *dicentra*, from the Greek, describes the flower structure: *di*, "two," and *kentron*, "spur," the way the flower looks before the white lady appears. Two white *dicentra* are also in flower in full shade. We only had pink bleeding hearts when I was a child. They remind me now of something you might expect to see embroidered in crewel-work on tapestry. The white *dicentra*, white as an egret's plumage, would be

my choice of one of the flowers at a baby's christening. Lilies of the valley would be another, white roses would be another, all flowering, of course, at different times.

In the cutting garden, there are hollyhocks, lavender, white phlox, Canterbury bells, *Platycodon* (balloon flowers), the blue ones, and of course, roses, roses, roses. Roses in the cutting garden are almost too much to take in. The 'Sea Foam' and 'New Dawn' roses, pale, blush-pink climbers growing on fencing behind the hydrangeas on the west side of the swimming pool are flowering as well. White rosa rugosa are in flower, and a few magenta ones on the bluff. The yellow rosa rugosa I planted along a shady path by the daylily bed flowered for a few weeks, but needs more sun to go on flowering.

Platycodon, or balloon flowers, in the cutting garden.

Hollyhocks in the cutting garden.

Drought protection begins with the earth.
The good soil you want holds water so
that plants' roots can absorb it as needed,
yet drains away...

Chapter 7

When in Drought:
Water Conservation, Flowers and Plants for Xeriscaping

At sunrise, on a late June morning, I looked out at the swimming pool and saw that a mallard mother duck was swimming around with seven ducklings following her. I'm always happy when wildlife enjoys our property. I like to see ducks and pheasants making use of stone and wooden steps, pecking up the corn Austin spreads on the lawn, driveway, and the low stone wall outside the downstairs guest room for them. I like to watch wild mallards and gadwalls swimming in the swimming pool. Austin is scrupulous about cleaning up after them. Our pool always looks crystal clear and clean.

I go out to photograph big white corymbs of the elderberry tree. It's a native tree, *Sambucus caprifoliaceae*, hardy in Zones 6 to 8, trouble free, happy in ordinary soil, needing only a late-winter pruning to keep its shape and within its modest 10' size. Ours has pinnate leaves. More ornamental varieties have colored foliage or variegated leaves, but I like our simple, ordinary ones with their lovely white flowers, presaging masses of purple-black berries on which the cardinals feast. I'm not one for elderberry wine, and I'd rather watch the cardinals eat the berries than go to the effort of making or having Isany, our talented Brazilian cook, make elderberry jelly. I look up at the beautiful white corymbs and imagine a Pequot Indian squaw having done the same hundreds of years past. There are also elderberry trees that are native to Europe and Asia. I've read that you can eat young shoots of elderberry as a substitute for asparagus and as a corrective for moodiness and anger. I've never tried this, but just looking at an elderberry tree imparts a sense of serenity.

José and his crew arrive. José says he wants his crew to plant some new Hidcote lavender bushes in the cutting

garden as ours were badly damaged by last year's rains. The rains drowned out other Mediterranean herbs we have, rosemary for example, José tells me, but he has new plants for replacements. It's no surprise that Scottish Austin says he'd rather have rain any day than a drought.

For me, with the calm waters of Long Island Sound lapping at our Starfish Point beach on one side, and on the other side, Block Island Sound and the Atlantic melding together in waves to roll in on our south-facing beach, in endless sibilance, with the gulls' cries and the oyster-catchers' skyborne roadrunners' cries of beep, beep, beep, ever in daytime earshot, it was difficult a few years ago even to conceive of a drought. I knew that saltwater is a plant-killer, but still, there always seemed to be mist, moisture, fog to dispel the thought of drought.

However, we experienced several summer droughts and concomitant needs to restrict water usage. I expect there will be more summer droughts and more water restrictions in the future.

Like all organic gardeners, I've had to plan about soil, plants, trees, orchards, areas of lawn, watering systems. For a water-wise garden, there are long-term and short-term solutions. Drought protection begins with the earth.

The good soil you want holds water so that plants' roots can absorb it as needed, yet drains away so that roots and soil microbes get the air necessary for their survival. How does your soil measure up? You can easily test it.

1. Dig a hole in your garden area about 6" wide and 12" deep. Fill it with water.
2. Let the water completely drain out of the hole.
3. Fill up the hole again. Clock how long it takes for the water to drain. If your soil drains too quickly, you could lose valuable earth nutrients. If your soil drains too slowly, your plants can become waterlogged and your bulbs rot.

Timing: 3 hours or less indicates that drainage is too fast, and that your soil is too sandy; 4 to 6 hours indicates that your soil is healthy, loamy, rich in organic matter, and just what you want; 8 hours or more indicates that drainage is too slow and that you have heavy clay soil. If your soil drains too quickly or too slowly, dig at least a 3" to 5" blanket of your good "black gold" compost in to the top 8" of your soil—a 5" blanket is recommended for sandy soils. Compost contains humus—the end product of the dissolution of organic matter that is the essential element of healthy soil.

Organic matter improves soil structure, and that affects water flow, opening up space in heavy clay soils for both water and air to circulate, encouraging the expansion of root systems, which augment plants' capacity for water intake. With light sandy soils, organic matter acts like a sponge, holding water until the plants' roots can absorb the requisite moisture.

Adding compost to your garden earth increases plants' root mass. The more extensive a plant's root system, the greater access it has to available water in the soil.

Most garden plants prefer a slightly acid soil (pH between 6.5 and 6.8). Poor drainage can lead to soils that are too acid (pH lower that 6.0) because base nutrients can dissolve in standing water. Alkaline soils (pH higher that 7.5) are often high in salts that dry out plants' roots. Adding compost, mixing it well into your garden soil, will solve both these problems, helping your soil hold water and giving your plants more time to drink it up. Amending porous, sandy soils through which water leaches quickly with the addition of compost improves their water retention so that they can absorb, not repel, moisture from the sky or sprinkler. Composted soil not only prevents erosion from wind and hurricane rain, but also helps plants develop better root systems that are more able to withstand drought.

The next step in drought-proofing a garden is to group plants together to cut down on areas that need supplemental water. **Water-dependent** plants such as hydrangeas and hostas should be in a community of their own. High visibility areas for attention-intensive plants in containers around decks, patios, and entries are other water-dependent locales. Moisture-loving plants will be best in your higher-water-use zones, and along north- or east-facing walls and slopes where water will not dry up as quickly as in sunnier south- and west-facing areas.

Transition-zone plants are plants that are moderately drought tolerant, plants that are adaptable to heat, wind, and soil, that can get along with normal rain, but which really thrive with extra watering and soil amendments, hallmarks of transition plants such as hollyhocks (*Alcea rosea*), coreopsis, aka tickweed (*Coreopsis tripteris*), coneflowers (*Echinacea* species), blanket flower (*Gaillardia* species), and dozens of others.

Then there are the **xeric plants**, tolerating an extremely dry habitat, requiring minimal water and able to withstand high heat, humidity and drought. For sensible **xeriscaping** (from the Greek word *xeros*, meaning dry, with the x pronounced like z), make use of these water-wise plants. Once established, xerics need little additional water or care. For the first year or two, to get established, these plants need regular watering and mulching. When they are established, they actually prefer to go without any extra watering or feeding. Their extensive root systems are wonderfully efficient at getting what little moisture there is out of dry soil. They tend to stay healthier with a lean diet. A selection of popular annuals, perennials, and other plants that fulfill these requirements in Zone 6/Zone 7 is listed on page 78. The Brooklyn Botanic Garden has an alternative list of drought-tolerant plants (See "Sources and Advice: Where to buy plants, seeds, garden furniture, pots and urns, both resin and clay, etc.").

Hollyhocks and birdhouse in the cutting garden.

XERICS

At Brillig, what xerics we may have I've lumped in with what I think of as "stalwarts," with a broad comfort range, that will hold up in dry conditions, all perennials, all cold hardy in Zones 6 to 7 and heat tolerant in Zones 8 to 10:

Anise or Hyssop (*Agastache cana, A. Barberi*), butterfly bush (*Buddleia davidii*), butterfly weed (*Asclepius tuberosa*), daylilies (*Hemerocallis*), gaura (*Gaura lindheimeri*), gloriosa daisies (*Rudbeckia hirta*); lavender (*Lavendula species*), rosemary (*Rosmarinus oficinalis*), thyme (*Thymus* species), and other Mediterranean herbs; penstemon (*Penstemon* species), pinks (*Dianthus* species), poppies (*Papavar* species), Russian sage (*Petrovskia atriplicifolia*), sea holly (*Eryngium bourgati*), sedums (*Sedum* species), yarrow (*Achillea* species) yucca (*Yucca filamentosa*).

Catmint (*Nepeta*) and sage (*Salvia* species) are true xerics, plants adapted to extremely dry habitat. Tough, dry-loving annuals include pot marigolds (*Calendula officinalis*); bachelor's buttons (*Centaurea cyanus*), which survive being overwatered among the thirsty roses in the cutting garden where they self-seed to the point that I've always considered them perennials; sunflowers (*Helianthus annus*); zinnias (*Zinnia augustifolia*).

Portulaca (*Portulaca* species) is a succulent with water-storing foliage—fat and spongy leaves that let it save water when water is abundant and use water up slowly during dry times, a trait that helps identify portulaca as a dry-condition survivor.

Plant species with *tomentose* or fuzzy carapaces are recommended for coastal gardens and water-wise gardens. A prototype tomentose plant is lamb's ear (*Stachys*), a favorite plant with all young children who like to caress their faces with its leaves. Among many other tomentose plants are woolly yarrow (*Achillea tomentosa*) and snow-in-summer (*Cerastium*). The downy coverings of tomentose plants form a mat to shade leaf surfaces. Evaporating water is also trapped and held in this thick flocculence. Like other drought-resistant plants, wormwood (*Artemesia* species) has silvery-colored leaves and stems to reflect bright light and avoid overheating. The silvery, gray-green foliage of lamb's ears and the silvery gray of artemesia make up for the insignificance of their flowers. Like the woolly yarrow which has yellow flowers, many other yarrows have brightly colored flowers but with less interesting foliage. All do well at Brillig. Too well, sometimes. They grow like weeds.

One of my cherished drought-resistant plants is creeping thyme, a low-growing, delicate-looking plant with tiny gray-green leaves and tiny rosy-lavender flowers that bloom from May to October. Cold hardy in Zones 3 to 9, it's a tough ground cover I've planted on steps leading to the swimming pool and beach. It smells delicious when stepped on.

Drought-tolerant ground covers we have at Brillig—bugleweed/bugloss/*Ajuga reptans*, call it what you will, snow-in-summer (*Cerastium tomentosum*), creeping juniper (*Juniperus horizontalis*), pachysandra (*Pachysandra procumbens*), the creeping thyme I've mentioned (*Thymus*)—do well.

Vines we have that are drought tolerant are honeysuckle, clematis, morning glories, wisteria.

Our drought-tolerant **evergreens** are our pine trees, holly, juniper.

For drought-tolerant **shrubs,** we have—surprise—our tree hydrangea (*Hydrangea grandiflora paniculata*), unlike our other water-guzzling hydrangeas; lavender (*Lavandula augustfolia 'Hidcote'*), Russian Sage (*Perovskia atriplicifolia*).

SENSIBLE WATER-WISE PLANTS FOR DRY CONDITIONS

A	Annual	**HP**	Hardy Perennial	**HB**	Hardy Biennial	**HB**	Herb
HA	Hardy Annual	**BI**	Biennial	**B**	Bulb	**D**	Deciduous
P	Perennial	**PB**	Perennial Bulb	**GRC**	Ground cover		

FLOWERS

Common name	Botanical name	Type
Artemisia/sea wormwood	*Artemisia stellariana*	P
Artemisia/wormwood	*Artemisia absinthium*	P
Black-eyed Susan	*Rudbeckia hirta*	HA/HB
Butterfly weed/milkweed	*Asclepias tuberosa*	P
Chicory	*Cichorium intybus* (naturalized wild flower)	P
Coreopsis/tickseed	*Coreopsis verticillata*	P
Coneflower, purple	*Echinacea purpurea*	P
Coneflower, yellow	*Rudbeckia*	P
Cushion spurge/milkwort	*Euphorbia epithymoides* (grows in clumps)	HP
Daylilies	*Hemerocallis hybrids*	PB
Dusty Miller	*Artemisia absinthium*, 'Lambrook silver'	P
Everlasting	*Helichrysum angustifolia* (aromatic)	P
	Helipterum manglesii/Rhodanthe manglesii	HA
Gaillardia/blanket flower	*Gaillardia artistata*	P
Globe Thistle	*Echinops ritro*	P
Goldenrod	*Solidago virgaurea*	P
Lamb's ears/tongue	*Stachys lanata/Stachys byzantina*	P
Liatris/gayfeather	*Liatris callilepsis/L. spicata*	P
Mallow	*Malva/Alcea 'fastigiata'*	P
Poppy Mallow	*Callirhoe involucrata* (naturalized wildflower; requires sandy soil; purple, red colors; 6 inches to 4 feet)	A
Poppy Mallow, fringed	*Callirhoe digitata* (height: 1 foot to 4 feet; requires sandy soil; color: rosy red to violet)	A
Mullein (yellow)	*Verbascum chaixii/V. vernale*	P
	Verbascum phoenicum	P
	Verbascum hybridum	P
(including varieties similar to pink hollyhocks and yellow delphiniums)		
Obedient plant/false dragonhead	*Physotegia virginiana*	P
Portulaca/purslane	*Portulaca grandiflorum*	HA
Queen Anne's lace	*Daucus carota* (naturalized wildflower)	P
Rudbeckia	*Rudbeckia sullivantii*, 'Goldsturm'	P

continued, next page

Russian statice	*Psylliostachys suworowii/Statice suworowii*	A
Sea holly	*Eryngium*	P
Sedum	*Sedum caeruleum* (blue, starlike, requires light sandy soil)	HA
Shasta daisy	*Chrysanthemum maximum*	P
Snow-in-summer/rock cress	*Arabis albida*	P
Spiderflower	*Cleome hasslerana*	HA
Spiderwort/Tradescantia	*Tradescantia virginiana* (soft violet blue, pale violet, deep blue, white hybrids)	P
Sunflower, common	*Helianthus annuus* (many hybrids, single and double forms, require watering)	HA
Statice/Sea lavender	*Limonium sinuatum* (parent of many hybrids)/*Statice sinuata*	A
Yarrow	*Achillea Millefolium*, 'Rosea'	P
Zinnia	*Zinnia elegans* (many colors)	HA
Zinnia, dwarf	*Zinnia angustafolia* (single, double blooms)	HA

SHRUBS, BUSHES, AND SMALL TREES

Oregon grape holly	*Mahonia aquifolium* (for dry shade)
Tamarisk (bush/tree)	*Tamarix pentandra* (In bloom, a cloud of pinky lavender, it grows particularly well in seaside areas)
Yucca (sub-shrub)	*Yucca filamentosa* (with spiky, glaucous leaves up to 15 feet, with a polelike stem on which creamy, bell-shaped flowers hang like giant lilies of the valley.)

NATIVE GRASSES

Bluestem	*Andropogon virginicus*
Buffalo grass	*Buchloe dactyloides*
Indian grass	*Sorgastrum nutans*
June grass	*Koeleriacristata*
Northern sea oats	*Chasmanthium latifolium*
Switch grass	*Panicum virgatum*

ORNAMENTAL GRASSES

Blue fescue	*Festuca ovina* 'Glauca'	P
Chinese silvergrass	*Miscanthus sinensis* 'Yaku Jima'	P
Fountain grass	*Pennisetum alopecuroides*	P
Quaking grass	*Briza maxima*	HA

Left: *Hemerocallis*, or daylilies, above the beach. Center: Yuccas flowering in July near the vista across from Fishers Island Sound. Right: Creeping juniper makes an excellent ground cover and is very low maintenance near the pool.

GROUND COVER

Bearberry, common	*Arctostaphylos uva-ursi*	P
Candytuft	*Iberis sempervirens*	P
Juniper, creeping	(see Evergreen shrubs)	
Lilyturf, blue	*Liriope muscari*	
Lilyturf, creeping	*Liriope spicata*	
Moss pink/moss phlox	*Phlox subulata* (many colors)	P
Periwinkle	*Vinca minor* (for dry shade)	
Sedum/stonecrop	*Sedum acre* (yellow, starlike)	P
Thyme	*Thymus* (fragrant)	P

EVERGREENS (SHRUBS & TREES)

Cotoneaster	*Cotoneaster cornubia* (to 15 or 20 feet; fruit and lower bearing)	
Juniper, creeping	*Juniperus horizontalis*, Bar Harbor (ground cover)	
	Other ground covers: *Juniperus prostrata* *Juniperus Sabina 'procumbens'*	
Yew	*Taxus* (wide-spreading up to 60 feet)	
Yucca	*Yucca Filamentosa*	P

DECIDUOUS TREES

Honey locust	*Gleditsia triacanthos*
Smoke tree	*Cotinus coggygria*

VINES

Hall's honeysuckle	*Lonicera japonica*

Long-term solutions to making the garden less vulnerable to future droughts by preserving supplies of fresh water would include reducing the size of our lawn area. Like all typical lawns, our lawn areas require regular irrigation to maintain their verdant charm. One can replace thirsty turf grass with water-thrifty shrubs and small deciduous trees like our shadbush/serviceberry (*Amelanchier arborea*) or hollies. Once established, trees and shrubs require less water than herbaceous plants. Some people are superb with ornamental grasses, but since I'm not

Sunflowers, the goldfinch's delight, bordering the generator house in the garage courtyard.

among them, I'd choose to fill in with drought-tolerant annuals, perennials, ground covers, and bulbs. A happy observation about bulbs and tubers is that their enlarged roots and stems store water and nutrition that the plants then use during the dry season. Many spring bulbs, such as tulip, daffodil and those stout, fussy, furbeloved little old-lady hyacinths that smell so sweetly, simply avoid dealing with the difficulties of summer heat and drought by going dormant. They actually thrive in dry summers.

Whether for the long or short term, add organic matter to your soil as you plant or whenever you have extra time. Compost and other organic matter such as chopped leaves and seaweed (well washed and cleansed of its salt), or grass clippings from the lawn mower will increase your soil's ability to retain moisture. Caution: Don't overdo too much. Instead of a 3" to 5" carpet of compost dug into the top 8" of soil, I got wildly enthusiastic about lavishing compost one summer on the site of the *Lycoris squamigeras* on the south-facing top of the bluff. That was the summer of heavy rains. When we walked there, we felt as though we were skating in mud.

Other Short-Term Tips for Water Conservation

Mulch your tree, shrub, and flowerbed plantings. Covering the soil surface helps retain moisture because it prevents water from evaporating in the hot sun by shading the soil, slowing water runoff, and enriching the soil as the 2" to 3" layer of organic mulch you have spread on your plantings—shredded bark, leaves, or compost—decomposes. Mulch also helps to catch rainwater before it runs off into drainage areas. For xeric plants that do best with minimal water, you can mulch with a 2" thick layer of 1½" crushed granite or limestone chips. The stone helps keep the soil moist and prevents disease by letting excess water drain away from the xeric plants. Use mulch or ground covers to moderate soil temperature and control the growth of weeds to reduce competition for water.

Collect and recycle water. With water used for steaming vegetables or boiling lobsters or pasta or whatever cools (as long as it has no salt added to it), use it to water plants near the kitchen. This "gray water" turned out to be a great tonic for plants in our kitchen's potted herb garden and dining deck plants. Friends of ours direct rain from the roof of their house by channeling it with flexible piping through the downspouts into compact mesh-screened or lidded 54-gallon containers (with a hole for piping) or rain barrels. If possible, always try to direct runoff from your downspouts, away from your house and from leaking into your cellar or washing onto your driveway, so that runoff is rechanneled into your landscape.

Site your garden on a flat surface. The more land slopes, the more quickly water will run off. When we planted on our bluff to prevent erosion, we flattened out terraces for planting so that rainwater, snowmelt, and the springtime emptying of the swimming pool water would soak into the plantings of the bluff on both sides, as well as into the roots of the pines on the west side so that no water would be wasted.

Shelter your garden from the wind. The wind can dry things out as quickly as can the simmering midday sun. A fence, a hedge, trees, bushes, or a wall can serve as efficient and attractive-looking windbreaks.

Locate plants with the heaviest water needs closest to your water source and those with the lightest water needs farthest away.

Put off planting projects until water is plentiful. Extra water is needed for seedlings and plants recently put in the ground to become healthily established. Outdoor container plants often require daily watering during summer heat. Create catch-water soil basins around newly transplanted trees, small plants, shrubs, and evergreens. For stabilized small trees, large plants, and shrubs, build an earth saucer around the base of each to catch and retain water,

Sea holly (*Eryngium*) by the steps leading down to the beach.

particularly rainwater, to get water to the plants' roots where it is needed.

Improve potting mixes. For container plants, you might want to try incorporating hydrogels into the potting soil. These water-retaining polymers hold several hundred times their weight in water and release it gradually to the plants' roots. If you presoak the hydrogels until they are fully expanded, they are easier to blend with the potting soil in the appropriate proper ratio. **Cautionary note:** Be careful not to add more than the designated amount of hydrogels. The crystals can expand to such a degree that your plants can be levitated right out of their containers.

Water wisely. Plants develop stronger, deeper roots where the earth stays moist longer if you water them thoroughly but not too frequently. Frequent, shallow waterings lead to weak, shallow-rooted plants. Avoid watering at times when wind and heat will cause evaporation. Water plants early in the morning. Mornings are cool, and water doesn't evaporate as quickly as it does in the heat of the afternoon. Evenings are also cool, but water remaining on leaves overnight can lead to fungal diseases. Water the soil, not the plants. Use soaker hoses, drip irrigation, a watering can, or other water-conserving irrigation techniques where less water is lost to evaporation to saturate the soil while leaving the foliage dry.

Surface-rooted plants like azaleas, blueberries, and dogwoods need extra water during hot, dry, summer droughts. Keep the earth around these plants moist at all times. Mulching them conserves moisture and cuts down on watering. Jerry Baker suggests his favorite mulch of 2" to 3" of shredded cypress. If that is hard to find, I've found that pine needles also work well and also increase desirable acidity in the soil for acid-loving plants.

Choose drought-tolerant plants mentioned previously for filling in existing plantings or for planting in containers to supplement ornamentals you already have. Pull out plants that are growing poorly. **Get rid of weeds!** Weeds compete with plants for moisture. Don't waste water caring for marginal or unattractive plants.

Tips to Keep Your Lawns Green and Healthy

To water a lawn the way it ought to be watered, you should soak the ground to half an inch below the grass's root system. Any more than this is wasteful, any less causes down-reaching roots to perish. You can check your lawn's moisture with a ruler. In hot summer months, most rye grass and blue grass lawns are going to need about 1½ inches of water weekly, either from rainfall or irrigation.

The amount of water a lawn gets is as important as the time of watering. The best time to water is in the morning between sunrise and 10 a.m., the coolest part of the day when there is less wind and heat to cause evaporation, and time to give the ground a chance to dry. Long periods of wetness or dampness bring about diseases, so don't water overnight. (Night rain is OK because rainwater, as our grandmothers believed, has been scientifically proven to contain tonic ingredients.)

When you mow the grass, leave the clippings, which return small but rewarding amounts of moisture to your lawn. Grass should be mowed from several directions,

so change the pattern every time. This will keep the grass blades from growing in one direction and help avoid soil compaction.

Keep your lawn mower blades sharp. Sharp blades make cleaner cuts that cause less water loss than cuts from dull blades. Dull mower blades can damage your lawn in normal, heavy-growing and drought conditions. Hone or otherwise sharpen blades after every third mowing, or keep at least two sharp blades on hand and switch every three weeks. Under normal growing conditions, you should cut your lawn every six to seven days. During the heavy growing season, you can cut it more often. During times of drought, cut your lawn less often.

Reduce fertilizer applications to slow growth rate of lawn grass so it will need less water.

Let lawn grass grow to 4" between mowings to shade the roots, reduce water evaporation, and then cut back to 3". This practice also encourages roots to grow longer to hunt for moisture deep in the soil.

Return clippings to the lawn to mulch grass roots, add nitrogen, and help retain moisture.

To aerate lawns and increase your lawn's water absorption, wear spiky golf shoes on your property walkabouts. Control traffic on lawns to prevent lawn stress and soil compaction.

Eliminate wasteful water runoff onto paved areas by matching your sprinkler's pattern with the shape of your lawn or garden beds. Keep all sprinkler heads clean to be sure of uniform water distribution.

Spray sprinklers, with evaporation rates as high as 70 percent on windy and dry days, are wasteful. You can lower your watering costs by 60 percent if you switch to drip irrigation, a system that delivers water where it is needed and in the proper amount directly into the ground versus imprecise airborne spraying. The technology of drip irrigation is unsurpassed at both saving water and promoting optimal plant growth. Your garden's soil neither dries out nor becomes waterlogged.

Companies that sell drip irrigation equipment will usually help you design a system and give you instructions on setting it up.

Drip systems can be permanent or semipermanent, and easily removed when regular cultivation is necessary for beds of bulbs or vegetables. The tubing can be disguised with wood chips or mulch. Drawbacks to drip irrigation? Occasionally, the tubes get clogged.

Soaker hoses, less expensive than elaborate drip irrigation systems and simpler to install, are an alternative. Soaker hoses can also be components of drip irrigation systems or they can be used on their own. They release water along their full length as seepage through tiny holes or as diminutive sprays. Soaker hoses conserve water, reduce evaporation, and don't wet flower leaves. Drawbacks to soaker hoses? There may be an uneven flow of water if the hose is laid on a slope or a water flow that is strongest closest to the source.

Drip systems and soaker hoses make sure your plants are watered deeply to encourage root growth. Plants will be watered thoroughly, and you won't waste any precious water as runoff.

For invisible watering, conventional pop-up rotors are the best, although wasteful (See "Sources and Advice: Where to buy plants, seeds, garden furniture, pots and urns, both resin and clay, etc.").

An extravagance of *Hemerocallis* (daylilies) on the south side facing the Atlantic.

...one hungry deer can transform a lush
border of hostas into a ravaged pathway
and decimate your most cherished roses
while you are having dinner with friends.

Chapter 8

Garden Pests:
Coping with Deer, Rabbits, Raccoons, Rodents, and Other Marauders

When we had a plague of pine beetles that killed a score or more of our pine trees as well as hundreds of island trees, I was unwilling to have our surviving pine trees treated with chemicals to "preserve" them. Our garden is organic. No chemicals allowed.

For a year or so, our place looked bare and bleak. Then dozens of new pines sprang up from pinecones scattered about. We succeeded in replanting a few. Other pine trees came up better and stronger on their own. Our landscape changed. We planted some deciduous trees and some evergreens. I liked the new landscape. All was well.

We've had and have other pests. For additional reading about pest controls that are safe for the user and the environment, I wholeheartedly recommend a practical guide: *Bugs, Slugs and Other Thugs*[1]

Rabbits in the garden: I used to have tender feelings about Flopsy, Mopsy, and Peter Cottontail. I now harbor the apoplectic wrath of Farmer MacGregor. Rabbits seldom range more than a few acres from their warrens. They breed often, reproduce copiously, eat ravenously.

In spring, summer, and autumn, rabbits feast on nearly all tender green shoots. Alfalfa, beans, beets, carrots, clover, newly planted grapevines, lettuce, peas, soybeans, strawberries, tomatoes, may be clipped off clean to the roots.

Members of the rose family such as apple trees, blackberries, raspberries, and, inevitably, stems of some of our most cherished roses are prey to their sharp buckteeth.

Looting Leporidae tunnel to lily, tulip, and other bulbs for their provender. If they don't gnaw the bulbs, they snap off stems and stalks of emerging flowers and nibble on their petals, wanton in their destruction of Casablanca and rubrum lilies as well as dianthus and many other flowers.

All during the year but mostly in winter, when sources of wild food are scarce, rabbits strip bark from bushes, saplings, and many trees, a practice that is wounding and destructive.

What to do?

Hot-tempered gardeners are apt to shoot, or try to shoot, any rabbit in sight. Other gardeners try scores of rabbit repellents with varying degrees of success. Using mulches of dog, cat, or human hair around plants is suggested. So are flings of mothballs, blood meal, rags soaked in human urine, wood ashes, laundry or deodorant soap tied to bushes and trees, powdered hot pepper flakes, chili peppers, black pepper, a mixture of eggs and Tabasco sauce, crushed limestone, talcum powder sprinkled over your vulnerable plants. Fresh applications of these and other repellents are recommended after every moderate rainfall. Needless to say, these deterrents don't work well in tandem with a sprinkler system.

I've read about Plant Pro-Tec units, small plastic vials that gradually release garlic odor over a period of six to eight months to discourage rabbits and deer from browsing plants (See "Sources and Advice: Where to buy plants, seeds, garden furniture, pots and urns, both resin and clay, etc."). If you don't mind the smell of garlic, this sounds like a good idea.

In dozens of garden books, I've found recommendations for fake owls and snakes; clear glass jugs filled with water set out in the garden, whose reflections are said to frighten rabbits; Mylar polyester film balloons, shiny colored ribbons, bells, pie tins that clang together like cymbals, things that move and clink and clank in the wind; rotten eggs, fish emulsions for target areas. Most of these suggestions are aesthetically disheartening and would be more offensive to me as they became predictable, after a while, for rabbits and other four-footed

marauders. As a bird lover, I shun anything that would scare birds or keep them away as most of these unbeauteous suggestions undoubtedly would.

To keep rabbits from chomping on the bark of your fruit trees in wintertime, Jerry Baker recommends mixing:

2 eggs
2 cloves of garlic
2 tbsp. of hot chili pepper
2 tbsp. of ammonia

in 2 cups of hot water. Let this mixture sit for 2 to 3 days, then paint it on the trunks of your fruit trees. Jerry Baker claims this veneer will help get your trees through the hungry bunny season and send those bunnies foraging elsewhere. You can also collar lower tree trunks with fine mesh fencing or spray on coyote or red fox urine-based repellents. In addition to mesh fencing, we have used commercial barriers such as plastic or metal tree wraps, but not fabric wraps as these can promote disease. Because rabbits are vegetarians, some people daub tree guards with animal fat or bacon grease: A dreadful mistake! What shoos away rabbits is a siren's lure to raccoons and rodents—more about these nasties shortly.

If you scoop up roadkill carcasses, or leave the bodies of rabbits you or someone else has shot on your property, live rabbits may be scared away. More generously inclined friends, and Jerry Baker as well, suggest tossing a few carrots or a bundle of hay into the snow as an alternative rabbit buffet. Some people place trimmings from their autumn pruning on the ground well away from cherished plants as a food source in the hope that rabbits will concentrate their feeding on these.

More effective, but also entailing a lot of time and work, are individual plant cages, row cages, and rabbit-proof fencing.

Before planting bulbs, dig a trench or a bed and line the bottom and sides with wire mesh, with openings no larger than 1". Add a handful of prickly gravel to the hole after planting the bulbs. Alternatively, you can plant bulbs in chicken wire mesh containers larger by an inch or two than the bulb.

To protect trees and bushes, encase trunks in cylinders of close-mesh woven wire, sunk into the ground 6", and held away from the trunk with stakes. Protection should reach 20" higher than the average snowfall line.

For cutting gardens and vegetable gardens, an enclosure of wooden fencing should have a border of heavy wire mesh at least 2' above the ground and 1' below the ground with an apron of several inches turned outward from the garden before the wiring is covered. **Note:** Protective individual caging of seedling plants also prevents them from flopping over as they fill out, and may help some plants to maintain attractive rounded shapes. Extra good news is that once plants pass the seedling stage, rabbits are more inclined to ignore them.

Espaliering flowering shrubs, fruit trees, and cherry tomato vines makes it easier to protect them from rabbit damage. Better yet, to foil rabbits, plant precious plants in tall resin or ceramic containers.

Best of all solutions to the rabbit problem, I've found, is to focus on plants rabbits dislike. Once garden crops are past the tender seedling stage, rabbits will tend to bypass them. Inter-planting garlic, onions, dusty miller and Mexican marigolds deters rabbits as they are put off by strong aromas and unsavory tastes. Rabbits aren't fond of corn, cucumbers, peppers, potatoes, squash, and tomatoes. Owing to a bitter-tasting phenol compound present in the stems and flowers of peonies, rabbits and deer spurn peonies. As for daffodils, these and irises seem to be about the only bulbs and corms I know that are safe from rabbit predation. Rhododendrons and azaleas aren't rabbit attractions. Jeff and Marilyn Cox, authors of *The Perennial Garden, Color Harmonies Through the Seasons,*[2] provide a rare and valuable list of rabbit-resistant perennials.

Protective fencing in wintertime around Roses of Sharon.

The following genera they suggest are guaranteed to make your garden a delight to you, but an unfavorite place of the local rabbit population.

PLANTS DISLIKED BY RABBITS

Achillea (Yarrow)	Papaver (Poppies)
Astilbe	Filipendula (Rosaceae)
Aconitum	Polygonatum (Solomon's seal)
Baptisia (False/Wild indigo)	Gentiana
Anaphalis (Pearly everlasting)	Polygonum (Knotweed)
Bergenia (Elephant's ears)	Geranium
Anemone	Salvia (Sages)
Cimicifuga	Helleborus
Aquilegia (Columbine)	Sedum
Colchicum (Autumn crocus)	Hemerocallis (Daylilies)
Artemisia	Stachys
Convallaria (Lily of the Valley)	Hosta
AsterCorydalis (Pseudofumaria)	Trillium (Wood lily)
Digitalis (Foxglove)]	Iris
Narcissus (Daffodils)	Trollius (Globeflower)
Doronicum (Leopard's bane)	Kniphofia (Red-hot poker)
Nepeta (Catmint)	Yucca
Epimedium (Barrenwort)	

In addition to this list, Suzanne Shutz, an ardent horticulturist and Fishers Island friend, offered me a list of some plants and flowers in her garden that rabbits also aren't keen about.

> Ajuga (Bugleweed)
> Alchemilla (Lady's mantle)
> Buddleia (Butterfly bush)
> Cleome
> Cosmos
> Nicotiana
> Pulmonaria
> Ruscus (Butcher's Broom)

Deer. Beautiful though deer are, and much as I love to watch them in faraway forests, I'm glad they aren't commonplace on Fishers Island. Insects and diseases tend to work slowly. Rabbits can nip a dozen magnificent Madonna lilies in two overnight, but one hungry deer can transform a lush border of hostas into a ravaged pathway and decimate your most cherished roses while you are having dinner with friends. I know. It's happened to me when I lived in Bucks County, Pennsylvania. Deer tear stems, take large ragged bites, and devour succulent new growth. They destroy apple, pear, and other fruit trees. They gorge on herbaceous ornamentals and garden vegetables.

To deter deer, you follow the same procedures as you do for rabbits, just on a larger scale—judicious fencing, selective plantings, plant caging, and, if you see fit, all the blood meal, deodorant soap, fluttering, and noisy ploys suggested to repel rabbits—and then some.

To win against deer, most people agree that the most effective, albeit expensive, solution, is fencing. An 8'-tall high-tensile 12.5 galvanized-steel fence stretched between 12' posts sunk 4' into the ground; a 10'-high electrical fence with 12 wires, every other wire carrying 8,000 volts (the alternating wires are grounds, necessary to complete the electrical circuit so that a deer will get a shock even if its feet are off the ground; wires strung 30' to 50' apart); a 10'-high polyethylene mesh fence, stretched on heavy-gauge cable strung between trees pinned down with giant sturdy wire hairpins were the subject of a column written by Anne Raver in the *New York Times*,[3] giving sources for fence installations in the American Northeast.

A properly designed and installed fence is the one control you can rely on, and in the long run, it's usually less work and less time-consuming than other techniques.

The most popular deer deterrent remedies call on a combination of offensive taste and smell. All those smelly concoctions of rotten eggs, fish, and garlic might work for a few days, but John Waite, who lives in Norway, Maine, sings the praises of human urine as a highly effective and

SOME DEER-RESISTANT PLANTS

Achillea (Yarrow)	Myrtle
Aconitum (Monkshood)	Narcissus
Agapanthus	Oleander
Ageratum	Pampas grass
Antirrhinum (Snapdragon)	Pentstemon
Aquilegia (Columbine)	Peonies
Asclepius (Butterfly weed)	*Perovskia atriplicifolia*
Ash	(Russian Sage)
Astilbe	Phlox
Black Locust	Pine
Boxwood	Poppies
Buddleia (Butterfly bush)	Rosemary
Canterbury bells	Rudbeckia
Chives	(Black-eyed Susan)
Clematis	Salvia
Cleome	Sedum
Coreopsis	Spruce Dicentra
Daffodils	(Bleeding Heart)
Dogwood	Digitalis (Foxglove)
Echinacea (Purple cornflower)	Yucca
Gas plant	Zinnia

enduring deer repellent.[4] Timing is all-important. Waite has been able to eliminate deer damage with just one spraying of a mixture of four parts water and one part

urine at the start of the growing season. Apparently, on the basis of their early-season experiences, the deer expect unpleasant-tasting foliage throughout the remainder of the growing season and avoid whatever they have tasted that has been sprayed. Just remember that if deer are hungry enough, they'll eat almost anything.

Raccoons. Although deer aren't a major problem on Fishers Island, raccoons are. Descendants of a pair of pets set free some 25 years ago, raccoons have now proliferated to overrun and plague the island. Terrestrial raccoons, who are also expert tree climbers, beachcombers, and bold as bandits, are *perpetually hungry*. With cunning little black hands, bushy tails, and black-masked foxy faces, they may look adorable, but they are especially aggressive, can carry rabies, terrorize bird life, rip through compost heaps, upend garbage pails, gouge holes in shingle roofs, walls, and siding, and uproot turf and lawn in search of toothsome grubs.

Buddleia is truly a butterfly bush.

Raccoons picnic on pheasant chicks and wolf down newly hatched cygnets and baby ducklings. They suck dry birds' eggs from arboreal, land, and beach nests and kill and eat all but the fiercest nesting parents. They pig out on mollusks, shellfish, and fish; everything growing in the garden; suet and peanut butter from bird feeders, and pet food. They like nothing better than fresh sweet corn and just-ripe fruit and berries.

Cotoneaster (*Pyracantha*, 'firethorn') and other brambles are a deterrent to sensitive-footed raccoons who also shy away from mothballs, blood meal, cayenne pepper, Tabasco sauce, ammonia, talcum powder, loud noises, blinking lights, pinwheels, streamers, barking dogs, and dog poop.

Leaving two-fingers-width of space, you can wrap a 30" section of galvanized duct pipe around the trunks of fruit trees to keep raccoons from climbing them.

Animal pests and animal bird-murderers are like weeds. They have a place in nature—just not in our gardens. Exclusion by fencing is the preferred solution, but if marauders aren't deterred by an ordinary fence, I have no intention of trying an electric or solar-powered fence with hot wires 3" off the ground to exclude rabbits, or 12" to 15" high to exclude raccoons and muskrats. A wire 3' to 4' high is effective against deer, but you have to bait the wire so that deer will take a lick and get a jolt that will usually discourage them from coming back. This sounds cruel, but I have been told it doesn't hurt them and it keeps them from trying to jump your electric fence. Researchers of wildlife have told me that live trapping and subsequent relocation stresses animals, disorients them, makes them vulnerable to predators, and offers a poor chance of survival. Harassed by raccoons forced by lack of habitat and their own proliferation to invade our garden and bird sanctuary, I wish we were living four score years ago. I fantasize about creating a market for replicas of the pre-PETA (People for the Ethical Treatment of Animals) men's winter great coats of the 1920s—racks and racks full of full-length raccoon coats beloved by F. Scott Fitzgerald.

Rats and mice don't carry rabies as raccoons do, but they can carry dangerous parasites and diseases such as trichinosis and salmonellosis. Rats can eat up to a half-pound of food daily and, like mice, damage far more than they eat, which is just about everything. Because rats need to blunt and shorten their fast-growing teeth, they can gnaw cement into dusty grit and cause electrical fires and serious structural damage. What is the best defense against rodents?

The Weitech Company manufactures ultrasonic devices that create stress in the bodies of rats and mice, sending them, they say, fleeing from your area. (See "Sources and Advice: Where to buy plants, seeds, garden furniture, pots and urns, both resin and clay, etc."). How far away and where would they go? This doesn't sound like a thoughtful thing for a neighbor to do, but it might be a good solution in a more isolated area than ours.

We had a terrible rat problem when I first came to live at Brillig some fourteen years ago. A previous caretaker had liberally spread rat poison pellets about the cellar and kitchen. Several rats had died within the walls of Brillig, which caused two rooms in the house to reek of dead rat for months and months and months. Rat poison is far too dangerous to have anywhere in a house or garden. Dead, poisoned rats in the house or garden could be fatal to dogs, cats, and birds, and contaminants of garden produce that could be seriously toxic to people. I laid down the law that absolutely no rat poison was ever to be used at Brillig again.

We prebaited traps in the house and garden for several days, letting rats see the traps, smell them, take the bait. Only then were the traps set. Rats aren't stupid. We caught over a dozen rats whose bodies were tossed on the beach for the gulls to eat. Dozens of other rats avoided the traps. It was only when Austin came to work as our caretaker that our rat problem was solved. He shot them when he caught them eating the cracked corn we offer our resident pheasants. He shot them when they raided our bird feeders, banqueted on bulbs, tunneled through the cutting garden, chewed on his fishing rod and plant roots, gourmandized on our delectable strawberries, blunted their teeth as they must on tree bark, roof shingles, cement, and hole-making in plant boxes and wooden steps.

Mice dislike mint. I send them packing with bundles of mint stems, their scent reinvigorated with mint oil. Austin sets traps for mice in the garage. Owls and hawks make off with the ones Austin doesn't get.

Dogs. When neighboring dogs leave urine-burned patches in the lawn, we spray the lawn with a cup of baby shampoo mixed with 20 gallons of water, and a week later, borrowing a page from Jerry Baker's homespun gardening advice, overspray the turf with a can of beer, a cup of ammonia, a can of regular (not Diet) Coca-Cola mixed in a bucket and poured into our 20-gallon hose-end sprayer. I've read that you can feed dogs Jerry Baker's Green-UM Neutralizer treats (Item 3612) that will "work wonders to eliminate the damaging effect of dog urine on the lawn." Your veterinarian may also be able to suggest brewer's yeast supplements or similar alkalinizing additives to your dog's diet for the same purpose.

A problem I have with dogs is that they can brush against poison ivy and then transfer the urushiol oil to your bare legs or bare arms.

Poison ivy was rampant when I first came to live at Brillig. Garden helpers dug it up, bagged it in Hefty sacks and carted the sacks off to the local dump (no longer located on Fishers Island, alas, and the cause of the rats' exodus from the west end to where we are). You never burn poison ivy, as the smoke, if inhaled, can be a serious problem, even fatal. To get rid of poison ivy, I used full-strength white vinegar. I just poured it over the whole plant, leaves and all, and bye-bye poison ivy. You have to amend the soil where the vinegar has been poured with compost later on so that the grass or whatever else has been growing around the site of the poison ivy will grow again.

Weeds/crabgrass. Vinegar poured over unwanted weeds or crabgrass has the same effect of getting rid of them with ease. You just have to take care not to get any vinegar on the surrounding plants.

Ants. Spraying ants with vinegar gets rid of them, too, as does a spray of a few drops of dishwashing liquid shaken up in a spray bottle. One good squirt right on the ants is all it takes to get rid of them. We keep ants away from our kitchen herbal garden with bunches of garden mint and an occasional slice of lemon or onion or a peeled clove of garlic.

Slugs and other garden predators. Six or seven years ago, I saw that slugs had made lacework out of Brillig's hydrangea and hosta leaves, with some leaves little more than an edging around a large, ragged hole. Trails of slime were smeared across mangled and mutilated young seedlings I had painstakingly planted the day before. We had an infestation of slugs.

Slugs are actually mollusks and belong to the subclass Pulmonata. They are closely related to clams and squid. During the day, these slimy predators hide anywhere that's cool and moist—under mulch, lettuce leaves, under boards, in the shade of large leaves. At night they come out and gluttonize on stems and leaves of tender plants. Hostas are a favorite. A slug can consume up to 30 to 40 times its own weight in 12 hours. Slugs lay eggs in the soil all through summer and autumn. They lay hundreds of eggs annually under fallen leaves, surface roots, around the compost pile, anywhere and everywhere that their eggs can be sheltered in batches that hatch in only three weeks, quickly ready to repeat the cycle. The eggs hatch during rainy weather and look like a slithery pink, parasitic mess, fortunately appealing to toads and our resident ducks.

I remember as a young girl watching my parents' gardener strewing lettuce and cabbage leaves on bare earth and laying lengths of board in the garden, later overturning the boards and the leaves to disclose a host of slugs, snails, grubs, cutworms that had sheltered beneath them that he captured. He troweled them into either

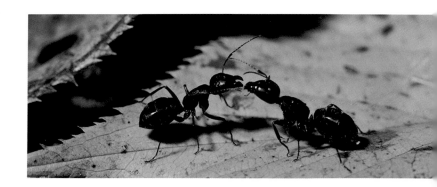

soapy water or a mild solution of rubbing alcohol for "the finishing touch," as he said, or "the cosmos solution," as my grandmother said when she handpicked Japanese beetles from roses and peonies in my uncle's garden in Scotland and dropped them into a bucket of soapy water or a pitcher containing a solution of rubbing alcohol.

These gambits were effective when I tried them at Brillig. Garden helpers suggested I set out pie tins pushed into the earth in the various garden areas and fill them with beer or grape juice to attract slugs that would fall in, drown, and furnish snacks for the pheasants. Or set out grapefruit halves for the slugs and other creepy crawlies to hide under and later to be captured and done away with. These suggestions weren't for me. I told the garden helpers I had no intention of uglifying the garden.

I stopped garden helpers from sprinkling salt on slugs, which left them dead and disintegrating, and also contaminated the soil with salt. I stopped garden helpers from scattering unsightly trails of crumbled eggshells around plants that injured slugs' skin, causing them to die from dehydration. I stopped one helper from throwing handfuls of ashes around, also an effective and lethal barrier for slugs, but unbalancing to our garden's pH when scattered about plants that preferred acid soils. Coffee grounds and sawdust were used successfully, but only on our strawberry beds.

Naturally occurring dustlike diatomaceous earth, I was told, effectively eradicates slugs when a handful is sprinkled around plants slugs feast on the most. Although diatomaceous earth is nontoxic to people and animals, I was also told that it is wise to use a mask to avoid breathing in the dust. Later I was informed that some types of diatomaceous earth were known to be toxic if inhaled or ingested. When I found out that not only does diatomaceous earth slice the undersides of slugs' bellies, making them uncomfortable, but causes them to dehydrate before they die, I decided diatomaceous earth was a thoroughly risky and unpleasant solution for dispensing of slugs.

Garden helpers kept telling me that slugs and snails don't like to crawl over irritating or rough surfaces, and advocated the use of sharp, crumbled eggshells, sharp gravel, ashes, diatomaceous earth, sawdust, coffee grounds, sand, even snippets of coarse horse hair. I would say no, the slugs would lay eggs and more eggs, and I began to see more and more intensive slug damage on leaves. I even saw slugs gorging on leaves in the daytime, a sure sign that something drastic had to be done.

The effective, happy solution? **Copper barrier tape edging.** Copper carries a weak electrical charge that repels slugs and snails naturally. You just wrap the adhesive-backed tape around planters and staple or clip it to the edging of flowerbeds and other areas, and voilà, simple, safe slug and snail repellents where you want and need them. Our hosta and hydrangea leaves, our tender, vulnerable plants are now undamaged. *Affordable and durable copper barrier tape edging in 20' rolls is available from Walt Nicke's Garden Talk* (See "Sources and Advice: Where to buy plants, seeds, garden furniture, pots and urns, both resin and clay, etc.").

Aphids are a nuisance. I often send for ladybugs and praying mantises. They both feed on aphids. Praying mantises also make meals of flies, caterpillars, and, alas, pollinating bees and wasps. They also cannibalize each other. Garden-friendly praying mantises are attracted to most leafy and woody plants and are happily at home in raspberry bushes and flowering cosmos. You can order both ladybugs and praying mantises from Gardens Alive (See "Sources and Advice: Where to buy plants, seeds, garden furniture, pots and urns, both resin and clay, etc.").

To make pleasant-smelling citrus spray to protect your plants from aphids: Boil 2 cups of water. Remove from heat. Add the peel of one lemon or one grapefruit. Cover the pot and let steep overnight. Make a solution of half citrus liquid and half water. Spray on plants as needed.

In a blender, you can purée peeled garlic cloves, mint, banana peel. Add water to make a spray to repel aphids.

A similar purée of strong-smelling roots and herbs and spices such as garlic, onion, ginger, horseradish, chili peppers, strained and diluted with water and decanted into a spray bottle, will repel aphids and other unwanted insect pests.

You can get rid of aphids on patio plants by applying rubbing alcohol to infected leaves with Q-tips or cotton balls.

To help control aphids, white flies, and mealy bugs, poke cloves of peeled garlic into the soil of potted plants. Spray the leaves and the soil three times in 10 days with a gallon of water mixed with a cup of light cooking oil and an ounce of liquid dishwashing soap. This spray smothers the insects and works like a charm, both indoors and out.

A teaspoonful of dishwashing soap added to a quart of water and decanted into a spray bottle is a simple and effective bug-off repellent for indoor and outdoor plants, for fruit trees, vegetables, trees, and lawn.

We also have used neem oil natural products and a mixture of mouthwash such as Listerine and water to get rid of insects.

Mosquitoes. To reduce the spread of West Nile Virus and to prevent other mosquito-borne infections, begin by eliminating all breeding areas for mosquitoes on your property.

Mosquitoes rest in moist, shaded grass and weeds, so keep these sites well clipped around your house and seating areas on your property. Every other day, empty water from flowerpot saucers, pool covers, splash pools—any place where water collects. Keep roof gutters clean. To control mosquitoes breeding in garden ponds, add a piece of Mosquito Dunk, a product that releases natural bacteria (BTI, or *Bacillus thuringiensis var. israelensis*) to kill mosquito larvae, harmless to frogs, fish, birds. For years, we sprayed ourselves with Muskol, an insect repellent containing DEET (N, N-diethyl-meta-toluamide), effective against biting insects and long lasting.

Then *mirabile dictu*, we discovered the Mosquito Magnet™, a commercial mosquito-abatement system used by the U.S. Coast Guard to reclaim its Bahamian station

that had become impossible to live in because of its swarming mosquitoes. Six Mosquito Magnets™ captured 1.5 million mosquitoes in six days. Mosquito Magnets™, electrically powered, or self-powered with propane, mimic human breath to trap and kill mosquitoes and other biting insects, covering half an acre, three-quarters of an acre or one acre.

We invested in three of them for our five acres. I thought they were expensive when we first got them, but to be free as I am from itching and scratching and worries about mosquito-borne viruses now is a blessing for which I would happily sacrifice or sell almost anything to own one of these miraculous systems (See "Sources and Advice: Where to buy plants, seeds, garden furniture, pots and urns, both resin and clay, etc.").

We ordered the most powerful (and most expensive) of the three Mosquito Magnet™ models offered by Frontgate (See "Sources and Advice: Where to buy plants, seeds, garden furniture, pots and urns, both resin and clay, etc."). Later, our local hardware store carried them.

Fungus, aphids, Japanese beetles: Howard Garrett says that if your foliage becomes afflicted with a fungus, such as black spot, powdery mildew, or brown patch, spray it with his organic fungicide early in the morning or late in the afternoon. Apply as needed— usually one spray clears fungus. We dissolve 3 tablespoons of baking soda per gallon of soapy water as a spray after rain. Applying regular cornmeal to soil at 2 pounds per 100 sq. ft., another Garrett suggestion, also quickly eliminates fungus. To control aphids, we zap them with jets of water or with a mild solution of dishwashing detergent, or wipe leaves with Q-tips or a washcloth dipped in rubbing alcohol. We used to use neem oil products to control Japanese beetles, or handpick them and drop them into a bucket of soapy water or a solution of water and rubbing alcohol, but for the past seven or eight years, we have been totally free of Japanese beetles because of our resident birds who eat them.

Slugs, snails, grubs, and cutworms: We use copper strips placed around the perimeter of flower, shrub, and vegetable beds as an excellent deterrent for the slugs and snails. Lengths of boards laid between garden rows or strewing lettuce or cabbage leaves on bare earth will attract a host of slugs, snails, grubs, and cutworms. Pests can then be captured and shaken into soapy water or a mild solution of water and rubbing alcohol and destroyed.

Strategies for safe pest control are outlined in the *Brooklyn Botanic Garden's Gardener's Desk Reference.*[5] This is a splendid book, always useful to have on hand.

Chapter 9

Increasing the Garden's Natural Charm with Bird- and Butterfly-Attracting Plants and Flowers

I wake up at dawn to the sound of the sea and the chiming of Latimer's Light in Long Island Sound. I pull up the shade of the north-facing window just as Majordomo, the sovereign of our three resident ring-necked pheasants, flies down from his roost in the roof-high blue spruce on the east side of the driveway. Sometimes he roosts there, sometimes in the pine tree on the west side of the driveway, sometimes in the center island of the driveway in one of the two honey locusts next to the fountain with the three hawthorns on the west side. Majordomo utters an awk-awk aubade, flapping his wings noisily for attention, then brisks down the driveway westward to the lawn where he pecks at the grass for grubs and insects. He is a beautiful bird, burnished, iridescent, his plumage a radiant toffee-amber in the early light, his head green and lavender, with a scarlet eye wattle and a white ring around his neck. I hope his dowdy brown-feathered mate can produce chicks this year. Last year's were eaten both in the shell and alive by a predatory raccoon.

A robin appears, hop-hop-hopping on the center island of the driveway, winging off with a worm for its fledglings nested in the junipers. The purple finches are awake and warbling. Eponymous Roger Peterson of my well-worn *Bird Guide* describes purple finches as looking like "sparrows dipped in raspberry juice."

There's a sudden shadow across the peripheral vision of my right eye. A pair of ducks are flying down to the swimming pool. I anticipate their skidding and coming to a stop in the water and move closer to the glass doors to watch them. They have landed. They are not the only ones in the pool. The pool is covered with marsh ducks. Black ducks, gadwalls, mallards. And ducks all lined up along the south side of the pool. And more ducks pecking up the cracked corn Austin has spread for them along the south side of the swimming pool lawn bordered with a hedge of white rosa rugosa. I try to count the ducks, but I can't. They keep moving about. There must be sixty or more.

Jocose July, joyful July. I breakfast on the dining deck and note in my Journal for July that the brugmansia in sight are still pale-leaved but that a white one and a yellow one are flowering. The white impatiens on its tiered rack on the dining deck is in full flower, but not at its August lushness. All the potted herbs on their stands on the deck by the kitchen door are flourishing. Apricot daylilies (*hemerocallis* to botanists) are blooming along the beach steps, and some in the daylily bed. The first blue agapanthus on the dining deck is in flower. There are a few daisies in view on the castle-side bluff. "Daisies, so fresh, so clean, so pure, so white, until like kudzu, they

*I wake up at dawn to the sound of the sea
and the chiming of Latimer's Light in
Long Island Sound. . . . Jocose July, joyful July.*

became a blight." I scribble in my journal, and note that there is purple clover growing on the castle-side bluff, good, and a few stalks of Queen Anne's Lace, bad, as they indicate poor soil. Two urns in sight are filled with neon-bright gold and orange nasturtiums, their color sharp, but a surprisingly pleasing contrast with the sumptuous bed of pastel yellow, pink, and white columbines along Brillig's house walls facing them. The yellow rosa rugosa bushes I planted along the shaded path by the daylily bed are no longer in flower. Rosa rugosas need sun for blooming and flowering well, and I planted these in the wrong spot. I hope in time that they will grow fuller and stay in flower longer. Because of their Herculean rooting system, they are difficult to dig up and transplant successfully. On the castle side bluff, the white rosa rugosa growing up the bluff from the beach and the magenta rosa rugosas growing by the first landing of the beach steps are in full flower.

I wish I could replace the magenta rosa rugosas with the yellow ones that would do much better on the bluff in the sun than where they are by the daylily bed in the shade. The magenta rosa rugosas are almost too large to think of digging them up. Even José and his crew could never dig up all the roots at one time. It would take several years to dig up all the roots and keep them from re-growing. That's the way gardening is. Wishful thinking. Projects one would like to do if one had more time or more help or more money or more space or more energy. A garden is never complete, never finished, always surprising, always a source for learning something new every day, sometimes frustrating, sometimes bliss.

After breakfast, I make my rounds, Journal and magic marker in hand. The climbing hydrangea on the west-facing living room patio is foaming with white flowers, totally luxuriant, but the ducks in the swimming pool hear me, see me, and *flap* they spring like rockets from the pool and swiftly wing west. I go back to my Journal notations. The potted white petunias are flowering nicely along the walled steps on the way to the swimming pool. The

The tamarisk tree by the steps leading to the swimming pool.

hydrangeas, white in the bud, blue in the flower, are more in the bud, less in the flower, but they look extravagantly green-leaved and healthy. By the downstairs guest room patio, some very young wisteria are flowering and one young lavender-blue ceanothus bush is in flower beneath a south-facing window. Looking west, I see the white

Siberian irises and the pale lavender-blue irises going to seed that José will collect to replant. The tamarisk is beginning to bloom, a great tree to have in a seaside garden. Its offshoot that we planted last year, across from it is still a sapling, a little treelet, but even it, is starting to flower, its feathering leaves already turning pinky lavender with sprays of tiny blossoms. The hostas are dense and luxuriant. The *Cimecifuga racemosa* on the west side of the gate to the driveway is in flower. The aruncus next to it, similar in appearance, is not yet in flower.

I make my way to the cutting garden. In the beds by the gate, the *ensata* irises are in flower, blue ones, purply ones, their flowers the size of cocktail napkins, a display I want to photograph to keep their beauty from vanishing away, but then, with the garden gate open, I see the zinnias coming up by the apple tree, and the foxgloves and the hollyhocks and the last of the peonies and the roses and the lavender in bud, a panorama drama of pink, purple, lavender, white, yellow, apricot, and peach stirring in the westerly breeze, and I want to dance, sing, and run around and play like a child, the way children become absolutely crazed with pleasure, as I do in my mind. I stand there transfixed.

July, that jewel of a month, when on the Fourth there will be fountains and cascades and showers of diamonds and rubies and golden drops in the night sky. The Fourth of July is when we shear away the withered mass of daffodils from the west side of the driveway. I think of the *narcissi*, those exquisite daffodils: 'Jonquille des Bois,' 'Soleil d'Or,' 'Extravagance,' 'Midas,' 'Buttercup,' 'April King,' 'Mount Hood.' Faded away now, they will return next year, bringing back beauty and loveliness and wonder. So scythe, mow, and use the weed eater, José and your crew, let everything look fresh and clean again in this jewel of a month.

In the cutting garden, we have two purple martin houses, multiple nesting boxes. Purple martins are the only colonial nesting birds we want to encourage, but house sparrows often usurp these houses. Starlings would like to, but the holes are too small. The house sparrow, *Passer domesticus*, is a weaver finch, introduced to the U.S. in the mid-nineteenth century, and not related to the song sparrows, chipping sparrows, fox sparrows, native to the U.S., that we also enjoy at Brillig. Insects make up 99 percent of the diet of our barn swallows, tree swallows, and rough-winged swallows. They are spectacular flyers and most of their food—gnats, flies, midges, no-see-ums, moths, dragonflies, beetles—is caught while they're aviating, performing acrobatics, jinking and diving with extraordinary speed and precision. Swallows and martins never visit our bird feeders, never visit our suet holders, never can be seen splashing in our fountain or pedestal- or ground-based birdbaths. What they do is fly over the swimming pool, dipping their wings in the pool as they go; they use the east-facing roof above the living room as a resting and preening site and a flight school for their fledglings; they use the roof's gutters to drink from; they like to rest and preen in the sun and in the shaded part of the roof where there is a light and slow-dripping runoff from the air-conditioning system. In the spring, I make mud puddles for them to get mud for their nests and they

I rarely see swallows resting.

do this, but they also use the artificial swallows' nests I ordered long ago and had Austin secure on a nesting shelf beneath the dining deck.

We've put out some two dozen or more nest boxes on the property, all used by swallows, wrens, sparrows, finches, chickadees. Swallows usually build their own nests, as do robins and catbirds. Except for nests of pheasants, which they assemble well hidden beneath bushes or dense planting of lilies, I've never come across any nests of the many other birds on our five-acre property.

I'm so besotted about birds that I've even made little dust-bath areas for the pheasants, and I'm glad we can afford our annual bills for cracked corn, birdseed, suet, raisins, and the grape jelly and the orange cups I put out for the Baltimore orioles I hope will stay—they don't, winging shoreward toward Connecticut—but catbirds and cardinals and other fruit-eating birds enjoy the luxury of fresh-halved oranges and serving bowls of grape jelly. The birds' happiness is my happiness.

Rachel Carson, the first and foremost among speakers against the use of pesticides, was my icon. I've believed fiercely in nontoxic solutions and noncontaminating products ever since I lived in Jamaica in the West Indies where a flock of guinea fowl I raised from chicks died because the gardener I employed at the time used a poisonous spray of DDT on a lime tree to which my guinea fowl and other birds were fatally exposed.

According to the National Audubon Society, 67 million pounds of pesticides are applied annually to home lawns; add school and golf turf and the amount rises to 73 million pounds. That equals 0.26 pounds of pesticide for every man, woman, and child in the U.S. or 8 pounds an acre. That is three times more pesticide than farmers use per acre.

USE OF PESTICIDES

❖ 5 billion pounds of pesticides are applied annually worldwide, 20 percent of them in the United States

❖ 672 million birds are exposed annually; 67 million birds die. This is a conservative estimate.

❖ 50 pesticide active ingredients currently used in the U.S. have caused documented bird kills.

❖ The Environmental Protection Agency registers 890 active ingredients in pesticides, but this does not mean that they are safe or that they were tested in combinations.

❖ 103,046 cases of human pesticide exposure were reported in the U.S.-certified regional poison control centers in 1998. But these centers serve less than half of the population and many cases are not reported since symptoms mimic the flu.

❖ Pesticides and herbicides have decimated butterfly and bee habitancy in the U.S., reduced the variety and quantity of our bird life; polluted, poisoned, and contaminated our ponds, lakes coastal areas, rivers, streams, drinking water.

❖ Current research is validating what J.I. Rodale reported during World War II: Organic produce contains more vitamins and minerals and fewer harmful nitrates and heavy metals than food grown with synthetic fertilizers and pesticides.

❖ First published in 2001 in the *Journal of Alternative and Complementary Medicine*, a study of nutritional data by Virginia Worthington, Sc.D. found that vegetables grown organically contained, on average, 27 percent more vitamin C, 21 percent more iron, 29 percent more magnesium, 14 percent more phosphorus, and 15 percent fewer nitrates than conventional produce. A study published the same year by the Soil Association in Britain drew similar conclusions. A recent posting on www.ORGANICGARDENING.com stated that researchers at the University of California discovered that organically grown produce is higher in cancer-fighting phenolics (antioxidants plants use to defend themselves) than produce sprayed with pesticides and herbicides.

❖ It is common knowledge that while DDT was banned in the U.S. in 1973, we now have chemicals that are just as toxic, and we have them in greater numbers than ever before.

Organic gardening requires no more work than gardening with chemical pesticides and synthetic fertilizers. No chemical sprays, no pesticides was my first edict about our Brillig garden.

Going organic creates healthier, more nutritious plants, builds up the soil, uses less water, and attracts more birds, bees, butterflies, and soil-aerating worms in to your garden, a garden that welcomes beneficial insects such as lacewings, praying mantises, ant lions, and ladybugs—ladybirds, as I used to call them as a child.

For advice about organic gardening, I think there is none better than Howard Garrett, landscape architect and organic horticulturist, author of *The Dirt Doctor's Guide to Organic Gardening*[1] and *J. Howard Garrett's Organic Manual*[2] (See "Sources and Advice: Where to buy plants, seeds, garden furniture, pots and urns, both resin and clay, etc."). In a fabulous newsletter to which I subscribe, *Bottom Line Personal*, he shared four of his secret gardening recipes that have worked like a charm for us at Brillig.

Here are his four organic gardening spray recipes:

Compost Tea
- Half fill a 5- to 15-gallon plastic bucket with compost
- Fill to the top with water
- Let mixture sit for 10 to 14 days
- Dilute with water until it takes on the appearance of iced tea
- Before using liquid to fertilize plants, strain any solid material from the tea through cheesecloth

Garrett Juice
- Combine 1 cup compost tea (see above)
- 1 oz. molasses
- 1 oz. natural apple cider vinegar
- 1 oz. liquid seaweed
- One gallon of water

Garlic Tea
- Liquefy two bulbs of garlic with some water in a blender
- Strain and pour juice into a one-gallon container

- Fill to the top with water
- Shake before using
- *To make garlic/pepper tea:* Add two cayenne or habañero peppers to the blender

Organic Fungicide
- 4 teaspoons baking soda or potassium bicarbonate
- 1 tablespoon horticultural oil (optional)
- 1 gallon of water

To get an organic garden started, here's what we did at Brillig: We tested our soil. Soil contains millions of diverse microorganisms critical to plant growth. Respecting the role of soil as a living ecosystem and nurturing it is the first step in organic gardening. Determine if your soil is acidic or alkaline, and the level of its organic matter and trace minerals. Autumn is an excellent time for soil testing, but you can test your soil anytime. Your local gardening center can give you information about nearby testing facilities. Make sure your soil is tested for

calcium, which is important for root growth and will also benefit beneficial soil bacteria. If the test results show you have a deficiency of calcium, you can apply calcitic lime to give your soil a boost. You might need other trace minerals, granite sand, zeolite, soft-rock phosphate, whatever. The exact amount and type of material your garden needs will depend on your soil analysis. If you don't have a local testing resource, Howard Garrett supplied information about his favorite testing resource: Texas Plant and Soil Lab, Inc. (See "Sources and Advice: Where to buy plants, seeds, garden furniture, pots and urns, both resin and clay, etc."). Garrett says that their tests are more thorough than those provided through most local garden centers, and available at affordable prices.

Mr. E.K. Chanler, the agronomist-microbiologist owner of Texas Plant and Soil Lab, Inc., well versed in the techniques of organic gardening and an expert about fertilizers, asks that you collect 2 measuring cups of soil samples from 4 to 6 locations, mixing them well together and putting the mixture into a plastic Ziploc bag with a written enclosure about your soil, what you have added to it

in the way of fertilizer, such as horse manure, seaweed, guano, chicken manure. If you are taking samples from turf areas, you should dig up soil from the top of the soil to 5". If you are collecting soil from a flowerbed, dig up the top of the soil to 12". It might be a good idea to talk with Mr. Chanler or one of his assistants before you send your representative composite mix of soil to be tested. There is a five-day turnaround, so you won't have to wait long to have the results of your soil's testing.

The prescription for soil health is supplied by the use of compost, manures, and mulches. E.K. Chanler recommends seaweed but would appreciate knowing just where your seaweed comes from, as there is a great deal of difference in seaweed that comes from Alaska or Australia or the Gulf of Texas.

An initial application of fertilizer is best done in early spring. If your plants are doing well, fertilize again every 60 to 90 days throughout the growing season. Howard Garrett's Garrett Juice is a nontoxic, highly effective fertilizer you can make yourself to apply to soil, shrub, and tree foliage, trunks, and limbs.

Compost is decomposed organic matter—some lawn clippings; rotted manure, vegetable peelings, well-washed chopped seaweed, kitchen scraps (everything except meat that attracts rodents); leaves, sawdust, dog, cat, and bird droppings. You can create a compost pile at any time of year in an unused area of your property. Compost takes about seven months to a year to be ready to use, when it is transformed to soft, crumbly, dark-brown humus, "brown gold," it's called, or "black gold," that smells the way a forest path smells, and is teeming with microorganisms that enrich the soil. If you need compost sooner, have several piles, as we do, or use a commercial rotating cylinder that can deliver compost in less than a month, sometimes within two weeks (See "Compost").

We use compost as a fertilizer on all our plants, and also use compost as a **mulch** to cut down on watering needs and to minimize weeds.

To prepare soil for planting, we hoe up grass and weeds, add a 4" to 6" layer of compost mixed in 3" to 8" of the soil.

Aerate your soil, poking it with a garden fork to get air to the microbes in the earth. Tilling the soil has the same effect of oxygenating the soil, but repeated tilling can damage the structure of the soil, which means that you'll have to add extra compost to help the soil life regroup and recuperate.

Native and ornamental grasses are top-notch anti-erosion plantings for road banks, cliff sides, beachfront. We have prevented erosion with plantings of bayberry and rosa rugosa, white and pink ones as well as the naturalized magenta ones. White rosa rugosa has a light, sweet fragrance. Yellow rosa rugosa has a more seductive scent. Vines and rosa rugosa don't mix well. We work hard to keep our rosa rugosas free of morning glories and ampelopsis.

When our compost heaps were maturing and I felt our soil was healthy and that no danger existed of poisons or contaminants, I thought the time had come to attract birds, bees, and butterflies to our garden by first providing **ready-made food, shelter,** and **birdbaths.**

Creating landscapes and gardens attractive to birds, butterflies, and bees improves plant pollenization and fertilization; ups the quality of local honey products; helps immeasurably to eliminate flies, midges, mosquitoes, bugs, slugs, and nasty garden pests that many birds consume daily in quantities equal to their body weight.

With the help of pollen spreaders like hummingbirds, butterflies, and bees, flowers make seeds that grow into new plants. Seeds also provide bird food. There's no denying that enchanting butterflies, as well as their larval caterpillars, are also a source of food for birds, just as birds are quarry for raptors and other predators.

Birds grant us pleasurable diversion with their patterns of flight and plumage, their colors, calls, and songs. Their rituals of courtship, nesting, feeding, territorial defense, bathing in water, preening can be mesmeric.

Adding bird feeders and birdhouses for nesting and shelter make your garden a more welcoming haven in exchange for exceptional bird-watching opportunities (See "Sources and Advice: Where to buy plants, seeds, garden furniture, pots and urns, both resin and clay, etc.").

The National Wildlife Federation encouraged us to include **native plants** in our landscape. Native plants are hardy, beautiful, and once established require less maintenance than exotic plants. Native flowers and grasses function like a natural system, with diverse plants offering food and shelter for birds, butterflies, and beneficial insects. Once established, native plants don't need pesticides, fertilizers, or water, saving a gardener money and time besides being beneficial for the environment. Landscaping with native wildflowers and grasses helps return the area to a healthy ecosystem, creates a sense of place, and enhances the biodiversity of the area. Native plants, like goldenrod, harbor insects, an excellent food source for some birds and, in the autumn, when the goldenrod fades, sparrows and finches will devour its seeds.

I like seeing native plants, knowing that they thrived on Fishers Island before that was its name, when the Pequots lived and fished here, before settlers arrived and

I grow milkweed especially for the monarch larvae to feed on.

introduced plants from other regions. Native plants have natural resistance to native pests and diseases. They have evolved and adapted to our climate and are accustomed to our soils and summers, our winters and our waters.

I like the idea that our orange coneflowers (*Echinacea fulgida*) and our purple coneflowers (*Echinacea purpurea*) are cousins of the narrow-leaf coneflower, much valued by the Indians of the Great Plains, the roots of which, Captain Meriwether Lewis wrote to Thomas Jefferson, are used to treat the bite "of the mad wolf or dog and also for the bite of the rattlesnake."[3] Our Amerlanchier trees are native, as are our ferns, butterfly weed (*Asclepias tuberosa*) beloved by butterflies, as are our drought-resistant black-eyed Susans (*Rudbeckia hirta*). Our junipers, Virginia creeper, winterberry (*Ilex verticillata*), our wild columbine (*Aquilegia candensis*), angelica, our *Cimecifuga racemosa*, turtlehead (*Chelone*), coreopsis, Joe-Pye weed (*Eupatorium*), sunflowers (*Helianthus spp*), penstemon, phlox, the late-summer flowering deciduous shrub, sometimes called summer sweet or spice bush (*Clethra alnifolia*), and bayberry with its fragrant leathery leaves and its waxy silvery berries are only a few of our native American plants, a joy to garden with. There are hundreds of other choices, of course, and the Brooklyn Botanic Garden can send you lists of nurseries supplying them in your area (See "Sources and Advice: Where to buy plants, seeds, garden furniture, pots and urns, both resin and clay, etc.").

Hummingbirds and butterflies are more reliable pollinators than the wind. To encourage hummingbirds, **plant nectar flowers so that something will always be in flower.** Columbines, agastache/anise hyssop, scarlet sage (*Salvia*) would be a splendid spring-through-autumn choice. Large groups attract the attention of hummingbirds better than a single plant.

Butterflies need access to water and mineral salts to strengthen the scent of male pheromones and increase the female's egg production. As well as enhancing lepidopteron reproductive success, water and minerals also help them maintain brilliant wing color, a defense against predation. One way to aid them do this is to dampen a compost pile, exposed to the open air that affords an area for butterflies to drink from, as they do from a seep of water over sand and a rock that I also provide for them, along with the requisite half-inch of water or less, furnished for hummingbirds to sip from and bathe in. On my mind's bulletin board I've pinned this quotation of Nathaniel Hawthorne: "Happiness is a butterfly, which, when pursued, is always just beyond your grasp, but

which, if you will sit down quietly, may alight upon you."[4] We have Eastern black swallowtails that actually range all the way to the Rocky Mountains where the Western black swallowtail takes over.  Parsley is a host plant for its larva, along with Queen Anne's lace, dill, carrots, and celery. Adult swallowtails like phlox and purple coneflowers. We have mourning cloaks and red admirals, monarchs for whom I've planted a large larval stand of milkweed. I've seen a great spangled fritillary feeding on a black-eyed Susan. I'm told they also like thistles and other nectar plants and that their larval host plants are violets. Butterflies really do flock to our butterfly bushes (*Buddleia*) and our butterfly weed (*Asclepias tuberosa*), described memorably in *Horticulture* magazine as "one of our zingiest native wildflowers."[5] Butterfly weed's deep, tuberous roots that render it drought tolerant also make it a pain in the neck to dig up and transplant, so where we've put it—on the bluff across from the stand of larval milkweed for the monarchs—there it stays, and now we have at least six plants of it, magnetic to butterflies and to hummingbirds.

Solitary bees pollinate our milkweeds (*Asclepias spp.*), Joe-Pye weeds (*Eupatorium spp.*), globe thistles (*Echinops spp.*), all native plants.

Bumblebees pollinate our lavender, foxgloves (*Digitalis spp.*), passionflowers (*Passiflora spp.*), catmints (*Nepeta*).

Butterflies pollinate our asters, bee balms (*Monarda spp.*), coneflowers (*Echinachea spp.*), honeysuckles (*Lonicera spp.*), milkweeds (*Asclepias spp.*), penstemons, yarrows (*Achillea spp.*).

Moths pollinate our yuccas, moonflowers (*Ipomea alba*), and flowering tobacco (*Nicotiana alata*).

Butterflies can't fight wind, don't like wind, and need a windbreak that can be anything from a stone wall to a trumpet vine hedge that provides nectar in summer and shelter in late autumn. Butterflies, like birds, only fly well when their wings are dry, but lack birds' ability to fly in the cold. Butterflies like sun, thrive in the sun and light, and like to rest on a warm rock, or a warm, dry railing. Butterflies are day-flying. Moths usually fly by night and are thus less commonly seen doing their important work of pollinating night-blooming flowers. Butterflies hold their wings vertically. Moths usually hold their wings in a V shape.

Things to remember, I reminded myself some fourteen years ago:

- To attract butterflies, it's important to provide food for their larval caterpillars as well as nectar for them. Plant artemesias, milkweed, nettles, Queen Anne's lace (a mistake, explained in the next chapter).
- Butterflies appreciate a water source, preferably a mist of water, or a film of water, something moist, like a juicy orange-half or a rotting pear or the compost heap after rain.

- Butterflies like asters, butterfly bushes, butterfly weeds, caryopteris, chives, purple coneflower, dianthus, honeysuckle, lavender, liatris, lilac, monarda, pansies, phlox, snapdragon, verbena, yarrow.
- To attract butterflies, avoid windy sites—impossible at Brillig. Provide windbreaks and shelter. Select brilliantly colored flowers. Nectar is more accessible in single flowers than double crinkly ones, like delphiniums. Butterflies are attracted to a quantity of a few plants rather than single specimens of many plants. Purple, yellow, orange, and red are butterfly favorites.

Fourteen years later my advice to myself holds up. We have many butterflies at Brillig in spite of the way their number has decreased nationally, owing to the use of pesticides and herbicides. For more information about butterflies and bees and the conservation of pollinators, visit the website of Xerces, an organization devoted to the health and preservation of invertebrates (See "Sources and Advice: Where to buy plants, seeds, garden furniture, pots and urns, both resin and clay, etc."). Here are two lists provided by the Xerces Society:

Black-eyed Susans flourish in the grape arbor.

Native Plants for Bees and other Pollinator Insects
(All good sources of nectar and pollen and all of which grow well at Brillig.)

Yarrow	*Achillea spp.*
Giant hyssop	*Agastache spp.*
Wild onion	*Allium spp.*
Aster	*Aster spp.*
Gaillardia	*Gaillardia spp.*
Geranium	*Geranium spp.*
Sunflower	*Helianthus spp.*
Flax	*Linum spp.*
Penstemon	*Penstemon spp.*
Currant/Gooseberry	*Ribes spp.*
Wild Rose	*Rosa spp.*
Willow	*Salix spp.*
Stonecrop	*Sedum spp.*
Groundsel	*Senecio spp.*
Goldenrod	*Solidago*
Mullein	*Verbascum spp.*

Garden Plants and Herbs for Bees and other Pollinator Insects (Which also all grow well at Brillig.)

Giant hyssop	*Agastache spp.*
Borage	*Borage spp.*
Ceonothus	*Ceonothus spp.*
Cleome	*Cleome spp.*
Cosmos	*Cosmos spp.*
Joe-pye weed	*Eupatorium spp.*
Sunflower	*Helianthus spp.*
Lavender	*Lavandula spp.*
Liatris	*Liatris spp.*
Mint	*Metha spp.*
Four o'clock	*Mirabilis jalapa*
Monarda	*Monarda spp.*
Basil	*Ocimum spp.*
Marjoram	*Origanum spp.*
Poppy	*Papavar spp.*
Rosemary	*Rosmarinus spp.*
Sage	*Salvia spp.*
Thyme	*Thymus spp.*
Mullein	*Verbascum spp.*
Verbena	*Verbena spp.*
Zinnia	*Zinnia spp.*

One of the reasons I regard butterflies as a fine rapture of our souls is that after Hurricane Bob in 1991 had uprooted and hurled trees to the ground, flung rocks like beach balls along the beach, strewn branches, leaves, twigs, flowers all over the grass, the rain stopped, the wind died down, and the first living creatures I saw from the living room window were a mourning dove and a yellow swallowtail butterfly lilting in the air toward a magenta rosa rugosa.

TO ATTRACT BUTTERFLIES

A	Annual	**P**	Perennial	**BI**	Biennial	**GRC**	Ground cover
HA	Hardy Annual	**HP**	Hardy Perennial	**B**	Bulb	**D**	Deciduous

FLOWERS FOR BUTTERFLIES

Ageratum/Floss Flower	*Ageratum spp.* *houstonianum mexicanum*	HA
Anise/hyssop	*Agastache foeniculum*	P
Asters	*Aster spp.*	P
Bachelor's button	*Centaurea cyanus*	A
Black-eyed Susan	*Rudbeckia hirta*	HA
Butterfly weed	*Asclepias tuberosa*	P
Cardinal flower	*Lobelia spp.*	P
China asters	*Callistephus chinensis* (Many kinds, colors)	A
Cleome	*Capparidaceae spp.*	A
Clover, red	*Trifolium pratense* (Naturalized herb that enriches soil)	P
Clover, white to pink	*Trifolium repens* (Naturalized wild flower that enriches the soil. There are 20 Eastern U.S. species of clover; some 250 species throughout the world)	P
Coneflower, purple	*Echinacea purpurea*	P
Coral bells	*Heuchera spp.*	P
Coreopsis/tickseed	*Coreopsis grandiflora*	P
Cosmos	*Cosmos spp.*	A
Dandelion	*Taraxcum officinale* (Naturalized herb, indicator of acid, compact soil)	A/P
Daylily	*Hemerocallis spp.*	B
Echinacea	(see Coneflower, purple)	
False Indigo	*Baptisia Australis*	P
Gaillardia x grandiflora	*Gaillardia spp.*	P
Globe thistle	*Echinops ritro*	P
Goldenrod	*Solidago spp.*	P
Hollyhock	*Alcea rosea spp.*	P/HA
Impatiens	*Impatiens spp.*	A
Joe-Pye weed	*Eupatorium spp.*	P
Knapweed/cornflower	*Centaurea spp.*	P
Liatris	*Liatris spp.*	P
Lupines	*Lupinus* 'Russell Hybrids' (Short lived: 3 years)	P
Mallow, marsh	*Malva, spp.* (Seashore, salt marshes, swampy, moist areas. *Alcea officinalis/* marsh mallow/pink mallow. Can be grown in ordinary garden soil, well-watered. Not to be confused with Rose of Sharon, *Hibiscus syriacus*, 'Diana')	P

Mallow, swamp	*Hibiscus moscheutos* (*Malva alcea officinalis* and *Hibiscus moscheutos* — Both genera thrive in damp locations)	P
Marigold	*Tagetes spp.*	A
Mexican sunflower	*Tithonia spp.*	A
Mint	*Menth spp.*	P
Milkweed/Butterfly weed	*Asclepias spp.* (Naturalized wildflower)	P
Monarda	*Monarda spp.*	P
Nicotiana	*Nicotiana spp.*	A
Pansy	*Viola tricolor*	P/BI
Petunias	*Petunia hybrida* (Good for pots, window boxes; many colors)	A
Phlox	*Phlox spp.*	P
Pinks	*Dianthus spp.*	P
Sage	*Salvia superba*	P
Scabiosa/pincushion flower	*Scabiosa spp.*	A/P
Sea holly	*Eryngium spp.*	P
Sedum	*Sedum spp.*	P/GRC
Shasta Daisy	*Chrysanthemum maximum*	P
Snapdragon	*Antirrhiniumm majus*	A
Snow-in-Summer/	*Ceraslium spp.*	P/GRC
Rock Cress	*Arabis albida*	P/GRC
Spirea (Blue)	*Caryopteris spp.*	
Sweet Alyssum	*Alyssum Maritimum/*	HA
	Lobularia maritima	HA
Tickseed	(see *Coreopsis*)	
Tobacco (flowering)	(see *Nicotiana*)	
Verbena	*Verbena spp.*	P
Veronica	*Viola spp.*	P/BI
Yarrow	*Achillea spp.*	P
Zinnia	*Zinnia spp.*	A

Veronica (*Viola spp.*)

HERBS FOR BUTTERFLIES

Chives
Dill
Fennel
Oregano
Parsley

VINES FOR BUTTERFLIES

Trumpet Vine	*Campsis radicans* (Climbing vine, bush up to 6 feet, orange flowers)	P
Honeysuckle	*Lonicera spp.*	P
Hops	*Humulus lupulus*, 'Americanus'	
Hops, Japanese	*Humulus Japonicus* (Dioecious; i.e., the male and female are produced on separate plants, so you need two plants which can be fertilized by bees, butterflies, and the wind)	
Passion flower	*Passiflora spp.* (hardy variety)	

DECIDUOUS TREES FOR BUTTERFLIES

Aspen

Wild Cherry

BUSHES/SHRUBS/SMALL TREES FOR BUTTERFLIES

Azalea	*Rhododendron spp.*
Butterfly bush	*Buddleia spp.* (Arches with age. Matures at 10 feet. Flowers: (white, pink, dark purple, reddish purple, bluish purple. Needs careful pruning. Flowers bloom off current season's growth)
	B. Alternifolia (Fountainlike, lavender colored blooms, needs careful pruning. Flowers bloom on branches of previous year's growth. Up to 20 feet. No other colors.)
Ceanothus	*Ceanothus spp.* (An attractive shrub with lavender-blue flowers)
Citrus trees, lemon and orange	
Clethra	*Clethra alnifolia*
Lavender	*Lavandula spp.*
Privet (shrub)	*Ligustrum spp*
Lilac	*Syringa Vulgaris*
Spice bush/Summersweet	(see *Clethra*)
Turtlehead	*Chelone lyonii*

TO ATTRACT HUMMINGBIRDS AND BEES

Bee balm/bergamot	*Monarda didyma*	P
Butterfly weed	*Asclepias Tuberosa*	P
Cardinal flower	*Lobelia cardinalis/Lobelia fulgens* (Requires protection from wet and frost) *Lobelia spp.*	P
Canterbury Bells	*Campanula spp.*	P
Cleome	*Cleome spinosa* (Also, greatly bee-loved for nectar and pollen)	HA
Columbine	*Aquilegia spp.*	P
Currant, flowering	*Ribes spp.* (Shrub/bush, many choices of form, and color, from white tinged with pink, to crimson red)	
Coneflower, orange	*Rudbeckia Fulgida*	
Coral bells	*Heuchera sanguinea* *Heuchera micantha* (purple-leaf)	P
Delphinium	*Delphinium spp.* (Belladonna hybrids)	P
Four o'clocks	*Mirabilis jalapa*	A
Foxglove	*Digitalis purpurea spp.*	P
Liatris	*Liatris spicata*	P
Lupine	*Lupinus*, 'Russell hybrids'	P
Monarda (see Bee Balm)	*Monarda spp.*	P
Morning glory	*Ipomea spp.* (Vines in pink, white, purple, blue, the latter most appealing)	A
Nasturtium	*Tropaeolum spp.* (Many climbing or trailing varieties, many colors)	A

Obedient plant	*Physotegia spp.*	P
Penstemon	*Penstemon spp.*	P
Petunia	*Petunia spp.*	.A
Phlox	*Phlox spp.*	P
Quince, ornamental	*Chaenomeles speciosa* (Scarlet-crimson flowers)	P
	Chaenomeles superba (Deciduous shrub or wall-climbing vine, orange-scarlet flowers; all varieties of quince flower on old wood and need hard pruning in early spring before they grow flowers)	
Rhododendron	*Rhododendron spp.*	
Salvla (sage)	*Salvia spp.*	
Scarlet sage	*Salvia splendens*	P
Summer Phlox	*Phlox spp.*	P
Tobacco plant (flowering)	*Nicotiana alata*, 'Daylight' (White, remains open all day)	A
	N. alata, 'sensation mixed,' Many colors, remains open all day)	
	N. hybrida (Hybrid cross of N. alata and N. langsdorffii, blooms summer to mid-autumn and remains open during the day. Most nicotiana, day- or night-opening, are intensely fragrant, appealing to bees.)	
	N. sylvestris (Strong night fragrance)	
Trumpet honeysuckle (vine)	*Lonicera spp.*	
Trumpet vine	*Campsis radicans,* *Tecoma radicans*	
Winterberry holly	*Ilex verticillata*	P
Yarrow	*Achillea x Moonshine* *Achillea spp.*	P
Zinnia	*Zinnia spp.*	A

OF SPECIAL INTEREST:

Hibiscus standards (in pots)	*Hibiscus, rosa sinensis* For sunny summer terraces and porches. Single or double flower forms. Colors: Pink, red, apricot. Yellow is less attractive to hummingbirds. Put outside after danger of frost is over. June is safe. Bring inside in October/November for overwintering. Expect loss of leaves and diminished flowering at lower temperatures, no less than 55 degrees. At 45 degrees, plant goes dormant and must be kept dry.

TO ATTRACT BIRDS

A	Annual	P	Perennial	BI	Biennial	GRC	Ground cover
HA	Hardy Annual	HP	Hardy Perennial	B	Bulb	D	Deciduous

BIRD-ATTRACTING FLOWERS

Ageratum/Floss Flower	*Ageratum houstonianum/A. mexicanum*	A
Alyssum, sweet alyssum	*Alyssum maritimum/Lobularia maritima*	HA
	(Many colors, including white, pink, violet, yellow hues, with silvery leaves prostrate, spreading, subshrubby habits)	
Asters	*Aster spp.*	P
Bachelor's button	*Centaurea cyanus*	A
Bee Balm	*Monarda spp.*	P
Black-eyed Susan	*Rudbeckia spp.*	P
Columbine	*Aquilegia spp.*	A
Coneflower, purple	*Echinacea purpurea*	P
Coreopsis	*Coreopsis grandiflora*	P
Cosmos	*Cosmos spp* (Many colors, from white to vermilion)	HA
Goldenrod	*Solidago spp.*	P
	Solidago canadensis (Hybrid forms in pink and many hues of yellow)	P
	Solidago vigaurea	P
Joe-Pye weed	*Eupatorium spp.*	P
Lily of the valley	*Convalleria majalis*	B
Marigold, African	*Tagetes erecta*	HA/BI
Marigold, pot	*Calendula officinalis*	A
Red-hot poker	*Kniphofia spp* (Great for seed-eating birds)	P
Roses	*Rosa spp* (Catbirds nest in our climbing 'New Dawn' roses)	P
Sage	*Salvia spp.*	P
Sea holly	*Eryngium amesthystinum*	P
	E. alpinum	
	E. tripartitum	
	E. variifolium	
Sedum	*Sedum spp.*	P
Shrub roses	*Rosa rugosa*, 'Hansa'	P
	R. virginiana	
Sunflower	*Helianthus spp.*	A/P
Sunflower, Mexican	*Tithonia rotundifolia*	A
Zinnia	*Zinnia elegans*	A
	Zinnia spp.	A

BIRD-ATTRACTING VINES
For Cover and Rest Sites

Bittersweet	*Celastrus scandens*
Clematis	*Clematis spp.*
Convolvulus, dwarf	*Convolvulus tricolor minor*
Grape	*Vitis spp.* (Autumn fruiting—is a lure for fruit eaten by more than 50 species of birds, including thrashers, mockingbirds, cardinals, catbirds and thrushes.)
Honeysuckles	*Lonicera spp.* (Catbirds, thrushes, towhees, thrashers, robins like honeysuckle for berries, resting, and shelter—attracts chipping sparrows, song sparrows, goldfinches, some, like towhees, for nesting)
Hop	*Humulus spp.*
Ivy	*Hedera spp.*
Morning glory	*Ipomoea spp.* (All varieties like full sun and soil after established)
Trumpet Vine	*Campsis radicans*
Virginia creeper	*Parthenocissus quinquefolia* (Autumn-fruiting, winter-persistent fruit, for berries and shelter— attracts mockingbirds, purple finches, robins, flickers, thrushes, catbirds, starlings, vireos, warblers, and many others)

BIRD-ATTRACTING DECIDUOUS TREES

Beech	*Fagus spp.*
Birches	*Betula* (silver birch and other species)
Bird Cherry	*Prunus padus*
Cherry, flowering	*Prunus avium plena*
Hackberry	*Celtis occidentalis*
Linden	*Tilia platyphyllos*
Mulberry	*Morus spp.*

(More than forty birds, including cardinals, robins and waxwings, find fruit and shelter among the mulberry. Position it where the falling fruit and bird droppings won't be a nuisance— away from walkways and far away from where you park your car. Fledglings need berries high in sugar in summer.)

BIRD-ATTRACTING BUSHES / FLOWERING, FRUITING SHRUBS / SMALL TREES

Barberry, Japanese	*Berberis thunbergii*, 'Golden Ring'
	B. Thunbergii, 'Rose Glow' (For protection, nesting, berries—attracts catbirds, juncos, hermit thrushes, song sparrows, tree sparrows, chipping sparrows)
Bayberry	*Myrica pensylvanica* (For nesting and high-fat berries—attracts catbirds, flickers, tree swallows, hermit thrush and many others)
Blackberry	*Rubus allegheniensis*
	Rubus spp. (More or less deciduous bramble, often naturalized, both erect and trailing. Highly flavored kinds for jelly-making are usually the erect-caned variety. Varieties include Lawton blackberries and Lucretia dewberries—attracts catbirds, robins, and many others)
Blueberry	*Vaccinium corymbosum*, Swamp-High Bush
	Vaccinium angustifolium, Low Bush-Dry Soil (For berries—attracts cardinals, chickadees, towhees, brown thrashers, thrushes, blue birds)
Buckthorn	*Rhamnus cathartica* (Fruits in summer and shelter for cardinals, finches, grosbeaks, blue jays, robins, sparrows, thrashers, thrushes, and quail)
Bush honeysuckle	*Lonicera tatarica*
Cherry, flowering	*Prunus tomentosa/Prunus spp.*
Chokecherry	*Prunus virginiana/Prunus spp.*

Chokeberry	*Aronia arbutifolia*
Cornelian cherry	*Cornus mas*
Cotoneaster	*Cotoneaster spp.* (Large shrub, up to 15 or 20 feet, wide-spreading. Provides cover and berries, loved for its scarlet berries by sparrows, robins, purple finches, wood thrushes, brown thrashers, cedar waxwings)
Crabapple, flowering	*Malus sargentii/Malus spp.* (Keep their fruits in winter and are beloved by catbirds, finches, robins, cardinals, thrushes, waxwings, grosbeaks, and many others)
Cranberry bush	*Vaccinium macrocarpon* (A woody plant with evergreen leaves, fruiting early in September, allied to the blueberries, mostly grown in the Northeast, in Massachusetts and New Jersey. Quite a few varieties, which grow in marshy land, acid soils of peat or vegetable molds free from loam or clay, cleared of turf and with a surface layer of sand. Protected from frost and winter injury by flooding)
Currant	*Ribes spp.*
Dogwood (flowering)	*Cornus spp.* *Cornus sericea* (Has attractive red branches for winter landscapes) *Cornus sibirica*, 'Kousa' (For berries—attracts cardinals, catbirds, finches, robins, juncos, king birds, vireos, thrushes, towhees, tanagers, grosbeaks, warblers, and others)
Elderberry	*Sambucas racemosa*, *Sambucus Canadensis* (Attractive to cardinals, kingbirds, mockingbirds, orioles, blue jays, common grackles, thrushes)
Firethorn	*Pyrecantha coccinea* (attracts cardinals, mockingbirds; catbirds nest in it)
Goldenrain tree	*Koelreuteria particulata*
Hawthorn	*Crataegus phaenopyrum* *C. crusgalli* (Keeps its berries in winter)
Holly/Inkberry/ Winterberry	*Ilex spp.* (Dioecious, i.e., for berries, you need male and female trees; bees, butterflies, and wind to pollinate. Attracts and provides winter food and shelter for cardinals, blue jays, grosbeaks, cedar waxwings, mockingbirds, robins, thrashers, thrushes, and towhees) *Ilex glabra* (The sort of small plant you see illustrated in medieval manuscripts, a symbol of sumptuous plenty, often regarded as a weed. Keep away from house porch and garden fence to avoid stains from bird droppings.) *Ilex verticillata* (For swampy and damp ground. A deciduous holly that holds on to its bright-red berries long after it loses its leaves. Attracts bluebirds, brown thrashers, catbirds, cedar waxwings, hermit thrushes, and purple finches)
Juniper	*Juniperus spp.* (Fruit-bearing)
Lavender	*Lavandula angustifolia/Lavendula spp.* (Attracts bees)
Lavender cotton	*Santolina chamae cyparissus* (Ever-gray foliage)
Mountain Ash	*Sorbus americana*
Mountain Ash, Sitka	*Sorbus sitchensis*
Plum	*Prunus americana*
Potentilla/Cinquefoil	*Potentilla arbuscula* (Flowering shrub) *Potentilla atrosanguinea* (Flowers that grow in a clump with branching stems) *Potentilla fruticosa* (Deciduous, dense, flowering bush) *Potentilla spp.*
Privet	*Ligustrum vulgari* (Used for hedges, small and large. When mature and tall, a good windbreak)

Raspberry, blackcap	*Rubus orientalis/Rubus spp.*
Raspberry, red	*Rubus strigosus/Rubus spp.*
Rosa rugosa/shrub rose	*Rosa rugosa spp.* (Many varieties and forms. Yellow ones are more strongly scented. Their varieties: colored pink, magenta, yellow, white. Most kinds naturalize readily)
Russian olive	*Elaeagnus angustifolia*
Russian sage	*Perovskia atriplicifolia*
Shad/Serviceberry/ June berry	*Amelanchier spp.* *Amelanchier canadensis* (Blooms mid-May when shad are running. Red-winged blackbirds love its berries as do woodpeckers, hermit thrushes, orioles, robins, cardinals, tangers, grosbeaks, vireos, waxwings, and others. Birds feast on dark-blue berries in June that earned it another name—juneberry.)
Snowberry	*Symphoricarpus albus* (Small, twiggy deciduous shrub up to 4 feet, pink flowers, large fruit berries. The variety laevigatus bears long-lasting berries. *S. orbiculatus* (a deciduous shrubby ground cover with scarlet berries in autumn. Good for covering bluffs and banks. Many new hybrid forms)
Staghorn Sumac	*Rhus typhina/Rhus spp.* (Autumn-fruiting, spiky clusters of hairy red fruits persist through winter that are important food for many birds. Attracts catbirds, cardinals, chickadees, robins, starlings, pheasants, thrushes, and many others)
Thimbleberry	*Rubus odoratus*
Vibernums	*Vibernum fragrans* (Small scarlet fruit, many other varieties, including cranberry bush vibernum) *Vibernum trilobum* (Retains berries through most of the winter) *Vibernum carlcephalo*, 'Fragrant snowball' (Is intensely fragrant up close) *Vibernum triloba* and *Viburnum ovata* (Hold on to their berries until early spring when food is scarce and migrating birds are in dire need) *Vibernum dentatum*/arrowwood (Attracts flickers, purple finches, robins, white-eyed vireos, Eastern bluebirds, rose-breasted grosbeaks, the latter three rarely seen on Fishers Island and never recorded at Brillig) *Viburnum spp.*

BIRD-ATTRACTING EVERGREENS

Arborvitae	*Thuja occidentalis* (Many cultivars)
Cedar	*Cedrus/Juniperus/Virginiana* (Autumn-fruiting, winter-persistent fruit, attracts waxwings and others)
Firs	*Abies spp.*
Hemlocks	*Tsuga spp.*
Hollies	*Ilex spp.*
Junipers	*Juniperus spp.* (Autumn berry-bearing, winter-persistent berries. Mourning doves, pheasants, quail, thrashers, thrushes, warblers, waxwings, finches, flickers, blue jays, mockingbirds, grosbeaks, phoebes, cardinals, robins, song sparrows, chipping sparrows, and fox sparrows all find food and shelter; some, like robins and others, nest in junipers.)
Pines	*Pinus spp.* (Provide shelter, seed inside the pinecones. Attractive to cardinals, chickadees, finches, flycatchers, hawks, blue jays, juncos, kinglets, nuthatches, owls, towhees, vireos, woodpeckers, warblers, and other birds who nest and shelter in them)
Spruces	*Picea spp.* (Autumn offers seed-bearing pinecones that appeal to seed-eating birds. Attracts migrating warblers and others, pheasants roost in them)

BIRD-ATTRACTING FRUITING GROUND COVER

Bearberry	*Arctostaphylos uva-ursi*
Huckleberry	*Gaylussacia baccata*
Strawberry, wild	*Fragaria*
Virginia creeper	*Parthenocissus quinquefolia*
Wintergreen, creeping	*Gaultheria procumbens* (For acid soil)

We have endured trials and tribulations.
...We shoveled, shoveled, shoveled...

Chapter 10

Coping with Mistakes, Triumphing in Disaster

We have endured trials and tribulations.

Ten years ago, garden helpers limed the lawn around the swimming pool with excess enthusiasm, thinking they would amend the compact acidic soil in which dandelions thrived. Hank asked the helpers to dig the dandelions up because he didn't like them, but they were hard to uproot, their fluffy seedballs parachuting far and wide. I happen to like dandelions, entertained by the British pronunciation of the French phrase *dent de lion*, or "lion's tooth," remembering also a French teacher who called a dandelion a *pissenlit*. A piss-a-bed, a pee-in-bedder, just like a naughty child, what a funny name for a flower. Why is it called that, I remember asking Mlle. Thiébaud, my French teacher in Senior One at Green Vale, where I was blessed with extraordinarily good English, French, and Latin teachers. "Because eating the leaves make people do that," she said. "The *racines* are good to clean the liver." The dandelion's botanical name, *Taraxacum officinale*, derives from a Greek word meaning to stimulate or unsettle, because the plant was used as an invigorating tonic. The Latin word *officinale* indicates the dandelion's availability in apothecary shops and is used as a medicinal plant. What Mlle. Thiébaud said still holds true. I recently read in a health magazine that dandelion roots are used as liver cleansers and purifiers. They stimulate the liver to produce bile, thus easing the digestive process, while the leaves produce taraxacin, which acts as a diuretic, stimulating the kidneys to produce urine. Because the dandelion is high in potassium, a vital nutrient often lost when the kidneys process their intake, herbalists prefer dandelion leaves to chemical diuretics. Young dandelion leaves, more nutritious than spinach, have more calcium, iron, and fiber than broccoli, and they are a rich source of beta-carotene, with 13 times the vitamin A of carrots. A tea made of dandelion roots and/or leaves is good for diabetics. Steamed young dandelion leaves as a vegetable with a little butter, cream, and a tad of vinegar are delicious.

The next year, there were no dandelions on the swimming pool lawn—there were some, thank heavens, on the front lawn—and the hydrangeas, emerging from alkalinized soil instead of their customary acid soil, had turned the color of tea-stained lace. I scissored off all the offending buckskin beige flowerheads and they went sackful after sackful to the compost heaps. We shoveled, shoveled, shoveled on coffee grounds and aluminum sulphate to re-acidify the soil around the hydrangeas. Instead of a great, thick L-shaped 'Nikko Blue' hydrangea hedge, we had a great, thick L-shaped leafy-green hedge that summer. The following year, we had blue hydrangeas again, somewhat paler, more mauve, lavender, some even blossoming pink. The latter we exiled from the pool area. The next year, all was well again with our wonderful blue hydrangea hedge. Few dandelions have returned in following years to the poolside lawn where they are most visible to Hank, who swims like a seal in the summer.

~ ~ ~ ~

During my early years at Brillig, before José came to bless our lives and garden, I had a fancy for Queen Anne's lace and daisies. I let myself be talked into growing Queen Anne's lace on the south-facing bluff by a part-time gardener who told me that a field of Queen Anne's lace blowing in the wind was "a breathtakingly beautiful sight, seeing wildflowers as they should be seen, blooming profusely in their natural state." Other wildflowers I can easily imagine marvelous en masse. Not so the wild carrot, Queen Anne's lace. When the wind blew, which it does almost continuously by the sea, looking at the swaying motion of a field of Queen Anne's lace induced an acute and extremely unpleasant nausea I'd never before experienced on any craft in any sea.

To queasiness-causing, add time-consuming nuisance as another problem. Long-stemmed blossoms of Queen Anne's lace, miracles of delicate complexity close-up, are tiresome as cut flowers. After a day, their flower heads waste away, sprinkling the surrounds with a profusion of white flower specks everywhere, all over everything, and under the furniture as well.

When I discovered that Queen Anne's lace, wherever it grows, is a reliable signifier of poor soil conditions, I had no qualms in ripping up all the Queen Anne's lace on the upper cliff face. I left a few plants of Queen Anne's lace thriving for the benefit of butterflies on the lower cliff face where it's hard to get anything to grow. Elsewhere,

Queen Anne's lace was banished, and the quality of our soil improved with the addition of compost.

In June, daisies look fresh and charming, white, bright, sunny-centered. Unlike Queen Anne's lace, daisies are attractive as cut flowers, but I've learned to watch out for daisies. They are killers and dangerously invasive. Not long ago, before José came to work at Brillig, these deceptively innocent-looking daisies choked out vinca and pachysandra, strangled new 1'-tall hostas, garroted new growth in a low hedge of potentilla, grabbed air and space that belonged to lilies and irises, all in such a sneaky way that I didn't notice until it was almost too late to repair the damage. We all know about the dangers of kudzu and loosestrife, but whoever would have suspected those charming daisies of harboring killer traits? They, too, have been exiled from the garden area, left to come up if they want on the road bank where I keep a wary eye on them, and a few find a place for themselves on the lower face of the bluff.

Daisies grow in profusion even in seemingly inhospitable sites.

Left: The rocks from the terminal moraine along the beach. Right: Wooden steps that are lifted in the winter or if endangered by hurricanes.

The bluff, those cliffs, the problems they have been! Brillig was built on top of an undulating rocky cliff underbraced with a concrete seawall and leftover boulders from glacial activity that ended about 20,000 years ago. The young son of a temporary cook we employed early on liked to play war games along the seawall, and circulated the rumor that Brillig was actually built over a gun emplacement and had been a bunker in World War II to stave off enemy submarines. Anyone hearing this fantasy could well believe that it was so, because that's the impression you easily could have when you looked up at Brillig from the beach. It did look as if it had been constructed over a bunker.

I was determined that the concrete wall and south-facing cliffs could be induced to support vegetation. "You can't grow nothing on them cliffs, ma'am," another so-called gardener told me. "Nothing's gonna grow on all them rocks and cement." Nonsense.

We pulled porcelain berry vines (*Ampelopsis brevipedulunca*), which were growing like weeds along the tops of the bluff, and about as invasive as kudzu, **down** the bluff face, rather than let them grow up, which they are

inclined to do. To hold them down, tendrils were twined with wild honeysuckle and secured with hairpins of my mother's, mementos of hers I'd kept after she died, that now were given a new and useful life.

We heaped compost, grass clippings, and chopped-up, hosed-down seaweed (to clean it of plant-killing salt) on the concrete wall. We bored holes for planting white rosa rugosa—plants so rugged they even survive immersion in seawater when hurricane waters rise high. Topsoil, sod, compost, and more grass clippings were layered annually across the cliffs and rocks. We planted milkweed we rescued from the island's roadside trimmers as larval food for monarch butterflies. We planted blush-pink rambling roses, white scilla, and pink *Lycoris squamigera*. Between our efforts, and those of the inevitable, eager, wild volunteers (mullein, blue flax, the Queen Anne's lace we uprooted, the daisies left to grow) grasses, goldenrod, and other wildflowers now cover the cliffs.

Because the cliffs were steep, I asked a contractor to build granite steps into the cliff that would connect with wooden stairs down to the beach that we could lift and store during the winter, or when threatened with a hurricane

Two views of our ugly granite steps to the beach and early plant camouflage.

that would wash them away. I wanted broad, gently graduating steps, like those I had seen in Francis H. Cabot's beautiful gardens at Les Quatres Vents, broad steps with low risers that would meander down the cliff in gentle curves. Yes, I was assured, of course, not to worry, all was understood, all would be done in the fullness of time over the winter when workers from the island and from the mainland were more readily available. That we would be gone from the island for several months was no problem. Trust him, the contractor assured me, all would be done just as I wanted.

We left in October. An expensive bill was paid. We returned in April. And what did I see? Short, narrow steps with high risers flanked with an ugly iron railing that went directly from the lawn down the cliff to a granite platform from which wooden stairs, yet to be built, could then slope down the cliff to the beach. The granite steps looked like the sort you find on public beaches with a sign that says, "This way to the men's room."

What to do? At huge expense, the offending steps could be removed, and with another huge expenditure, new steps could be created with the help of a landscaping architect whose fees are the equivalent of two years'

college tuition. I was brought up by a Scottish mother and a father of Dutch descent to "make do, or do without." So that was that.

The contractor couldn't understand why I was upset. What was the matter with the stairs? "They're serviceable," he said. "They get you up and down."

"They're ugly, ugly, ugly," I said. "Not what I wanted at all."

"If we'd built them the way you wanted us to, it would have been a lot more money," the contractor said. "I thought you'd be pleased that we saved you time and money."

When things are ugly, you try to camouflage them. We transplanted bayberry bushes from lower down on the cliffs to mask the railing posts. We repainted the iron railing dark green. A gardener we had at the time, who liked to mix colors, flower varieties, textures, different kinds of bulbs, told me he could create borders to the steps that he promised would embellish the steps in such a way that one might even think the cliff staircase was attractive.

I told him I didn't mind mixing shades or colors as we had with the border of daffodils along the driveway, or in the daylily bed, or in the rose garden with the same

planting and replace it with another takes time and the right foggy, misty day, and there are still hostas I see that I want to move, and I am determined I shall someday.

We have had disasters turn into dazzling successes. Hurricane Bob hit in 1991, felling trees and opening the view of the estuary of Long Island Sound where salty ocean water mixes with freshwater draining from the land. This view was so dramatically improved that we were inspired to cut a nature path from the wildwood of the vista area, where you can watch the sun setting across the Sound, to where you can walk above the beach on a south-facing ridge. This nature path and some of the others we created on our land and on the property of a cooperative neighbor led to the discovery of *Angelica lucida* and *Chenopodium rubrum*, both rare species in our area of New York state, the latter not known to be extant in the state of New York until our Fishers Island site was discovered. I was also pleased to find in the vista area two flowering crab apple trees, hidden before by the sumac, that are lovely to behold in bloom in June.

In the quarry area, the Pit, I was wrongly advised by garden helpers to lay down heavy black plastic and cover it with wood chips to keep out weeds while we planted native rhododendrons, a native paperbark birch tree (*Betula*), native winterberry (*Ilex verticillata*), a native turtle-head bush (*Chelone*), and Buddleia bushes, white, dark purple, lavender, said to grow up to 20', to replace the staghorn sumac felled by the hurricane.

The effect of the black plastic was horrid, like commercial/industrial landscaping. The black plastic kept on showing through the wood chips and was a grueling chore to remove. When we lifted it, there were colonies of earthworms trapped between the wood chips and the plastic and hard, compacted earth underneath. We encouraged Virginia creeper (*Parthenocissus quinquefolia*), another native plant, to grow as a ground cover. Instead of using black plastic, we liberated masses of wild and rare *Angelica lucida* we didn't know was there, wild straw-

species of flower, but I didn't like mixing different kinds of flowers together because it made it hard to cultivate them, to be sure each kind had the right soil and nutrition.

"Don't worry. Leave it to me," he said. "It will be fine."

Mirabile dictu, it was. He created a marvelous effect with all kinds of lilies I had left over from other parts of the garden. But his mixing different kinds of plantain lilies, as my grandmother called hostas, and planting them when I was away one weekend, was a mistake I'm still trying to repair. I don't like hostas with different shaped and colored leaves all jumbled together. I like the same kinds of plants planted together in drifts and borders. To undo a

berries and other plants and flowers brought to us by songbirds and pheasants.

We were so pleased with the nature path from the vista to the ridge that we cut a nature path through the tangled growth of wild honeysuckle, rugosa roses, blackberries, and poison ivy to the north-facing beach, Starfish Point, on Long Island Sound/Fishers Island Sound, an extension of Brillig's property across the narrow road that leads into the driveway. Later, we would make a clearing for a teak bench, table, and chair, with pine trees for windbreaks, and an unobstructed view of Connecticut across the water.

To survive the island's heavy, whipping winds and occasional hurricanes, plants must have strong root systems, aerodynamic design, an ability to bend with the suppleness of gymnasts, or the support of a wall or trellis.

A large-flowered white hybrid clematis (*Clematis* 'Henryii alba'), its apt botanical name one of the reasons I chose to grow it on the lattice-covered concrete walls in the swimming pool area, did poorly until I introduced silver-lace vine (*Polygonum aubertii*) as a screening shelter and lavender-blue flowered vinca as a ground cover to keep the clematis roots cool. When the silver-lace vine threatened to throttle the creeping juniper growing down over it from the banks above, we removed it, but by then, the white clematis was well established and flourishing.

In the swimming pool area, we added a pair of herons, cast in fiberglass, which looks like gray lead by Cecily Pennoyer of Locust Valley, Long Island, from molds of herons sculpted by Frederick Church for New York's Botanical Gardens. We also acquired Pennoyer decorative urns made of resin, easy to lift and move around, and a fiberglass birdbath for our daylily bed that we enlarged with hundreds of new bulbs that have now grown into thousands of bulbs. The herons, on either side of the steps leading from our west-facing patch of lawn to our swimming pool, greatly improved the scene by the smoky pink-mauve of a tamarisk, and suggested the addition of Siberian iris and pots of white petunias. By covering an ugly concrete wall with lattice and planting creeping juniper in a reverse C-shape around the swimming pool's lawn, we created an agreeably pleasing landscape from what I tactfully used to call a charm-challenged spot.

Whether you have to remedy someone else's, your own, or Nature's catastrophes, it always interests me that serendipity seems to take over.

Honeysuckle covered arches frame the entrance to the nature path in the vista.

Chapter 11

My Dream Garden:
A White Garden and a Moonlit Garden

Everyone has a dream garden, an image, never wholly fulfilled, from which to draw inspiration.

My dream garden is both a white garden and a moon
garden, a garden of annuals and perennials the color of
snow, cream, ivory, and milk, with flower textures delicate
as tissue paper, soft as velvet, smooth as silk, sleek as satin.
Consider beds of creamy white roses, clusters of lilies, car-
pets of white violets, clematis blossoms.

White is its own harmony, symbolizing light, purity,
glory, and joy. White speaks of passion and romance.
White reflects all the light rays of the visible spectrum
without any dominant wavelength of its own, which
makes it achromatic—having no chroma or color. This
reflective phenomenon allows any white garden to appear
larger and fuller than it actually is, with incandescent radi-
ance. Keats wrote in one of his sonnets, "O, what a power
hath white simplicity."

The most celebrated white garden of our time is at
Sissinghurst, the Elizabethan manor house in Kent, created in the 1930s by Harold Nicolson and Vita Sackville-
West. It became a British National Trust Property in 1967.
My dream garden borrows from it the white trumpets of
Regale lilies; white 'Helen Campbell' cleome, a yard tall;
spires of white 'Butterball' delphiniums; white pansies;
white irises; silvery-gray artemisia, *Cineraria maritima*; luminous 'Mrs. Sinkins' pinks; white *Veronica virginica alba*;
white eremuri; *Phlox paniculata*, 'Mother of Pearl;' the silver
willow-leaved pear, *Pyrus salicifolia pendula*; the fresh scent
of white tree peonies, *Paeonia suffruticosa*; and one of
Sissinghurt's many charming aspects, the *claire-voie*, a large
round hole cut in the lattice of a pergola or trellis, or an
evergreen hedge that provides a view to gardens beyond
and serves as a window to look up at the sky, the moon,
the clouds, and the stars.

I long for a white garden. Nothing as grand as
Sissinghurst, of course, but with white Oriental lilies, my
beloved Madonna lilies (*Lilium candida*), white astilbe,
white campanulas, white holly-
hocks, white hydrangeas, *Cimecifuga
racemosa* feathering above white iris
in a corner of the vista area where
you can sit and gaze at the heady
sunset views to the northwest.
Cimecifuga racemosa and astilbe, with
flowers that appear as delicate as
gauze, are as limber as the olean-
ders I used to grow in my Jamaican
garden. They survive high winds
far better than hot days with too
little water and too much sun. The

Claire-voie at
Sissinghurst castle.

Everyone has a dream garden, an image,
never wholly fulfilled, from which to draw
inspiration. . . . White is its own harmony,
symbolizing light, purity, glory, and joy.

Inspirational gardens at Sissinghurst.

I want butterflies by day and moths by night. Blossoms that lure day-flying butterflies rely on visual appeal and usually come in bright colors, with the exception of white buddleia (to me, the most appealing of all butterfly bushes). Flowers that attract nocturnal moths are typically glowing white with an intoxicating fragrance.

Lovely by day, pale-petaled scented flowers become magical by starlight, especially with a birdbath to reflect moonbeams, and the light of pierced brass Moroccan lanterns. Shimmering, glimmering flowers drench the air with sweet odors to attract pollinators. Night-foraging Luna moths with gossamery light-green wings and long, streamerlike tails, and hawk moths, with rapid wingbeats like those of a bird, and wing spreads of up to 6", leave their daytime hiding places to respond to the Lorelei perfumes of night-fragrant plants.

Victorians called this type of white garden, capturing the light of the moon and stars, with the added dimension of strong nocturnal fragrance, a "moon garden." For a moon garden's white, night-blooming flowers whose fragrances intensify at dusk to attract pollinators, there are inventories of hundreds of plants. One of my favorites is the moonflower (*Ipomoea alba*), a tropical vine that has been grown in American gardens as an annual since the eighteenth century. Just when morning glories close up for the night, pure white moonflowers begin to open. Moonflowers flourish in sultry midsummer weather. If watered frequently and fed occasionally—they prefer a soil that isn't rich—a moonflower vine can grow up to 15'. Tissue-fine flowers, some as large as butter plates, of luminescent white, will stay open through midmorning and are deeply scented. Night-scented stock (*Matthiola longipetala*, formerly *Matthiola bicornis*), tall plants, with jasmine-perfumed blossoms and yellow ones the color of whipped sweet butter; Mignonette (*Reseda odorata*); evening primrose (*Oenothera biennis*); large white petunia hybrids (*Petunia axillaris*, 'Rainmaster'); flowering tobacco (*Nicotiana alata*, 'Grandiflora' with star-shaped, five-petaled white flowers

sword-leaved yucca (*Yucca filimentosa*), on the other hand, is drought tolerant, loves the sun, tolerates its morning shower from the sprinkler system, endures rain, cold, hurricanes, everything.

The attraction of a white garden is that it gleams in the evening, looks cool, and adds distance to the perspective in the daytime. White butterfly bushes (*Buddleia*) live up to their promise and are mesmeric to watch midsummer when the monarchs, painted ladies, swallowtails, and mourning cloaks flitter about them. I want a swathe of pale-petaled daylilies, Asiatic lilies, Oriental lilies, all kinds of lilies to grow from late June through August.

on tall stems that opens early in the evening; *Nicotiana sylvestis*, a woodland tobacco plant, with nodding stems; tubular flowers on top of even taller stems; dame's rocket (*Hesperis matronalis*); white verbena with its lance-shaped leaves, four o'clocks (*Mirabilis jalapa*) sometimes called marvel-of-Peru, flourishing in European gardens since the sixteenth century, with clusters of trumpet shaped blossoms on 2'-stems opening in the late afternoon, giving off a light citrus fragrance; all these and more are annuals, attractive by day, which bloom at night in clouds of delicious scent.

Entrancing scentless plants are tall spider flowers (*Cleome*, 'White Queen') with oval white petals and delicate filaments, and cosmos, the same height, *Cosmos*, 'White Sonata,' or *Cosmos bipinnatus*, 'Purity,' are good choices for back-of-the-border plants, or where you want a tall grouping.

Other plants I find ravishing by day or night are *Phlox paniculata*, 'Miss Lingard,' and *Phlox paniculata*, 'David,' mildew resistant, tall and later blooming than 'Miss Lingard.' Both are night-flowering white phlox. The large pendent white-flowered angel's trumpet (*Brugmansia suave-*

Perennial hyacinths, cultivars of *Hyacinthus orientalis*, perennial gardenias, cultivars of *Gardenia augusta*, such as the "veitchii" variety, planted in the ground or in pots, and potted moonflowers (*Ipomoea alba*), an annual, are treasured for white gardens as well as moon gardens.

Native to Mexico, tuberoses (*Polianthes tuberosa*, 'The Pearl') are hardy only to Zone 8, so they need to be lifted and repotted for the following winter after they flower in midsummer and their leaves wither. I am so besotted by them that I have convinced myself they are worth all the extra effort. Their spires of waxy white flowers blossom when there is constant moisture in their soil—the soil kept moist, not wet, as too much water will rot their bulbs. They make graceful cut flowers, and their scent is as intoxicating to me as catnip is to a kitty cat.

olens) is poisonous if you eat any part of it, but in the evening, when it releases its seductive scent, all I want to do is immerse myself in its powerful perfume, not have it immerse itself in me. Among roses, *Rosa* 'Alba Maxima,' a great double white rose, a Jacobite rose, the white rose of York, with flat, double sweet-scented creamy-white flowers and gray-green leaves, is one of ten roses of different kinds I'd like to have, all with white flowers and all **deliciously fragrant.** There are three rampant ramblers: *Rosa filipes*, 'Kiftsgate,' with an abundance of glossy, light-green

Left: I like a mix of white and pink cosmos. Right: White violets can be a pleasing surprise.

leaves, bearing in early summer clusters of cupped, creamy white roses; *Rosa* 'Rambling Rector,' with gray-green foliage, many clusters of cupped, semidouble, creamy-white flowers borne in early summer, followed by spherical red hips in autumn; *Rosa* 'Seagull,' with many large clusters of flat to cupped, single to semidouble white flowers. *Rosa* 'Dupontii' is a shrub rose with gray-green leaves and cupped, single creamy-white flowers in early summer. *Rosa rugosa* 'Blanc Double de Courbet' flowers from spring to autumn, bearing semidouble white flowers followed by spherical red hips. *Rosa* 'Boule de Neige' is a Bourbon rose, flowering from spring to autumn with fully double-pink-touched white flowers with glossy dark-green leaves. *Rosa* 'Madame Harvey' is an early summer-flowering damask rose, vigorous, upright, with rounded, fully double white flowers and dark-green leaves. *Rosa* 'Paul's Lemon Pillar' is an upright climbing hybrid tea rose with dark-green leaves and fully double white flowers with a lemon fragrance, flowering in early summer. Three other climbers I fancy, because I like the look of roses arching over trellises and arbors, are *Rosa* 'Lamarque,' a vigorous noisette rose with smooth, strong stems, bright-green leaves, flowering from midsummer to autumn with fully double ivory-colored roses; another vigorous noisette climber, *Rosa* 'Madame Plantier,' with emerald-green leaves, bearing in early summer clusters of fully double lightly scented roses, the buds pink, the flowers white; and *Rosa* 'City of York,' a large-flowered climber with glossy bright-green leaves and clusters of lightly scented, semidouble, creamy-white flowers borne in spring and early summer.

Besides the perennial scented white violets (*Viola odorata*) as a ground cover, the annual sweet alyssum (*Lobularia maritime*) blooms all summer, is drought tolerant, perfumed by day and perfumed by night, and provides a noninvasive underplanting for lilies of the valley (*Convallaria majalis*) as well as white hyacinths and white narcissus that are also perfumed by day and night, as is the lovely white lilac (*Syringa vulgaris*, 'Madame Lemoine'). A drift of honey-

White roses enhance every garden.

I wish astilbe were longer-lived.

scented sweet peas (*Lathyrus odoratos*) are fragrant annual climbers that need a trellis or fence to climb on as well as mulch to keep their roots cool.

Flowers that aren't richly fragrant but are appealing for their forms and shapes and varied seasonal appearances that have white species and do well by the sea are many. Peonies, azaleas, hydrangeas, astilbe, bleeding hearts (*Dicentra spectabilis*), rhododendrons, foxgloves (*Digitalis alba*), veronica, hollyhocks, liatris (*Scarios* 'White Spires') *Echinacea purpurea*, 'White Swan'; large white-flowered *Clematis* 'Henryii.'

A moon garden should always have plantings of Casablanca lilies and Madonna lilies (*Lilium candida*), used in gardens since the Minoan culture flourished in 1500 B.C. Their steeples ascend during April and May, and by July "are ready to chime their scented praise to God," as Beverly Nichols wrote in *A Thatched Roof*.[1]

Mock orange (*Philadelphus*) can be almost sensually overpowering in its fragrance, as can some honeysuckles like *Lonicera fragrantissima* and the Italian woodbine (*Lonicera caprifolium*). I love the idea of gardenias planted in tubs that can be brought inside over the winter, but this is not practical at Brillig. Wind, sun, shade—I've never been able to get gardenias to cope with Brillig outdoors for more than a couple of weeks, then the buds drop off and no more flowers. To have a small portable pond with a fountain and a few nocturnal water lilies also seemed like

a feature that would be immensely pleasing, but I have yet to find a portable fountain and a little pool for water lilies. What I have found are scented geraniums (*Pelargoniums*: rose, citrus, strawberry, clove, and dozens of other varieties) whose foliage "wantons the air," as Sappho wrote in an ode to Aphrodite, "Luxuriant, like the flowing hair."

Charming small trees, such as *Viburnum carleseii*, and white-flowering almond (*Prunus glandulosa*), dwarf apples and cherries and crabapples are always pleasures, whether in bloom, fruiting, or just giving off their subtle scents.

To enjoy your moon garden in an intimate space, I think you must have comfortable seating and a table to hold glasses, a pitcher of iced tea, or a bottle of wine so that you can luxuriate in a sunlit white garden, or a garden that glows coral and pink at sunset. A true moon garden,

White azaleas along the nature path in the vista area.

though, is meant to be most cherished when it is bathed in moonlight, or illuminated by the soft light of candles, torches, or lanterns, when you and the pollinating moths can quietly share the exquisite fragrances of night-blooming flowers.

I dream of sitting beneath a Fishers Island summer moon, breathing the scent of vanilla orchids from Madagascar and a southeast Asian frangipani or plumeria tree, plants to grow in large fiberglass urns and capable of being successfully overwintered. These dreams have not materialized, as I haven't been able to find vanilla orchids in America and I've only managed to grow 2'-high frangipani that flowers not in our summer season, but in our winter season.

We have succeeded in putting bits and pieces, pieces and bits of the white garden and the moon garden together in the vista area, and as I lean over the railing of my bedroom balcony, inhaling the scents of nicotiana and potted tuberoses on the wall by the downstairs guest room beneath the balcony, it seems possible that the white garden and the moon garden I envisage will someday become realities.

On an autumn morning, four years ago, Rick
Patrick . . . gave me three seedlings of a passionflower. I thought back to the passionflowers I had
seen when living in Jamaica in the West Indies.

Chapter 12

Passiflora (Passionflower) and Other Vines

On an autumn morning four years ago, Rick Patrick, artist, collector of antique silver and furniture, gardener, gave me three seedlings of a passionflower, *Passiflora incarnata* (maypop). Rooted in the heavy clay soil in which he formerly grew them in Michigan, in five months the tendriling seedlings wound their way on strings to the top of my east-facing bathroom window in New York. Passionflowers must have a string, a trellis, another vine on which to twirl and climb. In May, I brought the pot with its three leafy vines to Brillig.

I thought back to the passionflowers I had seen when I was living in Jamaica in the West Indies. Exquisitely complex, these passionflowers were a flamboyant mix of deep purple, scarlet, and white. Marvelous flowers, a column rising from each flower stalk above petals topped with golden hammerlike anthers at the end of each of the five stamens, trumpet-shaped stigmata at the end of each of the three styles, an uptilting corona of multicolored filaments like a ruff of quills around the column beneath the anthers, and beneath the corona a corolla of ten petals. Each flower looked like a jeweled brooch, the treasure of an empress. When I first saw a tall-latticed fence extravagantly jeweled with passionflowers, I was incredulous. Nothing I had ever seen in glass houses or botanical gardens until then could compare with these extraordinary flowers. Perhaps I hadn't really looked; perhaps I had looked in the wrong season, because passionflowers really are not all that rare. The genus *Passifloraceae* comprises more than 500 species of mostly evergreen tendril climbers, a few annuals, perennials, shrubs, and trees, which generally occur in tropical woodland, on rocks and grassland in tropical North, Central, and South America, in Asia, Australia, New Zealand, the Pacific Islands, and the Caribbean.

The leaves are usually alternate, simple, or two- to nine-lobed, mainly three- or five-lobed, elliptical in shape or rounded or broadly ovate like a teardrop or a mango leaf in a Paisley pattern. The flowers appear singly, sometimes in racemes, from the upper leaf axils. Each flower has a wide, tubular base and sepals, sometimes five, sometimes ten, that are spread out flat, turned back, or form a saucer or bowl shape. A stalk in the center of each flower bears the ovary and five stamens and is surrounded by one or several rings of filaments (the corona). Many plants can grow 15' to 20' or more, depending on the species. In mild winter climates, some are evergreen. One species, incarnata or maypop, is cold hardy to Zone 6.

The *Passiflora* species of the passionflower family (*Passifloraceae*) galvanizes in diversity in the American tropics where you can find 95 percent of all passionflowers.

There is only a handful of temperate climate species, including *Passiflora incarnata* (maypop). The most common species of passionflower, called *Maracuja* in the Amazon, is the *Passiflora edulis*, which bears large white flowers with pink or purple centers and edible fruit. In the early twentieth century, in his *Thousand Mile Walk to the Gulf*, Scottish naturalist John Muir writes of the passionflower having "the most delicious fruit I have ever eaten." The passionflower fruit, round or egg-shaped, edible, usually yellow, varies in size. Since prehistoric times, the fruit of the passionflower has been eaten by Indian populations of North America—its seeds have been found at archaeological sites several thousand years old. The vine, leaves, and stem have been widely used by herbalists and health practitioners around the world for sedative, antispasmodic, and pain-relieving effects.

In Jamaica, Gladys, our household's cook at the time, told me that her church used the passionflower to teach lessons about Christ's crucifixion or passion. She showed me a printed card that noted that the stigmata were the nails by which Christ was attached to the cross, the anthers on top of the stamens the hammers used to drive the nails, the corona Christ's crown of thorns, and the corolla with ten petals represented the twelve apostles minus the disloyal Peter and Judas.

The formulation of the passionflower as an allegory to illustrate the crucifixion of Christ seemed simple to me then in the late 1950s. But the allegory's origins in the early seventeenth century were more complex. The key story is that in 1609, Jacobo Bosio, an ecclesiastical Spanish monastic scholar in Rome, was working on his treatise about the Cross of Calvary when an Augustan friar, Emmanuel de Villegas, a Mexican by birth, met him. He showed Bosio drawings of an extraordinary flower, but Bosio was not sure if he should include these drawings in his book to the glory of Christ, as he thought the drawings might not be accurate. After receiving more descriptions and images from priests in New Spain, and assurances from Mexican Jesuits passing through Rome that reports of the flower were true, and when he saw drawings, essays, and poems published by the Dominican Friars at Bologna, Bosio was satisfied that this astonishing flower did indeed exist. He called it the *Flora Passionis*, the flower of the passion.

Bosio wrote that although the insides of the petals are tawny in Peru, in New Spain, they are white tinged with rose-pink, to suggest the blood of our Lord, and the corona, or crown of thorns, tinged with blood-red, which suggest the "scourge with which our blessed Lord was tormented." Bosio describes the column rising in the center of the flower surrounded by the crown of thorns or scourge, and the three nails (stigmata) at the top of the column. There are seventy-two filaments surrounding the corona, which, according to tradition, is the number of thorns in the crown of thorns set upon Christ's head. "The abundant and beautiful leaves are shaped like the head of a lance, or pike, like the spear that pierced the side of our Savior, while the underside of the leaf is marked with dark round spots signifying the thirty pieces of silver that Judas was paid to betray Christ." Bosio interpreted the vines as symbolic of the whips of Christ's persecutors.

Later authors in Europe, who made use of passionflower as an example of the mysterious ways and wonders of Jesus, only had *Passiflora caerulea* as an example to work from, and not the *Passiflora edulis* that was Bosio's inspiration. Although the stamens, the anthers, the styles, and the stigmata are the same in both the *Passiflora caerulea* and the *Passiflora edulis* of the Amazon, the *caerulea* flowers lack the pink color Bosio saw as a representation of the blood of Christ. Omitting this part from their story, later authors wrote that the white petals of the *Passiflora caerulea* signified purity, and they wrote, as had Bosio, that the total of ten petals represented the ten apostles present at the crucifixion. The five-lobed or palmate leaves of the *Passiflora caerulea*, noticeably different from the spotted spearshaped leaves of the *edulis* species, were now said to represent the hands of Christ's persecutors, and the tightly twisting tendrils were a representation of the cords that bound Christ to the cross.

Neither *caerulea* nor *edulis*, the three passionflowers Rick Patrick gave me belong to the *incarnata* species, a fast-growing perennial vine occurring from Virginia to southern Illinois and southeast Kansas, south to Florida and Texas. Rick said that passionflowers grew exhuberantly in the garden of his schoolhouse studio in Jackson, in south central Michigan, so I hoped that they would do well at Brillig if I could find a fairly protected spot away from gusty winds, somewhere where they wouldn't freeze in the winter.

The fruits of the *incarnata* species, or maypop, ripen from yellowish to light brown in color. The aril covering the seeds is sweet and fruity when ripe. By mashing it in a sieve, the hard seeds can be separated from the pulp, or you can slit open the ripe fruit and suck the pulp from the fruit as I remembered often doing in India with seasonal mangoes, though overripe fruit can ferment easily and have a horrible taste.

You can propagate passionflowers by seeds, cuttings, or layering. Rick told me correctly that I didn't need to worry, that passionflowers, once flourishing, would send

Passionflower comes in many varieties—all uniquely beautiful; check Zone hardiness to find which is best for you.

up shoots from their roots all over the place, from a few yards to 20' from the original plant. A year later that's just what happened.

Ideal for covering a wall or trellis, maypops flourish in moderately fertile and moist but well-drained soil in full sun or partial shade with shelter from cold, drying winds. The species name, *incarnata*, means made of flesh or flesh-colored. A misnomer, and misleading, as the flowers, anticipated as tawny rose or pink or yellow or brown were none of these colors, but lavender. *Passiflora incarnata* is a tendril climber with three to five deeply lobed dark-green leaves up to 6" long. In summer, it bears bowl-shaped, lightly scented lavender flowers, 3" across, with purple

Amazon, I knew then where the passionflowers should be planted: in the garage courtyard border garden, with a palisade fence behind them, to ramble among the orange-flowered trumpet vines, which are beloved by our local hummingbirds. I planted the passionflowers in May, keeping their original clay soil matrix of potted earth around them as José and I posited them in deeper holes. They began to flower in late August and were thriving and still flowering at the end of September.

They have now been growing successfully at Brillig for three years, extending from the palisade fence across the adjacent generator house. They survived the generator house's roof being lifted off and replaced in order to put in

Left: Sweet peas smell sweetly in the cutting garden. Right: Hydrangea and potted *brugmansia* beneath the dining deck.

and white coronas, followed by ovoid, yellow, edible fruit to 2½" long. Passionflowers look rather like scabiosas with delusions of grandeur.

When I remembered seeing a nineteenth-century oil painting by American artist Martin Johnson Heade of green-feathered hummingbirds flying through scarlet passionflowers (*Passiflora coccinea*) in the jungles of the

a new generator required to power a recently installed air-conditioning system so that I could cope better with asthma and emphysema in humid weather. They attract butterflies and hummingbirds. They are an interesting contrast with the rampaging orange-flowered trumpet vines.

I like vines. They grow up but not outward. Vertical gardening expands your garden without taking up space.

Camouflaging the ugly, vines create beauty. Two or more vines rambling over the same support, as our trumpet vine (*Campsis radicans*) and passionflowers do, extends the flowering season of our garage courtyard with staggered blooming times, and achieves a full, lush, lovely look, mixed early in the summer with climbing red rambler roses that are strongly scented and flower before either the passionflowers or the trumpet vine.

The passionflowers are **curling vines, tendril vines**, which include the grapevines (*Vitis*) in our arbor; large-flowered white clematis, in the swimming pool area, growing on a lattice I had made to cover ugly concrete walls, a particularly successful solution to a difficult problem; sweet peas (*Lathyrus odoratus*), deliciously fragrant, romantically ruffled pastel charmers that are a fling of pleasure on a section of our cutting garden's western palisade fence; red, orange, yellow nasturtiums (*Tropaeolum majus*) that grow in our kitchen garden in a corner, hidden by a wall of our dining deck, grown for garnishes of salads and desserts. These vines depend on curling tendrils at the leaf joints. As the stems grow and lengthen, tender new tendrils reach for a hold on a rung of trellis or netting to anchor the stem for its next step of growth. They can also cling to other vines and shrubs. But, like "climbing" roses, "climbing" nasturtiums and "climbing" petunias also need to be coaxed up trellises or other supports by tying each stem or weaving them through trellis or other supports.

Twining vines need to get a grip on a vertical support so they can encircle, either to the left or to the right, any-

'Heavenly Blue' morning glories climb to the balcony above Brillig's entrance way.

thing from a length of string to posts, 6" across that we use to support wire fencing. Twining vines include our 'Heavenly Blue' morning glory (*Ipomea*) placed in pots to grow up the drainpipes by our front door; fragrant moonflower annuals (*Ipomea alba*) in pots on the downstairs guestroom patio, with bamboo rods to grow on; wisteria (*Wisteria floribunda*) that is growing on a trellis beneath the dining deck behind a marvelous hedge of hydrangeas, and as young plants in pots by the downstairs guest bedroom patio; honeysuckle (*Lonicera*), the native wild variety that spreads itself raggedly over our south-facing bluffs, preventing erosion, and smelling sweetly no matter what the weather, and also a scentless variety (*Lonicera sempivirens*) with tubular coral-colored flowers a gardener planted for me while I was away that turned out to be of some interest, at least, to hummingbirds and butterflies.

The **clinging or gripping vine** has many little rootlike sucker feet sprouting from its stems that attach to a brick wall or other flat surfaces and hold the vine tight. Both English ivy (*Hedera helix*), which covers the brick entrance walls to Brillig and fills two plant boxes by the steps of the outdoor part of our dining deck, and our climbing hydrangea (*Hydrangea anomala petiolaris*) on the west-facing brick wall outside the library, abutting the living room south- and west-facing patio, are clinging vines. Clinging or gripping vines are best used on materials that aren't prone to rot, because the sucker feet leave permanent marks on masonry and wood and can erode mortar as well as penetrating dried wood and causing rot by opening up hairline cracks for rain to seep in. Once clinging vines are attached, they can act like trellises for other vines. Virginia creeper (*Parthenocissus quinquefolia*), a native vine, scrambles along in the Pit in the vista area as a ground cover. But, just outside the little white gate leading from the driveway to the downstairs guest bedroom, there's a worn-out old pine around which a Virginia creeper has crept all the way to the top. From spring to autumn, when its brilliant red coloration is surprisingly attractive, the vine is a delight to me and to the birds who feed on its berries, and it certainly prettifies the skimpy foliaged pine.

Some "climbers" really aren't vines at all. "Climbing" roses need to lean on pillars or trellises and have to be encouraged to climb by tying their branches to these supports. Our blush-pink 'New Dawn' roses grow on wire fencing strung between posts that gives them air circulation and support as they and the 'Sea Foam' "climbers" next to them thrive and flourish where everyone told me no roses would grow because of wind and sea spray coming

off the bluffs. In back of the hydrangeas on the west side of the pool area, these roses seem to benefit from the leaching of acidic soil from the hydrangeas into their well-fertilized (with horse manure) beds. "Climbing" nasturtiums and "climbing" petunias also need to be coaxed to grow vertically by tying their stems to a trellis or other support.

Whether vigorous or recumbent, vines are adaptable and versatile, able like Virginia creeper and ampelopsis/porcelain berry to double as ground covers or drape themselves gracefully like a blanket over a fence as our sweet peas do. Some, like the unscented *Lonicera sempervirens*, are **tolerant of shade**, as are some varieties of clematis, like a deciduous twiner with lavender-blue spring-to-summer flowers, *Clematis macropetala*. We had it, I liked it, but then in the early years, a young man, trying out for a job as a garden helper, dug it up from where it was curling around a young birch tree in the Pit in the vista area and threw it in a leaf bag with the poison ivy that he

Floxgloves and honeysuckle growing inside the cutting garden.

thought it was. As long as its roots are cool and shaded and its leaves get full sun, many clematises bloom prolifically in the shade. As long as it gets bright indirect light, climbing hydrangea (*Hydrangea anomala petiolaris*) thrives.

There's a vine that will grow anywhere, sun, shade, in sandy soil, in rich earth, an almost indestructible vine with handsome grapelike glossy green leaves and berries progressing from jade green to pink, lavender, blue, and purple, like porcelain beads, in the autumn. Its botanical name is *Ampelopsis brevipedunculata*, and if you want to prevent erosion or to cover barren or rocky territory, ampelopsis is amazing in its growth. It needs nothing, no fertilizer, no water. Once it's established, it just takes off and grows. It would be great to cover a chain-link fence in a hurry, although lace vine (*Polygonum aubertii*) is another fast grower. We used lace vine to cover an ugly pool shed, which it did in a year, and we also used it to cover an area beneath the outside deck, next to the hydrangea hedge and the wisteria behind it.

It was a wonderful temporary fix. The lace vine blossomed in a fluffy blanket of white flowers, a lavish display. But the next year it got out of hand. It smothered clematis, it kept popping up through the outside dining deck, through the floor, through the benches. Before it could harm either the clematis or the hydrangeas, I asked José and his crew to pull most of it up and replant the area by the dining deck with more 'Nikko Blue' hydrangeas, and to leave the pool shed covered with the lace vine, but only

the pool shed. Contain the lace vine, I said. Don't let it get entangled with the clematis on the lattice covering the concrete wall or with the creeping juniper on the banks above the swimming pool. Two years later, so far so good.

Both the lace vine and the ampelopsis are curling, tendrilled vines. The ampelopsis is marvelous on the bluffs. It has covered the rocks, and we have cut a pathway between it and the white rosa rugosas, so that we can see and stop any entangling encroachment of the ampelopsis with the rosa rugosas.

We leave the ampelopsis to thrive on Starfish Point, where it provides cover for pheasant, quail, and nesting shorebirds. But last year, it escaped its boundaries and came rampaging into the arbor area, entangling itself with rosa rugosas, privet, grapes, daylilies, yucca, sunflowers, sumac, crocosmia, tradescantia, tulips—nothing escaped its clutches. We had to be ruthless in digging it up, getting rid of it, and putting it in the garbage, not the compost heaps. Ampelopsis can be **wildly** invasive. There is another species of ampelopsis, *Ampelopsis brevipedunculata*, 'Elegans,' said to be a docile version of the invasive *brevipedunculata* or "straight" species as some nursery growers refer to it. It has the same lobed, glossy, dark-green grapelike leaves and the same charming pale green-to-dark purple berries in the autumn, but it's more easily tamed. Just be warned about the "straight" species unless you are sure you can keep *Ampelopsis brevipedunculata* confined to the one area you wish it to cover.

Chapter 13

Volunteers

A volunteer, a gardener may say by way of identification, pointing to a flower or a plant that has sprung up unplanned, unplanted, unexpected, in an unlikely place. It's a versatile term that can express affection, indulgence, surprise, bafflement, wonder. Since I began to garden on Fishers Island some fifteen years ago, I've had two curious experiences with volunteers: *Lycoris squamigera* and Korean *Angelica gigas*, both of which bloom in August.

In the summer of 1991, I saw *Lycoris squamigera* growing on the south-facing beach cliffs of Brillig. I had no idea then what they were or what they were called. I just saw some pretty pink lilylike flowers. When I dug up the four of them, I saw that their sturdy, leafless stems were attached to bulbs that I quickly replanted farther along the beach cliffs, closer to the house.

The next summer, stalks shot up, seemingly overnight—one, two, three, four, five, six, just like that—naked stems with dark membrane-pink buds that magically burst into topknot clusters of pinky-lavender, frilly, lily-like trumpet-shaped blossoms. From the beach, looking up, the flowers shimmered. They looked iridescent. Close up, they had a subtle, fruity scent. When the wind or a wandering pheasant knocked over a few of the stalks, I gathered them for cut flowers that usually lasted for more than a week.

What were these marvelous plants? Flower catalogs and books appeared to be confused about their identity, referring to them as *Amaryllis belladonna, Belladonna Lily, Cape Belladonna, Jersey Lily, Naked-Lady Lily*, native to South Africa, hardy from Zones 7 to 11, or 8 to 10; and then again as *Lycoris squamigera, Magic Lily, Surprise Lily, Resurrection Lily, Hardy Amaryllis*, a variety of *Spider Lily*, and *Naked-Lady Lily* native to China and Japan, hardy to Zone 6, or hardy from Zones 5 to 10. Classified as bulbous perennial herbs belonging to the *Amaryllis* family, *Lycoris squamigera* and *Amaryllis belladonna* looked almost identical in colored photographs. Prices for a single bulb of either flower ranged from $3 to $5, sometimes more. I sent away for both kinds of bulbs, planted them, and saw no difference whatsoever between the flowers and their leaves (narrow and strap-shaped). The leaves of *Amaryllis belladonna* grow in autumn or early spring. The leaves of *Lycoris squamigera* come up in clumps in late winter to early spring and look like the leaves of daffodils, their relatives, as do those of *Amaryllis belladonna*. The leaves die back, fading, yellowing, drying, and looking messy until it is safe to trim them to the ground at the end of June when they have stored up sufficient nutrients from the sun.

Then, regular as clockwork, on the second day of August, fast-growing bud-tipped stalks begin to rocket up

A volunteer...a plant that has sprung up
unplanned, unplanted, unexpected, in an
unlikely place.

from 2' to 3' in height, topping out with light-pink flowers that appear in the day's changing light to be tinged with blue, lavender, and a thistle's vibrant mauve at sunset, two to eight blossoms to a stem.

Every year, I've discovered more volunteer *Lycoris squamigera*, not only on the cliffs almost hidden by bushes of rosa rugosa, but also here and there among the hydrangeas, daylilies, and blackberries. I've replanted them, as well as the bulblets or offsets growing around the larger bulbs, mostly in well-composted, alkaline soil of the sunny south-facing cliffs, additionally planting some in slightly acidic soil with partial shade along an east-facing stone wall. Although they don't like being transplanted and often will wait a year before they flower again, *Lycoris squamigera* don't seem to be fussy. They adapt, adjust, even burrow deeper into the earth if they have been planted in a too-shallow hole. They can be staked as a protection against strong winds, gamboling dogs, and roaming pheasants, and they should be protected in winter with a mulch

of compost and salt hay. With no more than this, *Lycoris squamigera* have multiplied so vigorously, self-sowing and naturalizing, that at last count in 2003, there were some 800 visible stems bearing blossoms, including no more than 75 new plants I've dug in over the years. After a flowering period of twenty days, the last petals wither as usual by the end of August.

If the bulbs had been the less hardy *Amaryllis belladonna*, they would have bloomed in early September or even October. Their blunt straplike leaves would have either appeared promptly after the flowers faded and persisted through the autumn and early winter, or come up in the spring like those of *Lycoris squamigera*. The bulb companies from which I ordered *Amaryllis belladonna* must have sent me *Lycoris squamigera* instead. Parenthetically, even the best bulb companies can slip up and ship bulbs that don't quite conform to specific orders, while other companies, either through carelessness or by intent, are known to ship bulbs that are not at all what the buyer ordered—American growers point the finger at the Dutch for this cavalier practice and vice versa. But to return to what's important, late winter or springtime foliage, hardiness to Zone 5, and a flowering period beginning by early to mid-August are characteristics that define *Lycoris squamigera*. I wouldn't have known this if Scott Kunst of Old House Gardens hadn't faxed me authentic information from the Royal Horticultural Society's *Manual of Bulbs*[1] (See "Sources and Advice: Where to buy plants, seeds, garden furniture, pots and urns, both resin and clay, etc.").

A friend, Richard Bell, enjoying his morning coffee among the *Lycoris squamigera* that match his pink shirt.

As for the Korean *Angelica gigas*, several national arboreta brought the first specimens to this country in 1988 after an Asian tour of a dozen or so of their member horticulturalists. In 1994, I had a specimen plant flowering by a nature path that our neighbors, the Bakers, share with Hank and me, on land they own and allow us to cultivate. **Question:** How could an arboretum's recent Asian acquisition make its way as a volunteer to a remote corner of Fishers Island? **Answer:** By a random bird's fortuitous dropping. (The route of a major Eastern seaboard avian migratory pathway passes right over Fishers Island.) What I didn't know, and was told by Lucy Cutler of the New York Botanical Garden, was that, prior to migration, "birds **stuff** themselves with **seeds** to fatten up and to store up strength for this grueling flight." Fruit, grain, nuts are all to the merry, but ornithologists have discovered that birds really go for seeds in a big way before their migration. Thanks to the enterprise of a bird about to take flight, compelled to go farther afield than usual to find an abundance of seeds to ingest and then excrete, we received a remarkable botanical gift that literally dropped from the skies. The plant's identification had both Ed Horning, the science teacher of a local elementary and high school, and Antonia Adezio buffaloed. Antonia Adezio is the president of the Garden Conservancy, a national organization located in Cold Spring, New York. Chairman of the Board is Frank Cabot, author of *The Greater Perfection*,[2] a history and description, beautifully illustrated, of his garden, Les Quatre Vents, in Charlevoix County, Quebec. Both Antonia Adezio and Ed Horning agreed that the plant belonged to the *Angelica* family, but to

which species? Neither of them had ever seen the plant before, not illustrated and certainly not growing. Months passed, and finally the plant's identity surfaced in a botanical newsletter. A biennial, *Angelica gigas* can grow up to 6' tall and 4' wide, with long-lasting, pinky-purple, dome-shaped umbels, or flower clusters, crowning stout dark red-purple stems, framed by large, glossy, serrated green leaves.

Flower sheaths grow directly from the main stalk, looking like miniature eggplants or little purple balloons ready to burst. Because it's a biennial, Korean *Angelica gigas* dies after it sets seeds, but it reseeds prolifically. It flourishes in moist soil, in part-shade, along with Joe-Pye

Angelica gigas, a gift from the birds.

weed (*Eupatorium*), *Buddleia*, and black-eyed Susans (*Rudbeckia hirta*). Hardy from Zones 4 to 9, it thrives in sun as well as in part-shade, is mound-forming with tall flower stems, attractive to bees as well as butterflies. *Garden Gate* magazine featured it as the Editor's Choice for an August flowering plant in their April 1998 issue, and provided a source for year-old bare root plants. They are available from Ambergate Gardens (See "Sources and Advice: Where to buy plants, seeds, garden furniture, pots and

Verbena canadensis, planted in the ground, only lasted for a season. Planted in pots, both annual and perennial varieties can be overwintered to rebloom in following years.

urns, both resin and clay, etc.") By now, *Angelica gigas* is available from many other sources. Strange, tropical, primitive in appearance, *Angelica gigas* has easily naturalized at Brillig in the Pit, a partially shaded area reached by either of two nature paths that intersect and lead from the vista area up to a south-facing ridge above the beach, with splendid views of Block Island Sound and the coastline of Long Island from the tip of Orient Point westward.

It was in the Pit also that migrating birds dropped the seed of *Verbena canadensis*, or Rose vervain, a plant barely 4" tall, its stems tasseled with panicles of rosy-pink flowers. I had no idea what it was either when I first saw it, but when I looked it up in *The American Horticultural Society Encyclopedia of Garden Plants*,[3] I found it was one of about 250 verbena species of annuals, perennials, and subshrubs.

According to Pliny, *Verbena*, or vervain, was held sacred by the Druids of Gaul and the Romans themselves. Its repute as a magical herb and as a protection against witchcraft survived through the Dark Ages into medieval times, even up to the twentieth century in Britain where it was called the Holy herb, its root tied around the neck of a child by a white satin ribbon as a charm to cure chills and fever.

John Gerard, an English herbalist and a surgeon, born in 1545, who died in 1612, author of *Herbal*,[4] the most famous of English herbals, illustrated with woodblocks, was skeptical about the magical virtues of vervain but mentioned that "guests will be the merrier in a dining room sprinkled with water in which the herb had been steeped." According to Gerard, vervain was also known as "Junos teares, mercuries moist bloude, Holie herb, and of some pigeons grasses, or columbine, because pigeons are delighted to be amongst it, as also to eat thereof as Apuleius writeth." Not to be confused with the columbine (*Aquilegia*), this rose vervain, or *Verbena canadensis*, is a scentless species of verbena, and unlike *Angelica gigas*, *Verbena canadensis* only lasted a season at Brillig, dying in the winter cold.

John Aubrey, antiquarian and author of *Brief Lives*,[5] one of my favorite books of all time with its entertaining accounts of personages of the seventeenth century, quotes in his *Miscellanies* a couplet (of unknown origin to me):

> Vervain and Dill
> Hinders witches from their will.

~ ~ ~ ~

This is August, a classical month of calm, August days, filled with volunteer plants and thoughts. July flowers linger on, and a few new arrivals first bloom in August. The *Lycoris squamigera* appears on the second of August, sometimes a day or two in advance, sometimes a day or two before, never more, later only if there are heavy unseasonal rains in July that can set everything back two weeks, or a fortnight, as my Scottish grandmother used to say. The *Angelica gigas* buds around August 10 or 11 and flowers soon thereafter. The daylilies that peaked in July are still flowering, as are the brugmansia. The Casablanca and Madonna lilies are freshly flowering by the dozens in the vista garden. They were tightly budded at the end of July, but now in the first week of August, you can smell their extraordinarily powerful fragrance the way you can smell lavender at a distance in Provence, or roses growing in Grasse. "Or onions boiling in the kitchen when you're in the attic," a visiting child says, who has come to swim in our pool.

What's new in August are the Rose of Sharon trees, a dozen of them, luxuriant with white flowers with scarlet centers, and with all white flowers planted in a double row in front of the cutting garden, and in back of the 'Sea Foam' and 'New Dawn' roses growing behind the hydrangeas on the west side of the swimming pool area, another in front of the daylily bed on the far side of the telephone pole platform bird feeder. Serene, pure, beautiful, voluptuously full-flowered, Roses of Sharon (*Hibiscus syriacus, Hypericum calycinum*) don't cling to their flowers but let them fall in blowsy swags beneath them, then bloom with fresh flowers the next day, extravagantly blooming, extravagantly discarding.

Our potted, overwintered *Hibiscus rosa-sinensis, Chinese hibiscus, Hawaiian hibiscus*, of which there are more than 5,000 hybrids known to grow in Hawaii where it is the state flower, have recovered from their indoor wintering over and are exuberantly leafing and flowering, their five-petaled red, pink, yellow, apricot blooms festive, evocative of the South Seas and the Orient, their petals between my fingers feeling like a mix of butterfly wing and fragile crêpe paper, waxy and not quite smooth, moist. I watch hummingbirds hovering above them as if tethered, then whizzing away on diagonal flights. We have half a dozen

Potted pink hibiscus on the downstairs guest bedroom patio.

2'-high bright scarlet hibiscus on the outdoor balcony of the living room, six pink ones the same size on the balcony of my bedroom facing the sliding doors, and two 6' ones at the south and north corners of the balcony. We have two bright scarlet six-footers on the living room patio, and three pink six-footers on the patio of the downstairs guest room in front of the sliding glass doors. By our entrance steps, we have ten apricot-colored flowering six-footers, and on the outside dining deck, three six-footers, one yellow-blossomed, two apricot-blossomed, and more small ones in the 2' to 3' coterie José has grown from cuttings in a mix of soil we have amended with compost, peat moss, a deep, rich, moisture-retentive matrix in which our tropical hibiscuses thrive. We've wintered over some of them for twelve years or more.

The lawn mower moves up and down in the distance, spurting little cascades of vivid green, while the cardinals beak up red berries from the cotoneaster in the southernmost of the driveway plantings, parallel with the two north-facing windows of the downstairs guest room.

The pink mallows in the Pit are in bud by mid-August, the same time the *Angelica gigas* is budding and flowering in the shadier southern side of the Pit across from them in the vista area. A starling fledgling fell into the swimming pool this morning, but Austin easily rescued it with the pool's long-handled net, and the fledgling flew back to its mother. I've filled the bedrooms, the TV room, the dining room with flowers. I've picked all the blue platycodon in the cutting garden and all the zinnias and filled four vases with *Lycoris squamigera* snapped off by the wind and pheasants who have a way of not walking between plants but shouldering their way through a path of their own desire, knocking over a stalky blossom or two every day or so. It doesn't matter. The *Lycoris squamigera* are wonderfully long-lasting cut flowers and can lie untended on the bluff, broken at the base of their stems, be brought in the house in the morning around nine o'clock by either Austin or José, be put in water and last a week.

The barn swallows and tree swallows gather on the eastern side of the roof above the living rooms while their fledglings practice flying and landing. The parent birds stretch their wings, rest on their sides, rest with their feet at their breasts, preening, relaxing, cooled by the sea breeze and the continuous dripping on the roof of the air-conditioning system's condensation. Sometimes there are as many as forty, fifty, sixty swallows on the roof, resting, then flying away, then returning. I watch them from the south-facing windows of the little blue room, the room my assistant, Jade Zapotocky Barrett, tells me she likes best of all the bedrooms.

Hibiscus on my bedroom balcony.

An annual is a plant that lives for only
one season, from the time its seed is sown.
It blooms, sets seeds, and dies.

Chapter 14

Annuals

My mother was a horticultural snob. Devoted to irises, roses, delphiniums, peonies, and other perennials and bulbs, she disdained annuals. She considered zinnias, sunflowers, petunias, and marigolds coarse and common, their colors a vulgarity.

For years, I also had little time for any flowers other than lilies and daffodils, and pink, white, blue, and lavender perennials. The notion of potting seeds, thinning seedlings, and pricking them out to transplant struck me as a waste of time and effort. That is, until I couldn't find enough six-packs of white impatiens at a local nursery to arrange on a tiered étagère for a floral extravagance I envisioned for a summer party. The extravagance has become an annual pleasure, and one of many examples of my newfound pleasure in **annuals** and **growing plants from seed**.

An annual is a plant that lives for only one season, from the time its seed is sown. It blooms, sets seeds, and dies. **Half-hardy annuals** are cold resistant. Their seeds can be planted in early May in our plant hardiness Zone 6 (0 to –10°F average yearly minimal temperature) and to Zone 7 (0 to +10°F average yearly minimal temperature). The seeds of **hardy annuals**, those that self-seed reliably, can be planted in the chill of autumn or in very early spring.

The seeds of many annual culinary herbs and flowering annuals can be sown directly in the garden in full sun as soon as all danger of frost is over. Dill (which rarely tolerates transplanting), cosmos, zinnias, and sunflowers are popular choices for this method. Some annuals, like morning glories, nasturtiums, sweet peas, and cilantro (a culinary herb that sets its seeds, known as coriander, in hot weather), do better if you give them a head start by potting them indoors in peat or humulus pots in which they can remain planted, their fragile roots undisturbed when they are replanted outdoors.

Cascading white impatiens and agapanthus on our dining deck.

A graceful pink cosmos leans against one of our many garden boulders.

I use peat or humulus pots for dill that I plop into an earth-filled terra-cotta pot to bring indoors with other kitchen herbs in the winter: basil, borage, cilantro, and chervil, which is best sowed both in the spring and late in the summer, as it grows quickly and prefers cool weather. I use peat or humulus pots both for potting perennial herb seeds and for seeds of perennial flowers—more about these soon.

You can prolong the life of flowering annuals by overwintering them. I use terra-cotta pots for annuals to overwinter as houseplants (before they are trotted outside again in the spring), such as scented geraniums, pelargoniums (Greek for "stork," a reference to the shape of their stork-billed seed capsules), along with evolvulus, a low-growing plant with cobalt-blue flowers, and others. Among annuals you might like to have outside or inside all year are: begonias, bouvardia, a summertime magnet for hummingbirds; fuchsia, heliotrope, lobelia, snapdragons, and verbena.

Before you start seeds indoors or organize them for sowing outdoors, **you have to have seeds.** There are **many catalogs that specialize in seeds,** but the seed catalog for vintage heirloom flowers, fragrant flowers, old-fashioned annuals, antique flowers, perennials, flowers from America, and flowers from Europe that I think you should have a look at first is Marilyn Barlow's *Select Seeds.*

(See "Sources and Advice: Where to buy plants, seeds, garden furniture, pots and urns, both resin and clay, etc.")

Suppose, though, that you want to gather your own seeds from your own garden. Sowing your own seeds from your own garden is one of many rewarding aspects of gardening. Some seeds are easy to collect, those of perennial Siberian irises are there for you in a neat packet at the tip of the stem. Seeds from flowering tobacco (*Nicotiana*), an annual, are just as easy. Petals of nicotiana wither and fall from little upright cups. When the cups are dry and brown, just pour the seeds into your flower-seed collecting container. The seeds of columbines are held in seedpods that look like vases, also easy to pour from. Seeds from heirloom, vintage, or open-pollinated varieties of flowers will grow into plants that look like the generations of plants before them. The seed of hybrids, plants bred from two separate but related species to produce a third variety, will revert back to one of the original plants and be different from the plant you grew from which you plucked the seeds. In other words, if you save the seeds of richly colored scarlet nasturtiums and plant them, they may come up orange or yellow or a mix with nary a scarlet one among them.

Columbines, or *Aquilegia* species, are notorious for bearing offspring quite different from their parents. Among named varieties, only a few will ever come true. Columbines may have leaves that look like baseball mits, according to sons, grandsons, and visiting boy children, but their seedpods are more poetic in appearance. They look like fluted vases, centrally joined. If you are afraid of missing the moment of ripening, or are going away for a few days, just cover the seedpods with little self-tying muslin bags and attach them to the columbine stems. When you come back, simply cut the stalk, turn it upside down to shake the pods and their seeds into its muslin bag. I was told you could do the same thing with paper bags, but they got wet with rain and our sprinkler system and disintegrated. I acquired dozens of little (2" by 3") muslin bags with thin cord ties at the top, ideal for seed gathering. Just what these little bags were originally used for and where I got them or even why I got them at the time are mysteries. If I had to get more now, I suppose I would instigate a search on the Internet.

Collect seeds from the healthiest plants in your garden, since some diseases can be passed along in a seed. Collect seed heads free and clear of insects. Be sure that the seeds you collect are mature. Immature seeds won't sprout. Leave the flower pod on the plant until it has dried on its own. If you think you'll forget, or a bird will get the seeds before you do, or the seedpod will pop and the seeds will wing away, tie a muslin bag or the foot of an outworn pair of pantyhose around the seedpod and secure with a twist tie. Be sure to use something that "breathes," so that the seeds can go on maturing and getting sun while on the plant. Check every couple of days to see how the seeds are coming along. Try always to collect seeds on a dry, sunny day. Collect seeds or seed heads in little brown paper bags. Put each bag inside a Ziploc bag that you can label, covering the label with Scotch tape to prevent smearing. Once collected, it's worthwhile to make an effort to label your seeds with scrupulous attention to the name of each plant, its collection date, or the date you received it, the company it came from if it's commercially grown, and the year, as well. Recording this information and protecting it with Scotch tape can save you, as it has for me, from wasting time and effort and making unnecesary mistakes.

Once back inside your house, spread the seeds on paper towels inside boxes without their tops in a warm, dry location out of direct sun (direct sun can cause seeds to degrade) and leave the seeds to dry in the paper towel-lined boxes, each type of seed labeled. Seeds may look and feel dry, but it's likely that they will contain enough moisture to spoil if stored. Depending on the humidity, it should take a few weeks for the seeds to dry.

To check if your seeds are dry enough to be stored, funnel the seeds into an airtight glass container, such as an old, clean jam jar with a screw-on lid, at room temperature. If you see condensation inside after a few hours, your seeds need more drying time.

Seeds are easier to store, and less likely to rot, if they are separated from the **chaff**, the dry flower parts, like the seed pods, petals, or withered leaves, surrounding the seeds. The perennial *Echinacea purpurea*, or *Rudbeckia purpurea* as some refer to it, is hard to **thresh (separating the seed from what is holding it)**, as are some types of zinnias, those easily grown annuals. If you only have a few seeds, try rubbing them between two butter paddles or between two plain boards, but be careful not to press too hard as you might damage the seeds. When I had sacks of Siberian iris seeds, some in their pods, some out of their pods, someone told me to put everything into a pillowcase and whack the knotted pillowcase on the kitchen table to thresh the seeds. The next step is **winnowing the seeds from the chaff**, removing the seeds from the loosened chaff. You can put everything into a pillowcase and shake

Potted herbs thrive on a sunny deck outside our kitchen.

it up. Sometimes, all the seeds fall to the bottom. But if they don't, then you can either tweeze out the seeds with a tweezer, or just leave the chaff mixed in with the seeds. Just be sure that the seed-chaff mix is dry before you store it to pot indoors or to sow outdoors in the spring.

After your seeds are dry, to store them as viable living organisms, resting and dormant until you give them the signal to sprout when you plant them, store your seeds so that they will remain cool, dark, and dry in airtight containers, preferably at a temperature from 40 to 45°F. Jelly jars or Ziploc plastic bags make good storage containers, if you put these carefully labeled jars and plastic envelopes in a cardboard box or a suitcase, to maintain the dark components of cool, dark, and dry.

What do you do with seeds someone has given you, or seeds left over from last year's planting, or seeds you don't know will grow? **To check seeds' viability** or potential to germinate, moisten a paper towel with some warm water so that the paper is damp, but not wringing wet, then scatter 10 seeds on half of the paper towel, folding the towel in a Ziploc bag, and store in a warm place, such as the top of a refrigerator, for about ten days. Then count the number of seeds that sprouted or germinated after ten days. If six or more seeds sprouted, plant them in pots or sow them outdoors when the weather is appropriate. If less than six seeds germinated, toss them and the remainder into your compost pile. Why waste space with seeds that aren't going to germinate successfully?

Many of us just send for seeds from catalogs. Each seed packet tells you what kind of seed it is, annual or perennial, hardy annual, half-hardy annual, with planting dates, time until bloom, special needs, instructions. It's all there, even if you have to get out a magnifying glass to read it. When seeds are harvested commercially, they don't get to experience natural seasonal cold, heat, and rain and usually have to be coaxed into growing.

Now that you have your seeds, you'll need a place to work and materials to work with.

Columbines (*Aquilegia*) ornament the garden with their delicate jewel colors.

You'll need bags of commercial "**soilless**" **seed-starting mix**, a lightweight **sterile** mix of sphagnum peat moss, vermiculite, perlite, and other components that help prevent damping-off disease, a fungal problem that causes seedlings to wither and die. **Do not use potting soil, which is often too rich and doesn't drain well enough for seedlings.**

- You'll need peat or humulus pots. How many depends on how many seeds you have to pot. Figure on two or three seeds to a pot. For tiny seeds, try to plant only a few in a pot.
- Although you don't really need them, see if you can find cell packs of nine little containers each into which you can fit your peat pots or humulus pots. I like them as holders for peat or humulus pots.
- You'll need shallow trays or edged cookie sheets on which to set your planted peat or humulus pots, so that you can water seedlings from the bottom by

adding water to the tray rather than risking disturbing seedlings by watering them from the top.

- If you have south- or east-facing windowsills, place your trays of pots on them, or on supplementary tables in front of the windows. Otherwise, set up your workspace in the cellar or anywhere else indoors and rig up one or two 2'- to 4'-long shop lights with two cool white fluorescent tubes and chains to mount them on so that you can move them easily up or down. Seedlings need 14 to 16 hours of artificial light a day.

- Some people find the cellar much easier for planting seeds. You can make a mess in the cellar and not worry that your seedlings will be bumped into or knocked over by visitors, children or dogs. Whatever your modus operandi, you'll require a work surface and space for supplies and space for seed-starting equipment.

- You'll need lots of sticks for inserting into pots for attaching seed packet labels or written labels enclosed in heavy-duty plastic bags, as you will be moving the pots outside in the spring.

Presoaking is the number one technique for successful germination of both annual and perennial seeds. This simple but vital procedure exposes the seed embryo to moisture, the primary impetus for making a seed grow. José and I pour hot water, hot but not boiling hot, into shallow ceramic containers, empty a packet of seeds into each, spread out the seeds, and let them sit for up to 24 hours. Soak the seeds for any longer than two days and they can spoil. The seeds swell as the water penetrates the aril, or seed coating, and the embryo inside begins to plump up. Be sure not to presoak seeds until the night before you plant them in peat or humulus pots, or plant them outside in the garden. Once the seeds have

Evolvulus with its lovely blue flowers, an annual, can be over wintered to re-bloom in the spring and summer.

plumped up, you have to get them into moist earth instantly, pronto, right away, then keep them well-watered until they are up, green, and growing, growing, growing.

Other procedures sometimes needed to break the dormancy of stubborn seeds are **scarification** and **stratification.** "Scarification" just means nicking the aril, or seed coat, with your fingernail, a knife, or sandpaper so that moisture, vital to a seed's life, can more easily reach the seed's embryo. You only need to remove a tiny slice or section of the seed coat, so don't be too fierce with your fingernail or knife. You can also line a Mason jar or other glass jar having a screw-on lid with a sheet of coarse grit sandpaper to fit. Insert the sheet of sandpaper so that it curls right around inside, put in the seeds that need to be scarified, screw back the lid, and shake the Mason jar until the seed coats are abraded but still protect the embryo inside the seed. Again, don't overdo. Scarify seeds just before planting as seeds nicked too long before planting can easily dry out and be infertile by the time you pot them up or sow them. When the seeds are scarified, soak them overnight in lukewarm water before planting them. Sow them immediately after soaking them or they will wither and die. Morning glories and the entire Ipomoea species should be presoaked before planting, of course, but also, the seed packet may tell you to scarify them, which you should. The seeds of sweet peas, morning glories, and nasturtiums germinate more easily if their hard seed coats are nicked, or scarified, so that they can soak up more water.

If you are venturing out into the world of seed planting for the first time, don't worry, most annual flowers need only to be presoaked, rarely scarified, and now that we all know what scarification is, starting annuals from seed is hardly a problem. Annuals are quick and easy and provide welcome beauty and color only a few months after planting. Hardy annuals such as sunflowers should be sown directly into the outdoor soil, while tender annuals such as petunias, which are actually perennials in their native tropics and require a much longer growing season to come to fruition than we can give them in the north, need to be started indoors beginning six to eight weeks before the last frost. This timing can vary, however, and you should follow directions on your seed packets. To be sure of the best possible germination, keep your seed packets away from heat and moisture in a cool, dark, and dry place until you are ready to sow.

Stratification, an old term for breaking the dormancy of seeds outdoors under natural conditions by exposing seeds to extreme temperature changes, supplying a period of moist cold to trick seeds into falsely experiencing winter, sounded like an odd thing to do when I first heard of it, but it makes sense. The seeds of many plants that are native to regions with cold winters germinate most readily after a period of moist chilling in a dark place. In the wild, that's what winter furnishes for them. During the seeds' deep sleep, their seed coats soften until the warmth and moisture of spring encourage them into growth.

If you're sowing indoors in spring, presoak the seeds, put them in pots, and put the pots in a Ziploc bag. Top off the seeds with another inch of moist medium, and then put the bag in an undisturbed corner of the refrigerator (at 34 to 41°F). Check weekly for germination. When the seeds begin to sprout roots, they will sprout a tiny green delicate new growth. Then, care for them as you would any other seedlings. If you don't put the seedlings in peat or humulus pots filled with moist seed-starting medium but just put the seeds in zip-top plastic—sandwich bags filled halfway with moist seed-starting medium—and top off the seeds with another inch of moist medium and store the bag(s) in an undisturbed corner of the refrigerator, as many gardeners suggest, then you would have to spoon

each seedling out of the bag when it began to sprout roots and carefully transfer the seedling with its sprouting root to a peat or humulus pot, being extremely careful neither to disturb the fragile root nor the fragile new growth. I just think it's easier to plant the seeds in the peat or humulus pots to begin with.

Seeds of perennials that require stratification can also be planted outdoors in the autumn or stored in the refrigerator through autumn and winter, and then be planted in pots and started indoors or out in spring. For outdoor seed-starting in autumn or winter, plant the seeds in peat or humulus pots filled with seed-starting medium and plant these pots in larger terra-cotta pots in a wooden box with fine metal mesh screening tacked on top to help distribute raindrops and prevent hail from falling like bombs on the seeds. If you overwinter the pots in a cold frame or against the wall of a garage, you should bury the pots to their rims in a level layer of moist sand, keeping the pots close together to insulate them from severe cold. Having the pots close together in a wooden box also prevents them from tipping over and spilling, or being knocked over by roaming raccoons or feral cats or neighboring dogs.

If the weather is warm, you can expect the seeds to germinate in about two months. If the waiting period is unusually dry, water the pots carefully from a watering can with the smallest of watering holes so that you can sprinkle the potted seeds gently. If you have labeled your outdoor potted plants with a label in a plastic bag on a stick (the best way I know of guaranteeing that the labeling will be legible at all times), you can pull out the stick and feel the bottom end of it for moisture, or if the pot feels heavy, there probably is sufficient moisture in it. If the pot is light, it's probably time to water.

When there was no more room for flats of potted seedlings on tables in front of all south-facing and east-facing windows when I first came to Brillig, and we had fewer refrigerators than we now have and a cook who wouldn't tolerate a refrigerator full of seeds, what could

Seedlings sprout in the living room converted in the winter to a greenhouse.

we do? Our gardener at the time, who later turned out to be a con man who duped all his clients, shrugged, muttered an untranslatable obscenity, sowed seeds into dark-green plastic cell packs, set the cell packs in wooden flats, stacked the wooden flats in a black Hefty leaf bag, and set everything into the garage where the temperature is cold but almost never much below freezing. Once the seeds had received the recommended period of stratification, he brought the flats into the cellar and set them under lights for germination. He came up with the idea of attaching aluminum foil as reflectors to the fluorescent tubes to catch the light that would otherwise just get uselessly dispersed in the darkness. He attached wide strips of foil to the left side of one light and to the right side of the other as well as a strip of foil between the two fluorescent fix-

tures that provided a lighted space and a source of warmth for three trays instead of two. He used wooden clothespins with metal fixtures to attach the aluminum foil to the lighting fixtures. When I complimented him on this brilliant idea, he said it wasn't his idea, but one he'd seen used on the New Jersey coast. When this intelligent, resourceful, and seemingly honest fellow was later exposed as a con man, a regular scamp about money, who kited checks, padded bills, used his clients' cars when they were off the island, I was sorry that the lust for money should have been his downfall, but, at the same time, grateful to him for his resourcefulness in solving seed-growing problems.

Old-time traditional information advises you to plant seeds thickly in a flat or tray, then "prick out" individual seedlings and repot them into larger containers. I'd rather eliminate the need for transplanting, and prefer to plant two or three seeds in a pot 2¼" in diameter or a larger pot.

First of all, pour the seed-starting mix into a plastic pail, moisten with hot water, and mix well with a wooden spoon or one of those rubber-tipped kitchen utensil thingies. Fill each pot with the moistened soil mix, water thoroughly with warm water, and smooth the soil surface in each pot.

Select your seeds and be sure to read all the directions on the packets.

Distribute large seeds evenly and cover with dry planting mix, three times the thickness of the seed, unless the directions tell you the plant needs light to germinate, in which case, follow the directions given for columbines and cleome following shortly.

Seedlings are carefully labeled in the wintertime living room greenhouse.

For fine seeds, the trick is to sow them sparingly. Try creasing the flap of the glassine envelope and tapping the envelope to get the seeds to move slowly. Overcrowding in a pot or tray can result in disease and weaken seedlings. If you do seed too heavily by mistake, tweeze out the extras among the freshly germinated seed with tweezers. Try to leave ¼" to ½" between seedlings in the tray or pot.

Be sure to label the pots as you proceed and protect the labels with plastic envelopes.

I think pots are the only way to raise slow-growing perennials and annuals (the ones you are told to start indoors eight to ten weeks before the last frost date). It's easier to care for seedlings that way and there's no weeding.

How deep to plant? If the seed packet doesn't tell you, a good rule is to plant a seed three times as deep as its smallest diameter. Some seeds, like spider flowers (*Cleome*) and columbines (*Aquilegia*), need light to germinate, and these you don't cover at all. Scatter them directly on the top dressing by tapping them gently from the seed envelope, trying to avoid letting the seeds clump together. Tap them softly with your fingers to settle them, or you can also tap the pot against your workbench or other surface to settle the seed. Then set the pot in a shallow basin of water for five minutes or until you see moisture on the surface of the sterile seed-starting mix.

After you have planted your seeds, immediately cover the potted seeds on their trays with transparent plastic to seal in moisture and create a humid greenhouselike atmosphere to prevent the surface from drying out. Cover the seeds loosely but securely. Place the plastic over the top of the pot. At 65 to 75 °F, seeds should sprout without additional heat. Bottom heat jump-starts seedlings by speeding germination and stimulating root growth by keeping the soil at about 70°F. Some people do this by putting their seed trays on the warm tops of their refrigerator(s) or investing in thermostatically controlled heating pads or propagation mats attached to six-foot power cords, (10" by 20" for one flat, 20 watts—or 48" by 20", 107 watts for four flats.) I recommend a visit to the Gardener's Supply Company website. (See "Sources and Advice: Where to buy plants, seeds, garden furniture, pots and urns, both resin and clay, etc.")

Read your seed packets or reference material carefully to see whether your seeds require light during the germination process. Some may prefer total darkness until the plants sprout from the soil. If your seeds require darkness, cover them with a black plastic garbage bag. For your light-requiring seeds, plug in the fluorescent lights, which you should adjust to about 4" from the surface of the seed-starting mix. If your seedlings get leggy, lower the lights an inch. Lights must remain on for 14 to 16 hours a day, with a period of complete darkness at night. You may want to use a timer. Some people prefer to check their pots twice a day as they turn the lights on and off. Remember to water occasionally, from beneath, rather than above the pots, and don't ever allow the pots to dry out completely. Keep an electric fan or two on low to keep air circulating to encourage seedlings to become strong and sturdy.

Most annuals will germinate in a week, perennials in two weeks. Some seeds take as long as a month to sprout. Once your seeds have germinated, take off the plastic wrap or humidity dome and keep about 2" to 3" from the fluorescent grow lights to keep them from getting leggy. As the seedlings rise, keep the lights at the proper distance and water carefully, using water from the bottom and a water mister on top.

The stems of your seedlings will first bear a twin set of thick little seed leaves called cotyledons, not true leaves, which will soon be replaced with fine, lobed leaves. José uses a weak solution of water-soluble fish emulsion fertilizer weekly to encourage the growth of seedlings. He mixes the fertilizer at a ratio recommended for indoor container plants or cuts the amount of fertilizer recommended for outdoor use in half, about a teaspoon of fertilizer for each gallon of water.

As soon as seedlings have two or three pairs of leaves, they are ready to go out into the garden, but before they are subjected to the rigors of wind, sun, rain, fog, good or wretched weather, higher or lower temperatures than they are used to, they need time to adapt to their new surroundings, to get acclimated, to "harden off," to be introduced gradually to the conditions in your garden, a process that will take about two weeks.

Begin by taking trays of seedlings outside to a protected shaded place close to a wall or put them in a south-

facing cold frame for a few hours on mild days until, after about a week, you gradually work up to a full day, then overnight. This hardening-off process is vital to assure that your seedlings adjust to a coastal climate. Gradually move the seedlings into a sunnier spot or to the exposure where you will plant them. **For horse owners, if you don't have a cold frame, you can put a simple one together** using four bales of hay placed in a square, with an old window as the cover. Prop the lid up during sunny days, or your seedlings will bake. Gradually remove the cover for a few more hours each day until your seedlings are hardened off, and transplant them into your garden after all danger of frost is past. After the requisite two-week period of hardening off, hope for an overcast, misty, foggy, drizzly, gray day with rain in the forecast and no heat waves or frosts expected for transplanting. Without the drying effect of the sun and with additional moisture, seeds will get off to a fine start. If the weather is unremittingly sunny, plant late in the afternoon so your seedlings will get their start in the cool of the evening and minimize the time the seedlings roast in the sun.

Rake the area a few times to break up the earth's crust, if there is one, and maybe weed if necessary, in the plot where you are going to plant the seedlings. Keep the seedlings in the shade or shaded until you are actually ready to plant each one. First, dig a hole for it. Carefully cut into the peat or humulus pot with a sharp knife to give the seedling's roots a chance to escape easily if the pot doesn't break down quickly enough. Once the pot is in the ground, cut off any part of it that is above the soil line as it can dry out and pull moisture from the earth.

If you didn't use biodegradable pots and are transplanting, plant your seedling at about the depth it was in the pot or a little deeper, not too deep, because if your soil is soggy, wet, or cold, planting too deeply could rot the stem.

IMPORTANT: **Always handle seedlings by their leaves, never by their stems. Leaves can and will grow back. The stem is the seedling's—any plant's—lifeline, its fragile spinal column, which can be easily damaged.**

Be sure to identify your seedlings with a seed packet or label attached to a stick with a plastic bag slipped over the packet cover or label to keep it dry and legible. Firm the soil around your seedlings, but don't press so hard that you compact the soil.

Sunflowers

I have often used plastic-mesh strawberry containers as covers for newly transplanted seedlings, covering each plant with a container, leaving it in place for several days until the plant becomes thoroughly acclimated to its new home outside. You can water the covered seedlings right through the mesh container. The mesh containers may look awful—they do to me—but they are wonderful seedling protectors where the winds are sharp and there are predator rabbits.

Seedlings become established when you see new growth, anywhere from a few days to a week, depending on your seedling and the weather. Your seedlings may wilt, droop, or experience the shock of transplanting if they weren't hardened off completely or if the weather is unseasonably hot, cold, rainy, or windy. Most young plants recover in a few days, but be sure that the earth is firmed around them so that there's no danger of air pockets drying out the roots. Water only if the top inch of garden soil is dry. Don't water if the soil is already wet. Be sure to keep the soil moist until the plants start growing well. Wait about a week to ten days after transplanting before fertilizing your seedlings. They will have sent out new feeder roots by then and will be beginning their more intensely active stage of growth.

In our Zone area—Zone 6 to Zone 7 area—you can also sow seeds directly outdoors in full sun in late April, early May, in a seedbed you have prepared beforehand by clearing away any weeds or any existing vegetation and loosening the soil to at least the depth of a garden spade. Add 2" of well-rotted compost to the bed, turn it, and hoe it at least 6" under. Remove any rocks and debris from your seedbed to make it easier and simpler for tender seedlings to sprout through the earth. The soil texture should be moisture-retentive and light and minus any lumps or clots. Mark your seedbeds for direct sowing with weather-proof labels, using a stick and an enveloping plastic bag for your seed packet or handwritten labels.

Your best bets for seeds to sow directly are quick-germinating, fast-blooming plants, such as perennial black-eyed Susans (*Rudbeckia hirta*) or trustworthy annuals such as zinnias (*Zinnia spp.*), marigolds (*Tagetes spp.*), cosmos (*Cosmos spp.*), sunflowers (*Helianthus spp.*), or perennial purple coneflowers (*Echinacea purpurea*). For most seeds, moisture and soil warmth are all that are necessary to start growth. The weather as well as the soil has to be warm enough to support the plant. Sowing quick-germinating seeds such as cosmos too early could expose young seedlings to a damaging frost. If you want to grow a large drift of flowers,

Potted begonias on our dining deck.

scratch the surface of the soil with a garden rake, broadcast the seed, scattering the seed with a fling of your wrist, then gently go back over the area **with the back of a rake** to work the seeds into the soil and smooth the soil.

IMPORTANT: **Delay planting seeds outdoors until after the last projected frost date in your area.**

You'll usually find the ideal soil temperature listed on the seed packet. If you stick a soil thermometer into the soil about 2", you'll see if your garden soil is the right temperature for planting.

Seeds need moisture to germinate. To keep them from being washed away when you water, you can cover the seedbed with porous material of some sort; porous foam rubber is a reliable suggestion, the sort of material used as an antislip rug-backing, which usually comes in an ugly light-gray or tan color, but you, the gardener, are the only one who sees it, because the minute you're finished watering your seeds, you roll the porous stuff up and get it out of sight.

After the cotyledons appear and the first true leaves, you may find that your outdoor seedbed is too crowded. Overcrowded plants don't do as well as those that have a little room for branching out. Scissoring or pulling up healthy plants is difficult, but you can always pot up the rejects, keep them, or give them away as presents to friends.

Some annuals to consider sowing directly are: Bachelor's buttons or cornflowers (*Centaurea spp.*); calendulas (*Calendula spp.*); California poppies—mix their tiny seeds with sand for easier sowing (*Papavar spp.*); cosmos (*Cosmos spp.*); forget-me-nots (*Myosotis spp.*), which like

Among their other uses, I rely on petunias that flower all summer long to line the steps leading to the swimming pool.

A word to the wise: Remember not to fertilize columbines, cosmos, mock orange plants, and nasturtiums. They need lean, nitrogen-light soil to starve them into more intense efflorescence. If you fertilize them, you'll have abundant foliage at the expense of fewer flowers. Remember that fragrant annuals such as four-o'clocks (*Mirabilis jalapa spp.*), night-scented stock (*Matthiola spp.*), jasmine tobacco (*Nicotiana alata*), and other night-flowering plants only release their seductive scent after the sun goes down.

Although they need a regular supply of water until their root systems are established, when mature, California poppies, cosmos, marigolds, and zinnias are remarkably drought resistant. If you are stuck with common rosa rugosa bushes with purply-red flowers, a rather harsh magenta color, you can improve the scene by planting cosmos casually around and about. Cosmos' slender grace, delicate airy foliage, and both pink- and raspberry-colored flowers make an amazing difference.

Fast-growing perennials recommended for direct sowing are: Black-eyed Susans (*Rudbeckia hirta*); butterfly weed (*Asclepias tuberosa*); China pinks (*Dianthus chinesis*); Columbine (*Aquilegia vulgaris*); coreopsis (*Coreopsis spp.*); feverfew (*Tanacetum parthenium*); gaillardia (*Gaillardia spp.*); kniphofia (*Kniphofia spp.*); mallow (*Malva spp.*); purple coneflower (*Echinacea purpurea*).

Transplants are best for: Ageratums, Canterbury bells, English daisies, heliotrope, impatiens, lisianthus, lobelia, pansies/violas, petunias.

We propagate our scented geraniums, properly called pelargoniums, from root cuttings, not seeds.

In early autumn before your annual scented pelargonium dies in the cold, look for roots that are about the diameter of a drinking straw or pencil. With a sterilized knife (dip it in rubbing alcohol or Clorox and rinse well in water), trim and discard the fibrous parts from the long roots and start making 2" cuttings. Keep track of which end goes up! Make an angled cut at the bottom and a straight cut at the top so that you'll know which end to

constant moisture; four-o'clocks (*Mirabilis jalapa spp.*); snapdragons (*Antirrhinum sp.*); sunflowers (*Helianthus spp.*), beloved by goldfinches; sweet alyssum (*Lobularia maritime*); zinnias (*Zinnia spp.*).

Among annuals for shaded areas are: begonias, caladiums, ginger, impatiens, nicotianas, all species known by their botanical names. *Abelmoschus esculentus* is an ornamental okra, somewhat like a hollyhock, but shorter, an impressive player for one-upmanship horticulturalists.

poke into the soil. The angled cut points down. New growth sprouts only from the top piece. Plant the cuttings. Dip each cutting in growth hormone to help stimulate rooting. Use a straw or a pencil to poke a hole and then insert the root cutting, angled end down, into a pot filled with moist, "soilless" seed-starting potting mix. The top of each cutting should be flush with the soil. Firm each one in place and water the seed-starting mix thoroughly by putting the pot in a basin of water and waiting five minutes or so for water to be drawn up to the top, or by gently sprinkling water on the top until water leaks out of the bottom of the pot. Place the pot with your cuttings in a coldframe or in a cool spot in your cellar or garage. The cuttings don't need much light. It will probably be spring before tender new shoots emerge. Individually repot these little pelargoniums, give them

lots of sunlight in a south-facing windowsill, and keep the soil slightly moist.

You can also take root cuttings from perennial plants before they go into dormancy in late autumn or early winter by following this basic procedure.

I found it was simpler for me to overwinter the majority of our scented pelargoniums and our other pelargoniums in our sunny, many-windowed living room, an ideal room to jury-rig as a greenhouse. However, José and I are responsible for quite a few scented pelargoniums that we've replicated with root cuttings.

Until you've done it, the maternal or paternal interest you take in growing plants from seed or root cuttings is hard to define, hard to explain, but never underestimate the nice sense of joy you get when you see the seeds or root cuttings you planted in full flower.

Chapter 15

The Cutting Garden

How can you prolong the life of cut flowers? Florists' bouquets? Flowering branches?

Charles Masson, proprietor of **La Grenouille**, a New York restaurant known for its flower arrangements as well as its food, told me that he believes the main requirements are fresh flowers, sufficient **fresh** water and nourishment for them, and **clean** flower holders **filled daily** with fresh, room-temperature water. My grandmother's Scottish kitchen maid obeyed this fiat when using glass or crystal vases. Her flower arrangements never failed to be decorative and long lasting. Her secret? She preferred using porcelain vases into which she would ladle two cups of earth, pour in lukewarm water and then put in the flowers.

She wouldn't clean the vase until the flowers died. I use a "frog" for arranging flowers. She just dumped in garden soil, which serves the purpose equally well (as long as you don't see it.)

Don't use metal flower holders, use "neutral" flower holders of glass or porcelain or china or earthenware. You can use brass or silver containers if you use a jar or a glass or a plastic quart/gallon freezer bag as a liner for flower holding. To avoid contamination, stains, and leaks, use the same precautions with porcelain, china, and earthenware containers.

In his book, *The Flowers of La Grenouille*[1], Mr. Masson describes how plants and flowers need to be conditioned and maintained in different ways, and tells how to accomplish this with professional expertise. **Conditioning** is what you do to flowers and branches to firm their stems and revivify their leaves and blossoms before you put them out on view. First, cut and trim stalks and branches, using clean, sharp clippers or a knife so that you don't fray the stems with dull blades. Remove less-than-perfect upper leaves and all leaves and side shoots from the lower part of the stem that will be submerged in water. Set aside side shoots and branch cuttings with buds in a water-filled plastic bucket until the buds open up and offer you flowers for other arrangements. The stems under water should always

The key to conditioning cut flowers and branches
is to help them absorb as much water as possible.
The longer the stem ends of flowers and branches
are exposed to air, the sooner they wither.

be leafless. Leaves on stems under water rot and cause that awful "pong" smell, as my Scottish cousins said instead of "stinky," the reek of poorly maintained cut flowers.

Whenever you cut a flower stem or a branch, always cut above the node, a little green bump, which is an embryonic bud. If stems are forked or multibranched, cut them the way you think looks best and be sure that each stem can absorb extra water.

- **For amaryllis, anemones, daffodils, narcissus, and other flowers with tubular stems,** which look like drinking straws, cut straight across.
- **For flowers and plants with milky sap such as hollyhocks, milkweed, poppies, and poinsettias,** burn the stems by flicking them over a gas burner or candle flame. N.B. **Hydrangeas** are an exception. Treat them as branches, mentioned subsequently.
- **For roses and most flowers,** cut stem ends diagonally on about a 45° slant.

The key to conditioning cut flowers and branches is to help them absorb as much water as possible. Immediately after cutting the stem of a flower or branch, plunge it in water. The longer the stem ends of flowers and branches are exposed to air, the sooner they wither.

Try to leave flowers and branches for about 12 hours in their conditioning water, in a cool place—ideal temperature is 48°F—before you arrange them with fresh water and flower food such as Floralife or Chrysal.

Every morning, when you change your flowers' or branches' water, snip a smidgen from each stem end until the blossoms fade. If you don't want to rearrange a large bouquet, tip out the old water completely before you pour in fresh water to which you have already added Floralife or whatever, and stirred well to mix.

Water evaporates, so don't forget to check the water level of your vases from time to time during the day and evening.

Remember to keep your finished bouquet cool and away from sources of heat including overdoses of direct sunlight, electric light, and candlelight.

Tip: *For decorative accents, choose herbs, slips of lavender, mint, rosemary, or edible flowers like nasturtiums—to decorate fruit, cheese, or shelled or unshelled nuts. For potpourri, evergreens, wreaths, and garlands, choose any flowers that please you and put them in water-filled plastic tubes ideal for this purpose that you can get from your florist. Condition and maintain your choices in these water-filled tubes.*

Branches: Forced inside, early-blossoming branches are welcome harbingers of spring. Witch hazel, pussy willow, star magnolia, flowering pale-pink quince—a favorite of mine—and fruiting tree branches are among many choices that can be forced. Cut branches from trees or shrubs when the flower buds are just beginning to plump up—they're a bit larger that the leaf buds. Make a pruning cut flush with a main branch, clean the branch at the bottom by scraping off the bark. Remove all dead shoots. Cut off stems that might draw too much water from the main branch. Hammer the bottom ends of the branches to fray them. Then, make vertical cuts with clippers or pruning shears of an inch or a little more, depending on the length of the branch. This helps the wood absorb water for abundant flowering.

Place the branches in a large nonmetal container of water. Add a commercial food as directed. A plastic dry cleaner's bag tied over the top of the container will provide the right amount of humidity until the buds swell before opening. Branches will force easily in a brightly lit room. (Avoid direct sunlight).

For evergreens of all types, add 1 tablespoon of glycerin for each quart of water.

To clean apple blossom branches, add 2 tablespoons of ammonia for each gallon of conditioning water.

CAUTION: **Never pull off a green leaf or leaves at the branch top, near the flowering heads of lilacs, as these are water conductors to the blossoms.**

Ferns: Submerge in water for 12 hours. Gently shake off excess water before arranging.

In the spring, a pussy willow bursts into bloom like popcorn.

Flowers

Anemones: To freshen drooping flowers, place in a "neutral" flower holder filled with water and ice cubes up to the base of their heads. After flowers revive, use ½ cup vinegar to 1 gallon of water. Never spray.

Carnations and Pinks: Submerge up to their heads in chilled water. After their 12-hour guzzle in a cool place, the buds will open when you bring them to a warmer place.

Chrysanthemums: For every 2 quarts of water, use 10 drops of oil of cloves.

Clematis: Use 3 tablespoons of rubbing alcohol or vodka or gin or other clear liquor, plus a pinch of baking soda for each quart of water.

Cosmos: Use a teaspoon of sugar for each quart of water.

Daffodils, Jonquils, and Narcissus: Use small quantities of water for conditioning and arrangements. Do not combine with other flowers because members of the Narcissus family exude a mucilaginous sap, which can shorten the vase life of vase companions.

Daisies (all types): Mix 3 drops of oil of peppermint for each quart of water.

Daylilies: For each 2 cups of cold water, add ½ cup of vinegar.

Delphiniums: Use 1 tablespoon of rubbing alcohol or gin or vodka or other clear liquor for each pint of water. With large hybrid delphiniums, carefully remove lower side shoots, not cutting too close to the stem. Upend delphinium, cut stem straight across, and fill hollow stem with water mixed with rubbing alcohol or clear liquor mentioned above in given proportions. Plug opening with cotton wool, turn flower right side up, and instantly place in a water-filled holder with the same ratio of rubbing alcohol or clear liquor. Leave in the cotton plug.

Gardenias: Keep moist, misted. Wrap in wet tissue paper to rest in a cool place until you wear them or "float" them in water or on other surfaces. Gardenias never drink after they are cut, so there is no point in putting stems or branches in a water-filled vase.

Hollyhocks: After burning stem ends, plunge flowers into 2 quarts of water, to which you've added a handful of salt.

Iris: Add 3 drops of oil of peppermint for each quart of water.

Lilies: Place in a gallon of water with ½ cup of vinegar. Use less vinegar if stems are weak or thin. For safe disposal, gently pull pollen from the anthers over a newspaper-lined sink. Like grape juice, lily-pollen stains can be close to indelible on certain kinds of material, including Formica countertops.

Milkweed: Treat as hollyhocks.

Pansies/Violas: Submerge flowers in water for an hour, then place in a holder filled with ice water and allow to warm to room temperature.

Peonies: Rush water to blossoms by placing them in shallow hot water, then in a pint of water with 3 tablespoons of sugar. Peonies are quick to wilt, so keep them cool. If you are lucky enough to have an extra refrigerator, you can try cold storage to prolong the bloom of cut peonies. (If you put peonies or any flowers in the same refrigerator as fruits and vegetables, the ethylene gas emitted naturally from the produce will wreck your flowers). Cut your peonies while they are still in the bud stage, when the flowers haven't opened but the green sepals have separated so you can see the color of the petals, and the buds feel soft and squeezable. Be sure to leave at least one leaf on the part of the stem that remains on the plant; leave at least one third to one half of the original foliage on the entire plant. In other words, don't cut every flower on the plant. The plant needs leaves to collect solar energy to make flowers the following year.

Chill in a refrigerator. Don't place the cut flowers immediately in water. Let the stems rest for about 20 minutes, then put them in a container of clear water and set the container in a vegetable- and fruit-free refrigerator for 2 hours.

Then take the container and peonies out of the refrigerator, empty the water from the container, and let stems dry. Then swaddle the stems and the buds completely in Saran or other plastic wrap. Lay the wrapped cuttings on their sides in the refrigerator where they will keep for as long as a month.

When you are ready to bring the buds into bloom, take the flowers out of the refrigerator, unwrap them, and arrange in a vase of lukewarm water. Within 8 hours, they will open and you will have peonies in all their glamorous beauty weeks after other peonies in neighboring gardens have died.

Petunias: Use a teaspoon of sugar for each pint of water.

Poinsettias: Treat as hollyhocks.

Poppies: Treat as hollyhocks.

Roses: Remove lower leaves on the part of the stem that will be submerged in water. To rush water into the stems, plunge roses immediately into a Pyrex measuring cup or similar flower holder with enough boiling water (!) to cover stems about halfway. When water cools, add a gallon of water at room temperature well mixed with 2 tablespoons of salt. To force rosebuds to open, add a lump of sugar to the vase water.

New York authors Lance and Susan Brind Morrow were once given a generous bundle of Christmas roses, all with sagging heads and leaves curled from the cold. The Morrows told me they plunged the roses' stems midway up in boiling water, as I'd once advised them, waited until the water cooled, and then added vodka. "The roses revived like magic and lasted well over a week," Susan reported. The vodka was their idea, not mine. I asked how much vodka they had added. "Maybe a quarter of a bottle," Lance said. "The roses looked magnificent."

Snapdragons: Pinch off flower tips with your fingers. Place flowers in 2 quarts of water well-mixed with 2 tablespoons of salt.

Tulips: If you get tulips from the florist, cut off the lower leaves and the white part of the stem. With garden tulips, spray off dirt before placing them in cold water up to the base of their heads. Place tulips in shallow warm

water with ½ tablespoon of sugar for each quart of water if you want the flowers to open and bend gracefully. When you pick tulips from your garden, only cut the stems and leave as many leaves as you can. The leaves are needed, like those of peonies and daffodils, as a conduit of nourishment for next year's plants. A copper penny placed in a vase with cut tulips will keep them from opening wide. Unlike most flowers, tulips' stems continue to grow after cutting, sometimes as much as 1" to 2". Tulips are particularly thirsty flowers and enjoy fresh water daily, even more than most flowers do. They prefer cool room temperatures and often curve and bend toward sources of light. Do not combine tulips with daffodils, jonquils, or narcissi, which may be flowering at the same time. Members of the Narcissus family exude a mucilaginous sap, which can shorten the vase life of tulips and other flowers.

Violets: Treat as pansies.

~ ~ ~ ~

These stratagems will add at least two to three days to the life of flowers and branches and will sometimes even triple their vase life. I've listed a number of beneficial additives for cut flowers that are happy to help guarantee a long life in a vase. Focus always on keeping the vase or plastic liner clean, the water fresh, and recutting the stem ends daily. Most cut flowers are better for the addition of sugars and antibacterials to their vase water. Sugars feed the cut flowers, antibacterial agents keep the water fresher longer by lessening bacterial growth. Citric acids make it easier for a flower to suck up water into its stem. Floralife, or Chrysal liquid, both highly recommended preservatives, provide cut flowers with the right acid balance, nutrition, and bacterial control, helping the vase water to stay clear and bright. (As well as Floralife and Chrysal liquid, I use many of the home remedies listed previously). Diluted with a cup of water, lemon-lime drinks such as 7-Up furnish both citric acid and sugar but lack an antibacterial agent. Adding half a teaspoon of Clorox or other bleaching agent to 2 cups of liquid is a useful antibacterial. Pennies and aspirin are good as a touch of acid. Your local tap water may be "soft" or "hard." I like experimenting. Floralife and Chrysal liquid both extend the life of cut flowers by four to eight days, even more, I've found, with the use of other additives.

Conditioning and maintaining flowers properly may seem like more effort and time than you wish to expend, yet many of us experience the sight and scent of fresh-cut flowers in prime condition as one of life's memorable blessings.

Hank and I celebrated our tenth wedding anniversary by vacationing in Maui, a paradisaical Hawaiian island where the whale watching and snorkeling were extraordinarily rewarding and the trade winds carpeted our hotel corridor with rosy-pink leaflets of bougainvillea. As much as I love delphiniums, hydrangeas, irises, lilies of the valley, velvety pansies, and roses, there are times when I feel like steeping myself like a tea bag in the glamour and exoticism of tropical flowers. Giant-size king proteas, (*Protea cynararoides*) as well as the smaller pincushion proteas, the *leucospermum* species, which look like gentle sea urchins, both species native to South Africa, are successfully farmed on Maui. So are the white or orange birds of paradise (*Strelitzia reginae*), lobsterclaw heliconia, heart-shaped anthuriums, many kinds of white and red ginger, and an abundance of dendrobium and phalenopsis orchids. You can have these delivered fresh as the dawn to you as well as glossy *ti* (pronounced tea) leaves (*Cordyline fruticosa*), either a handsome lush green or a dark-red, used for food wrapping, hula skirts, thatch, sandals, raincoats, and religious ceremonies; or fragrant leis of the indigenous soft red feathery *ohia a lehua* (*Metrosideras polymorpha*) mixed with white *pikake* for its delicious scent. (See "Sources and Advice: Where to buy plants, seeds, garden furniture, pots and urns, both resin and clay, etc.")

A white cloud of springtime flowers, an
effervescence of pink blossoms presaging a later
harvest of fruit with crisp and buttery textures,
sweet and rich flavors, aromatic flesh...

Chapter 16

Peaches, Pears, Grapes, and Berries

A white cloud of springtime flowers, an effervescence of delicate pink blossoms presaging a later harvest of fruit with crisp and buttery textures, sweet and rich flavors, aromatic flesh—fruit trees are the stuff dreams are made of. Apples, blueberries, crab apples, currants, elderberries, figs, gooseberries, grapes, passionflowers, peaches, pears, raspberries, and strawberries, we have planted them all, and they all have good features. Even the fig trees, which look strangely ectopic (because they are, and have to be overwintered), furnish a useful supply of attractive leaves for decorating trays of cheese and biscuits or hors d'oeuvres.

Our outstanding successes are our raspberries, our strawberries, and our espaliered pear tree. Blackberries grow wild all over Fishers Island, along roadsides, in woods, and around the areas of several freshwater ponds. Like blackberries, with their tart, sunwarmed seedy fruit that I found in the vista area when I first came to Brillig, raspberries belong to the genus *Rubus*, a species commonly referred to as brambles. Their root systems are perennial and long-lived, but their canes are biennial, dying off every two years.

Raspberries, cold hardy in USDA Zones 3 to 8, are less sensitive to cold than blackberries, which are cold hardy in USDA Zones 5 to 8. Raspberries require full sun, well-drained soil, a little fertilizer, periodic pruning, and are divided into two types: summer-bearing and autumn-bearing, or primocane-fruiting, which bear fruit at the tips of new canes the first year and farther down those canes the second summer. Summer-bearing varieties form a new cane the first year and don't bear fruit on this cane until the next summer when the cane dies after it fruits. Raspberries are less thorny than blackberries, but a raspberry patch is not something you can prune without getting scratched unless you wear long sleeves and sturdy trousers or blue jeans. If you neglect a raspberry patch and don't prune it, it will still bear fruit, but the yield will be skimpy because of the messy congestion caused by excess canes, dead growth, and weeds. Raspberries have a shallow root system, so you have to be careful when you clean out grass and other weeds. In the autumn, José prunes and mulches our raspberry patch in the cutting garden, using free-draining wood chips to help prevent weeds from coming back.

We all delight in the bounties of our raspberry patch. Handpicked berries, luscious and warmed by the sun, are a summer treat that Austin, José and his crew, Isany, our Brazilian cook, and I revel in. Hank, the traditionalist, prefers his served in a bowl with cream and a teaspoon of sugar. Birds beak-pick their choices. There are always enough raspberries for breakfast and desserts as well as

We share delicious raspberries in the cutting garden with the birds.

sauces for ice cream. Wine-red berries strongly scented with raspberry aroma spring from a variety of cultivars, including Heritage, Killarney, Latham, and Titan. My favorites are the autumnal Fall Gold which ripen in early August.

Strawberries (*Fragaria*) also grow wild on Fishers Island, *fraise des bois*, American style. I began our strawberry patch in our cutting garden by transplanting some of these delicious, delicate little strawberries. I added everbearing varieties. I prefer everbearing to Junebearing. Junebearers are strawberries that yield their first harvest a year after planting and require thinning. Everbearing varieties fruit the first year and don't need to be thinned. Strawberry plants spread by runners, horizontal stems that make new plants at their nodes. For winter protection, we cover the strawberries with a mulch of straw and pine needles as soon as the soil freezes to about an inch deep in the autumn. Expert horticulturalists at the Brooklyn Botanic Garden, responsible for putting together the *Gardener's Desk Reference*[1], an extraordinarily helpful book, believe that the "straw" in "strawberry" may be derived from the recommended usage of straw mulch associated with the plant. I hope a later edition of the *Oxford English Dictionary* than mine[2] will pick up on this logical and thoughtful explanation. In my edition, the two conjectures about runners being like straw, or achenes, the little specks in the coating of the strawberry, being like straw, seemed quite improbable and lacking the sense of the suggestion put

forward in the sine qua non *Brooklyn Botanic Garden's Gardener's Desk Reference*. Annually, we add pine needles from our Christmas tree. When growth begins in the spring, José, his crew, and/or I gently rake off the mulch with our fingers and hand-spread it around the plants. Strawberries are easy to grow and bear quickly.

What started as half a dozen little plants in front of the raspberry patch has now become a wide L-shaped border from the east gate of the cutting garden, all around to the west side, south of the lavender and the roses. Hank prefers raspberries to strawberries, but the rest of us, including the birds, founder on fresh-picked strawberries. I think pine needles do something special for strawberries, increasing their aroma, as they acidify the soil which strawberries prefer and deepening their flavor. Cultivars we've planted include 'Midway,' 'Pocahontas,' and 'Redchief.'

Both our raspberries and our strawberries thrive in mists, fogs, salt spray, winds, humidity. As does our espaliered Bosc pear tree, 'Beurre Bosc,' with large russet-skinned fruit that has an extremely high sugar content, a spicy flavor, and a somewhat fibrous texture. I would have preferred having a 'Seckel' or sugar pear, espaliered. 'Seckel,' an American cultivar introduced in 1790, often called a favorite heirloom because it is easy to grow, richly flavored, juicy, sweet, finely textured, prized both for eating fresh and for cooking. But the Bosc tree was in place when I arrived at Brillig, and so I thought I would make do and let it be. I now wish I had started more espaliered trees. The ancient art of espalier, the horticultural practice of pruning tree branches into fanciful shapes like candelabra or horizontal cordons, or diamond shapes, called Belgian fencing, or fan shapes, the simplest, which our Bosc pear tree is, is a marvelous idea. In Egyptian tomb paintings, you can see espaliered fig trees growing in the Pharaoh's garden. In monastic gardens of medieval times, monks trained nut and fruit trees to grow flat against cloistered stone walls. In the seventeenth century, the art of espalier appeared both in elaborate configurations in the

Our espaliered Bosc pear tree with alternating sumptuous and mingy harvests.

kitchen garden of Louis XIV at Versailles, as well as in simpler styles on the walls of villagers' gardens.

Apples, crab apples, and pears, trained as espaliers, make good use of limited spaces so that a great deal can be fitted into a small garden or garden room. The bonus is that training the branches in a certain pattern makes the fruit easier to pick. Trained branches have an excellent cropping rate, and the fruit is far more accessible at picking time. Espaliered trees **don't cast shadows**, allowing a gardener to plant right up to the tree without lowering light levels. Our espaliered pear grows up from a planting box flung across with a rug of silvery green creeping juniper. We could have planted flowers there instead. As it is, the south-facing espaliered pear is a joy to behold. In spring, the espalier is a confetti cloud of white blossoms, with glossy, dark-green foliage in summer, as the budding pears take shape along the branches. In autumn, there is the fruiting finale as we harvest dozens and dozens of pears in years of bounty, and perhaps less than two dozen pears in alternate lean years. I'm told I can balance this

harvest by nipping off many pears in the bountiful years, but I prefer the feast-or-famine aspect of our Bosc pear harvest. With espaliers, though, it's always a feast. Espaliered plants produce more abundant fruits and flowers because the roots of the clipped plants have less area to nourish.

Depending on the desired size and shape of a tree, or trees, it takes about four to five years to hand-sculpt a tree into precise and geometric classical European forms like the candelabra, the Belgian fence, or the horizontal cordons. The fan shapes, with a central trunk and two or more branches on either side, are the simplest and easiest, and can be a slightly looser and more romantic arrangement. Espaliered trees are low maintenance, as they only require retying and formative pruning once or twice a year. Knowing where to prune, where to bend, and how far to bend without breaking a stem are the keys to success in espaliering, an artistic style ideal for seaside fruit trees, as you get large crops and branches that have support and a wall to lean against so that they can resist fierce winds without damage. A few leaves of our espaliered pear were scorched with salt spray in 1991 during Hurricane Bob, but otherwise, our espaliered fan-shaped pear tree came through almost unscarred.

Since we have just started our grape arbor, there hasn't been enough time to tell what the grapes will do. How cold hardy they are, when they can be relied upon to ripen, what grows best are unanswerable mysteries at the moment, but I have hopes that the grape arbor will be the joy I trust it will be.

Chapter 17

Houseplants

Houseplants have a homebody sound, safe and cheerful, bringing to mind the virtues of a nursery cup of cocoa and the images, perhaps, of an ancient Boston fern in a brass cachepot on a gueridon or a pot of African violets on a bathroom window sill. Interior container gardening, a sophisticated synonym, sounds somewhat more daunting, although wider in its possibilities. Whichever phrase you prefer, archaeologists have discovered that indoor gardening existed some 7,000 years ago. China was the birthplace of penzai (potted flowers and trees), the prototype of the cutting and clipping art known as bonsai, and penjing (potted miniature landscapes featuring rocks, water, aquatic plants; the mini-illusion of a forest.)

A study of the popular tastes and preferences of seventeenth-century China revealed a hierarchy for the species commonly used in penzai and penjing, ranking plants in order of public preference: the Four Great Masters (Broom, Boxwood, Jasmine, Juniper); the Seven Sages (Pine, Weeping Cypress, Elm, Maple, Holly, Gingko, Hedge Sageretia); the Eighteen Scholars (including Plum, Peach, Barberry, Cherry, Azalea, Quince, Camellia, Yew, Crabapple, Bamboo, Crape Myrtle, Pomegranate, Gardenia); and the Four Refined Gentleman (Orchid, Chrysanthemum, Narcissus, Calamus). Friends interested in miniature plants tell me that the Michigan

Bulb Company features a selection of starter plants for bonsai training. (See "Sources and Advice: Where to buy plants, seeds, garden furniture, pots and urns, both resin and clay, etc.")

A century ago, Tibetans considered potted herbs and plants a sign of wealth—the more the merrier. European colonizers potted the plants in their gardens so that they could take them to their next posting and enjoy the plants indoors or out.

The National Aeronautics and Space Agency has scientifically proven that houseplants are a fabulous way to filter indoor air of volatile organic chemicals such as ammonia, formaldehyde, carbon dioxide, benzene, and other pollutants released by home furnishings that can cause fatigue, headaches, sinus congestion, burning eyes, scratchy throats. Plants remove carbon dioxide from the air, along with chemicals such as formaldehyde. Two plants for each 100 sq. ft. will clean and freshen the air in your indoor breathing zone. Double that, and your indoor environment will become healthier in a week. Plants help absorb unwelcome odors of cooking as well as stale and stuffy air. Highly recommended for rapid vapor removal of the fumes of hazardous household products as well as the fumes caused by dry cleaning clothes, upholstery, and rugs are: chrysanthemums, gerbera daisies, ficus, bamboo,

An Alfred Jensen oil painting is a striking
and vivid background for spathiphyllum
(peace lilies), sturdy air-cleaning houseplants.

palms, English ivy, spathiphyllum (peace lily), Schefflera arboricola, philodendron, Dieffenbachia 'Camille.' I use spathiphyllum in the kitchen at Brillig as well as in the front hall where I sometimes have as many as twenty plants. I also recommend using Hepa air filters in every room, in the country, by the sea, as well as in town.

Over-wintering Amaryllis in foreground and Frangipani (*plumeria*) in background.

I strongly recommend *The Naturally Clean Home: 101 Safe and Easy Herbal Formulas for Nontoxic Cleansers*[1]. The author, Karen Siegel-Maier, is a herbal researcher and writer for numerous newspapers and national magazines such as *Natural Living Today*. She has written a wonderfully thorough bible of herbal and other nontoxic alternatives to commercial cleaning products by combining the antibacterial properties of herbs and essential oils with other natural ingredients such as baking soda, vinegar, lemon juice, and borax. I recommend this book unconditionally as a sine qua non for everyone interested in health, cleanliness, and a safe environment.

Besides cleaning and purifying the air, I want houseplants to look attractive and have a pleasing scent. One of my favorite flowers is the gardenia. No *parfumier* ever quite seems to capture its scent, or perhaps it's the combination of its visual appeal in addition to its fragrance that gives it its extraordinary evocative power for me. Once cut, gardenias don't absorb water, so you can float them in a bowl of water as a table centerpiece if you like, or just spread them over the top layer of a basket filled with grasses and fern leaves—they will do well either way. I first knew gardenias as a pair bound together, with their glossy dark-green leaves decorated with a white ribbon bow or a silver tinsel ribbon bow, and supplied with two faux pearl-topped steel pins, one to use and one as a spare, to pin on the left shoulder of a lace-collared party dress for the Miss Robinson or the Junior Holiday Dances. The gardenias would arrive from the boy I was going with on the afternoon of the evening dance in a white pasteboard box. The gardenias would be wrapped in a special kind of glazed paper, a seeming blend of waxed paper and tissue paper. One of the maids would carefully put them in the icebox, the Kelvinator, the fridge, the refridgeeraytor, a rectangular white enameled box with a cylindrical humming coil on its top, too high for me to touch. We had a real icebox in the kitchen pantry, a large affair made of oak with four chrome-hinged and chrome-handled doors, but the cooling contraption in the dining room pantry was also an ice-box to me, because that's what my parents called it. Sometimes the boy I was going with to the dance would come with the white pasteboard box in hand. After the dance, I would put my corsage gardenias in the icebox to chill and turn yellow and it still smelled wonderfully two or three days later. Gardenias smelled as exciting as the Christmas perfume of balsam, brandy, oranges stuck with cloves (the pomander balls I made for my mother), nutmeg on the eggnog, the strong peppermint fragrance of the candy canes on the Christmas tree. An exciting smell, a delicious smell I associated forever after with being loved and given to, of loving, giving, and pleasure, the exciting odor carrying with it a secret scent, intoxicating, sensual, a special *frisson*. If I had known about sex when I was twelve, I would have described it as "sexy," but I knew nothing about sex then, not even when I married at the age of seventeen. All I knew was that I liked to bury my nose in a gardenia and inhale deeply until I felt dizzy with pleasure.

Alas, gardenias remain a short-lived extravagance at Brillig as houseplants. Summer days are too hot for them outside, nights too cool, the weather or site too draughty or too muggy, the salt spray toxic for them. Something there is that is not good at Brillig for gardenias outdoors in either light sun or shade in the summer. They do better indoors, but there's no place for them in any of the bathrooms where they can get the humidity they like, or elsewhere posited on trays of pebbles and water for humidifying them. If they're in flower when they arrive, their flowers are sparse and not long lasting. Sometimes I buy a few sprays of gardenias from the florist in New London, have them delivered by ferry, and float them in shallow bowls, an extravagant indulgence that makes me feel too guilty to repeat more than once or twice a summer.

Friends who are all-year residents on Fishers have also been unlucky with their potted gardenia plants. I'd suggested that the plants might do well in winter if they

Potted begonias on top of an antique Indian cabinet.

placed them in a sunny window in their large airy bathroom adjoining their bedroom, an ideal location for many houseplants in the winter. But the gardenia leaves of both plants turned yellow and died "with no bugs noted." My friends thought they had either overwatered or underwatered their gardenias. This was not the problem.

Gardenias require evenly moist soil, a temperature of 70 to 75°F in the day, 60 to 65°F at night. A humid atmosphere is a major requirement, fulfilled by lightly misting branches and leaves with water two or three times daily, or keeping plants in a bathroom where you shower or luxuriate in a hot bath, or else elevating gardenias on trays of pebbles covered with water.

Yellowing leaves (chlorosis) result from alkaline soil. So you never apply lime or wood ash to a gardenia's soil. Gardenias require acidic soil with a pH of 5 to 5.5. A soil mixture custom-made for gardenias comprises one part sphagnum peat moss to two parts rich loam, ½ part dried cow manure, ½ part beach sand (washed in a cheesecloth bag to get the salt out of it). To this mix, add a 4" pot of superphosphate to prevent chlorosis (leaf yellowing) and a heaping tablespoon of iron sulphate (copperas FeSO4 7H2O), to each bushel basket.

A deficiency of iron also causes chlorosis. To prevent this condition or cure it, add ½ teaspoon of ferrous or iron sulphate (Copperas FeSO4 7H2O, a green crystalline substance used for making ink and dye) to the soil.

Water, if possible, by putting the pot in a pail or pan filled with water to within an inch of the pot rim. Wait about 30 minutes until enough moisture has been drawn up to make the surface soil feel moist. Then lift out the pot. Your gardenia, thoroughly watered, will be beautifully refreshed, especially if, at the same time, you mist the top leaves and branches.

To keep gardenias flourishing, apply ½ teaspoon of fertilizing nutrients labeled 4-12-4 or 5-10-5 every six weeks. These numbers refer to the three basic elements: nitrogen, which stimulates growth; phosphorus, which improves leaf and flower color, strengthens the root system, and pushes flower and seed production; potash, which wards off disease, stabilizes growth, and intensifies color.

Temperature must be kept above 65°F to maintain healthy foliage and flower buds. Gardenias can't stand drafts. They need lots of light, but avoid strong sunlight that can burn the leaves. Their soil must be kept moist all of the time without becoming soggy.

Scented-leaf pelargoniums (See Chapter Four: "Geraniums and Pelargoniums") are easy-maintenance houseplants. They come in a bevy of delicious fragrances that you can sample by rubbing your thumb on the underside of their leaves. Rose geranium is the best known and most popular of the scented leaf pelargoniums, or geraniums, but there are at least five different rose scents that I know of, as well as the varieties with fruity, spicy, citrusy, minty, or pine-scented perfumes. The favorite for potpourri and for flavoring syrups, cakes, and cookies is pelargonium 'True Rose,' the cherished "rose-scented geranium" that has been beloved since Colonial days. Logee's Greenhouses and Ballek's Garden Center have the best and most varied assortment of scented-leaf pelargoniums/geraniums that I've found. (See "Sources and Advice: Where to buy plants, seeds, garden furniture, pots and urns, both resin and clay, etc.")

Lily of the valley (*Convallaria majalis*) and tuberoses (*Polianthes tuberosa*) are both intensely fragrant. Easy to grow, easy to maintain, their flowers last longer than those of a gardenia. I think lilies of the valley are more beautiful as flowers than the larger, showier tuberoses, and they are perennial, so they can be planted outdoors when they have ceased to bloom indoors. They flourish at Brillig where I have a mixed bed of them, richly scented, an excellent ground cover for a shaded border on the north

A view of pink hibiscus and the blue sea from my bedroom balcony.

side of the downstairs guest room. Lilies of the valley have an irresistible sweet, delicate, fresh scent said to enhance one's alertness. My response is a sense of languor, the feeling that if I had a hammock, I'd just want to swing slowly side to side in it, watching the clouds, a bouquet of lilies of the valley by my cheek, mindless until I fell asleep. I wondered if I could get lilies of the valley, one of springtime's most appealing flowers, to bloom in early summer indoors.

No problem. I ordered some large pips (dormant root-stocks) guaranteed to bloom the first year, whether I planted them outside or forced them to bloom inside, from White Flower Farm. (See "Sources and Advice: Where to buy plants, seeds, garden furniture, pots and urns, both resin and clay, etc.") One could use a 9" or 12" terra-cotta bulb pan or a deep pot or pots for planting. I chose two deep pots, covered the drainage holes in the bottom of the pots with small squares of window screen—sometimes I use pebbles or styrofoam peanuts for this—and then filled the pots two-thirds full with potting soil. I arranged the pips with their tips upright on top of the soil, poked holes for the long roots with a thick marking pencil, and then gently pushed the roots down into the holes and soil to pack around them. I covered the pips with additional potting soil until only the tips showed. I firmed the soil with my fingers and gave each pot a thorough watering. Another time, I used shallow bulb pans, filling them one-third full of potting soil, then arranged the roots of the pips in a tangled mat on top, with the tips of the pips pointed up and barely showing after I covered them with the rest of the soil. This method also worked. I put the pots on a tray in a sunny and bright window ledge. I kept the soil evenly moist. In about a month, the lilies of the valley sprouted and the bell-like flowers appeared among the glossy-green oval leaves. I wish that lilies of the valley were edible flowers, as their perfume is one I would like to taste, but that is literally to die for. **Lilies of the valley, alas, are poisonous to eat. Don't use them to garnish desserts, no matter how beautiful they look.**

Polianthes tuberosa, 'The Pearl,' is a classic southern bulb that is fully hardy in Zone 8. In Zone 6, tuberoses have to be treated as annuals, brought inside to overwinter after they have flowered. I cut them back, stop watering, and keep the bulbs in their pots to let them rest and dry. In May, when all danger of frost is past, out they go in their pots to be watered and fertilized and to flower again. Their scent is as heady as that of gardenias. When they bloom, they have 3 to 4' spikes of 2" star-shaped blooms that open in August and carry on until October. I grew masses of them in Jamaica in the West Indies. Their legendary scent makes me feel a bit giddy and unguarded, a remembered freedom of a child's conscious craziness. I smell their fragrance in the daytime and I want to leap up and down on one toe with joy, to sing, to laugh, to dance, to say whatever comes to mind. They make me feel radiant and smiley. I grow pots of them that I place outdoors on the low walls by the steps to the swimming pool, dead-heading the white, waxy, tubular flowers as they begin to fade to encourage more to grow. Then I bring the pots inside when they flower to place in the hallway along with pots of spathiphyllum, or in the bedrooms. In the evening, the scent of tuberoses takes on a sensual frisson, not unlike that of gardenias. To smell them outdoors in the evening is intoxicating. White Flower Farm offers the double-flowered form of bulbs, the kind I like best. (See "Sources and Advice: Where to buy plants, seeds, garden furniture, pots and urns, both resin and clay, etc.")

~ ~ ~ ~

Around Thanksgiving and Christmastime, friends often send me pots of sweetly scented paper-white narcissus, either bulbs to force to bloom in about a month's time, or flowers already blooming. All you have to do is to plant the bulbs in a potting mix. Put the bulbs in the soil so that they are almost touching and the tips barely beneath the surface, and water them in. With an 8" diameter pot, you can fit about seven or eight bulbs.

If you can keep potted bulbs in a cool dark place around 60°F for ten days, the bulbs have a better chance of growing strong roots, and you'll get better plants. The garage, the cellar or a cool coat closet will do the trick nicely. If you don't have such a place, not to worry, the bulbs will grow anyway. During this time, just keep the soil evenly moist—not soggy, just dampish.

After ten days, put the container(s) on a sunny window ledge or nearby on a table. Water the soil to keep it moist, but don't overwater as that will rot the bulbs. You'll have flowers in about a month. Once they bloom, move them away from direct sun and move to a cooler spot, which will help the flowers to last for about two weeks. Continue to water and feed them with a commercial houseplant fertilizer. I cut the stems of the flowers when they wither and the leaves as they yellow. I cut down on the water as I cut back the yellowing leaves until the last one dies. It's true that once the bulbs have been forced that they can't be forced again. Some people say that forced bulbs won't flower if you plant them outside. Wrong. I've found that I can plant bulbs that have been forced and grown, flowered, withered, and cut back to dry, from August until the ground freezes in the autumn. They will sprout leaves the following year and flower the next year, provided that you allow their leaves to soak up nutritious sunshine for at least two months after they have grown, before cutting them back in early July. I've often imagined solving the messy-leaf problem by interplanting narcissi and daffodils with Asiatic, Oriental, and daylilies whose growing leaves will hide

Potted agapanthus going to seed on the dining deck in August.

their dying ones. This solution didn't occur to me until after I organized the digging and planting of a wide border of daffodils and narcissus along the west side of the driveway all the way up to the lawn facing Brillig's front entrance. Digging in this border to interplant lilies seemed too risky a project to undertake. "I should have thought of doing this when I first had the idea of having a border of daffodils and narcissus," I said. A garden helper, trying to console me, said, "There are always things one should have done and didn't do." Like Fiddler Jones in *Spoon River Anthology*, I don't like having regrets. I realize

daylilies wouldn't look right growing along the driveway. I tell myself I was right the first time and just have to put up with a mess of withered leaves for six weeks.

Flowering winter houseplants such as amaryllis, African violets, and orchids are city flowers in my mind, and I have them all in our apartment in New York where they have flourished for fifteen years. They just don't seem to be right for the country. Cyclamen also doesn't work at Brillig. Given pots of it in New York, I took the pots to Brillig, replanted the cyclamen in a shady spot in the vista area where they didn't survive the winter. I brought other pots of cyclamen to put out on our dining deck and those just sat there during the summer, looking stunted and miserable. Back those three pots came to New York in the autumn. I put them on the marble doorsills in front of the French doors in the dining room. There are double glass doors for the French windows so that you can open or close the inner doors as insulation for the cold air leaking through the outer doors. The cool air is pleasant in a steam-heated apartment, and I like it. So did the cyclamen. To my astonishment, the three picayune plants thrived in this location, bloomed with a luxuriant profusion of white flowers that were complementary to the red hibiscus in pots that were also placed in front of the French doors of both the dining room and the living room.

I've tried ficus trees as large houseplants in both New York and Brillig and I've learned to dislike them. They drip little sticky puddles of some unknown (to me) exudation on the floor or rug beneath them and seem to attract aphids even though no other plant in the apartment or house has been known to attract aphids.

The one plant that seems worth the effort of transporting from New York to Brillig and back again is a legendary yellow clivia given to me by Frederick Delos Reynolds III, also known as Renny Reynolds, organizer of superb parties and a marvelous landscape architect and florist as well. The yellow clivia, the Holy Grail of the horticultural elite around the world, costing between $100 and $750 for a blooming-size plant, far more than the more common orange clivia, both indigenous to South Africa, was a plant I never thought I would own. Why so expensive? Renny explained that if you cross-pollinate two naturally occurring yellow forms of clivia, you won't really know what the flowers will look like for four, five, even six years. If the cross-pollinization is successful, you can propagate by division, and then it will be another two, three, four years before the divisions are ready to be divided again. Of course, you can buy seeds for yellow flowering clivia for about $18 for two seeds, but there is a chance that the seeds won't come true to their yellow parents, and you will end up not having yellow flowers. Blooming size isn't achieved until the fourth or fifth year after sowing, so it requires lots of patience. Seed sources include Park Seed that ships seed only in March—at the peak of freshness—at which time it must be planted immediately. (See "Sources and Advice: Where to buy plants, seeds, garden furniture, pots and urns, both resin and clay, etc.") The yellow clivia, which looked dazzling when it bloomed in our New York apartment's living room this February, has another spike that may bloom during the summer when the clivia plant is placed on our dining deck. Renny assures me that germination by seed is easy, that clivia are easy to grow and are superb, long-lived houseplants. He has a few yellow clivia plants for sale, as does the Louisiana Nursery. (See "Sources and Advice: Where to buy plants, seeds, garden furniture, pots and urns, both resin and clay, etc.")

Our dining deck, with its screened ceiling, screened front and side, with a cushioned banquette along the front extending outside to a small unscreened deck, and a place for flowering plants. A heavy-gauge metal three-tiered plant stand, some 5' across with 2'-wide corner units, holds sixty pots of white impatiens. Started from seed, sprouting in early May, a flowery cascade of white and green by July. Our étagère of tiered white impatiens is in bloom during the entire late spring and summer and remains in flower until November. Inexpensive, easy to maintain with watering and plant-food feeding, these shade-loving impatiens, originating in east Africa, were popularized in America by Claude Hope, a Texan known

In mid-June, agapanthus burst into blossom and potted impatiens are beginning to leaf out.

as the father of impatiens, in 1969. They are an unfailing decorative mainstay, "the same pleasing shape as a low Georgian stairway," artist Rick Patrick observed.

In the dining area, there are urns and pots of blue agapanthus and white agapanthus, perennial African lilies that are flowers I've seen growing like weeds in California and along the roadsides of the Portuguese island of Madeira. They have taken four years to grow from bulbs at Brillig, and are hardy only in Zones 9 to 10. Centered on tables are pots of blue evolvulus, an annual that flowers for most of the summer. Massed on an antique Indian cabinet are other semi-tropicals—pots of *rhizomatous Rex* begonias with dark-red and green leaves. They rot if overwatered but otherwise are totally trouble free. From time to time, they bear insignificant little pink flowers about the same size as the flowers of scented-leaf pelargoniums. I like to use the leaves of both plants to decorate baskets of bread or biscuits or plates of cookies, or to poke into small glass vases with other flowers and leaves for the table or for trays.

We have pots of moonflower vines (*Ipomoea alba*, 'Giant White') on the patio of the downstairs guest room, and pots of white morning glories (*Ipomoea Alba*) and blue morning glories (*Ipomoea tricolor*, 'Heavenly Blue') there as well as growing up the drainpipes by the front entrance. The moonflowers are night-blooming and smell sweetly. The morning glories flower during the day. The blue ones are a truly heavenly blue. The blossoms of moonflowers and morning glories both live for little more than twelve hours. José starts them both from seed in early March indoors and places them outside in May when all danger of frost is past. The majority of our potted plants are hibiscus, absolutely ideal for seaside summers.

We also have a miniature forest of wildly poisonous *Brugmansia suaveolens* growing in large pots. A mild euphoria is said to result from smelling their glorious white trumpet-shaped flowers. I started our forest with seedlings in little 3" pots, and now they are 4' high. Cousins of the equally poisonous Datura or Jamestown weed or Jimsonweed or Angel's trumpet, *Brugmansia suaveolens* can be grown outdoors in a temperate climate in a pot, then cut back hard in the autumn and brought inside to overwinter in a cool (45°F) place. Their fragrance, pronounced at night, faint in the day, is Easter lilylike and their flower colors, the color of pastel Easter eggs. **Every part of the plant is poisonous to ingest.** I even scurry to the kitchen to wash my hands after I touch one of the flowers to lift it to my nose to smell it. Even so, *Brugmansia suaveolens* are a joy to behold when in bloom. I hear from friends who have mature plants over 6' tall that their brugmansia have as many as three dozen flowers all at one time on a single treelike plant. I would not recommend having them around with very young children, but brugmansia please me immensely.

Also, in the growing stage are *ti* leaves and frangipani (*Plumeria*) plants, brought back as rootstock from Hilo Hattie's in Lahaina from a Maui vacation. These also have to be brought inside to overwinter. *Ti* leaves are what the Hawaiians use for dancing "grass" skirts, and they are also used in Hawaii to wrap food as we might wrap food in paper or plastic. I like the idea of using *ti* leaves instead of lace paper doilies underneath hors d'oeuvres and cakes and cookies. (See "Sources and Advice: Where to buy plants, seeds, garden furniture, pots and urns, both resin and clay, etc".)

I'm not sure where I got my aloe vera from, but no kitchen should ever be without this marvelous plant. Just snap off a piece of its green and white leaves to use its gel as an ointment for minor cuts and burns. Gladys, our cook in Jamaica in the West Indies, first introduced me to the wonders of aloe vera, and since then I've rarely been without it.

A potted aloe plant hovers over the shells in my shell table in the living room.

*Early September, a clear bright sky deepens
to an endless blue arching overhead, the sea
all diamonds and sparkling…*

Chapter 18

The Autumn Garden

Early September, a clear bright sky deepened to an endless blue arching overhead, the sea all diamonds and sparkling, and in the cutting garden, dragonflies are darting, golden, catching the light. They streak across the purple-blue platycodon and disappear into the Hidcote lavender.

In comparison, monarch butterflies are slow—flutterbys, as the children used to call them. I've just driven in the golf cart on a sightseeing expedition from the vista area, seeing monarchs among the buddleia bushes and trees in the Pit, monarchs enjoying the marzipan pink flowers of the turtlehead bushes (*Chelone*), monarchs clustered about the Joe-Pye weed (*Eupatorium*), and monarchs feeding on the goldenrod (*Solidago*).

Seaside goldenrod (*Solidago sempervirens*) grows wild along the coastal dunes of New York and New Jersey with clusters of incandescent yellow flowers blooming on 5' to 7' stalks. It flourishes in full sun and in lean, well-drained soil. We have goldenrod growing here and there on the bluffs and here and there along the shaded wooded area next to the vista. Goldenrod is one of the best autumn plants for monarchs, and I'm glad we have as much of it growing wild as we do. On the bluffs, just for the butterflies, I've planted swamp milkweed (*Asclapias incarnata*) and butterfly milkweed (*Asclapias tuberosa*). In July, monarchs are still mating and laying eggs. Stands of swamp milkweed do double duty in late summer and early autumn, providing leaves for this new generation of monarch larvae and nectar for the butterflies that are migrating south. Migrants begin to arrive as early as August.

Monarchs migrate thousands and thousands of miles and need good nectar sources along the way to arrive successfully at their overwintering sites of Mexico and California. Other butterflies overwinter as eggs, and the adults that lay them need an extra nutritional boost at the end of the season to produce large numbers of healthy eggs that can withstand the rigors of winter. Late-blooming flowers or even a second round of summer nectar plants help these butterflies get the energy they need.

In the cutting garden, I watch a red admiral tonguing up minerals and acids from a rotting peach. I hope we have enough flowers for the monarchs to use for nutritional fuel before they take off on their exhausting migration. Autumn-blooming plants are invaluable nectar sources for migrating hummingbirds and butterflies. I've seen dark swallowtails, their wings bordered with blue spots, taking nectar from our honeysuckle and Joe-Pye weed and little brown skippers flying about the lavender and the faded hollyhocks and the French marigolds (*Tagetes patula*). Skippers, to me, are like the unidentifiable LBJ (little brown job) birds that I notice among our resident finches and warblers.

I watched a hummingbird and a yellow swallowtail, both attracted to the nectar of several anise hyssop (*Agastache*) plants, and wrote a note to myself to be sure to get some agastache with lovely peach-pink flowers, called 'Summer Breeze,' said to do well in full sun, well-drained soil, where the agastache we have is already posited.

I saw an Eastern kingbird sitting close by on the cutting garden fence. Kingbirds are said to have a red patch on their crown, but I've never been close enough to see it. This time I thought I glimpsed it, but then again, perhaps I imagined it, as I was more focused on butterflies at the moment than on birds.

Sun-loving, sea-loving hibiscus are still vibrant and colorful in the autumn.

As I was watching the mallards and the gadwalls, by now a customary but ever-mesmeric outlook, I suddenly saw in the ocean not far from the beach a considerable number of mottled brown and black-and-white ducks drifting past, headed west. The mottled brown ones were obviously the females, but looking at the drakes with my field glasses I could see that they had white backs, black bellies, black-crowned white heads, yellow bills, and gray-green napes. What could they be? Identified by *Peterson's Field Guide* as common eiders (*Somateria mollisima*), they were totally uncommon to me. "The only duck in our area with a black belly and a white back," according to Roger Tory Peterson.

I try to learn something new every day, but to see an unknown bird, an unknown flower, anything totally different from what I've known before evokes a feeling that is somewhere between a happy surprise and wonder, by Samuel Johnson's definition: All wonder is the effect of novelty upon ignorance—a humbling experience, in its way, but pleasingly humbling.

Our pots of standard hibiscus are looking marvelous in September—I always wish they could evolve to this peak of perfection earlier in the summer and not wait for early autumn to show off like beauty queens—but that's how it is with hibiscus, and hummingbirds are still feeding from them. Our pink *Lycoris squamigera* died off before the first of September, but our cosmos and cleome are still flowering in abundance and an attraction as always for painted ladies, red admirals, swallowtails, and monarchs. Our Autumn Joy Sedum, pleasing in the spring and summer, with its green and pale mauve flowers, now has floppy flowers, the pale reddish, blackish color of squashed blackberries, an unpleasant color. I was going to cut off their flowers when I relegated them to the grape arbor area, but fortunately, I didn't. They attract butterflies and hummingbirds, and they're in the grape arbor area where I don't have to look at them all the time. One problem solved with no downside.

Early autumn is the reverse of early spring. In spring, you are looking for first appearances. In early autumn, you're looking for survivors, the lingering flowers of July and August. In August, we stopped deadheading cleome, cosmos, morning glories, daylilies, nicotiana, and others leaving on seedheads for the birds and myself. A cardinal, brilliant scarlet against the blue sky, is pulling plump, ripe rose hips the size of cherry tomatoes, off the rosa rugosa bordering the swimming pool area. Cardinals, jays, catbirds, thrashers, mockingbirds, the whole fruit-eating avian group resident on our place has stripped the native shads (*Amelanchier*) of their serviceberries and the viburnums of their fruit, or all of it that is ripe. I hope there is plenty for the birds besides the food we put out for them. There are orange berries on the bittersweet growing wild on the ridge and some in the wooded area next to the vista. I haven't noticed any berries on our winterberry (*Ilex verticillata*) yet, a dioecious shrub that requires both a male and female plant for bright-red berries, but they will appear soon. There are red berries on the Virginia creeper, growing some 25' up a pine tree near the front entrance of Brillig, and more scrambling about as a ground cover in the wooded area off the vista garden. The firethorn or pyrecanthus (*Pyrecantha cocinnea*), growing on the upper level of one side of the garage wall so that you can see it from the south-facing dining room window, has bright-orange berries that are just beginning to ripen. I hope a catbird who built her nest in this tall-climbing vine will get a chance to have a go at the berries before she migrates south.

But back to butterflies. Are there enough flowers for them? Roses are still flowering in the cutting garden, and can last even up to mid-December as they sometimes do. Black-eyed Susans and pink marsh mallows are still flowering in the wooded area by the vista garden, along with the primeval-looking *Angelica gigas*, its dark-purple florets attracting dozens of bumblebees. Nearby are the lovely fresh pink flowers of turtleheads or chelone, and tall stands of Joe-Pye weed with their flowers the color of

Summer roses last through November.

Bees and I both love fragrant lavender in the cutting garden. Lavender is wonderful for cookies and potpourri.

bushes of purple lilac I remember from my childhood, the color I see when I read Walt Whitman's poem about the lilacs that last in the dooryard bloomed. Scented pelargoniums are flowering with their tiny blossoms. The crocosmia in the grape arbor area is flaming like a torch. There are still sunflowers of different heights and widths in the grape arbor area and in the garage courtyard where the passionflowers continue to flower and attract hummingbirds and butterflies. There are still a few Oriental lilies in the vista area and a few in the upper driveway garden. The silverlace polygonum vine is in its second flowering, covering the ugliness of the swimming pool shed with a lacy blanket. A few white blossoms and a few red-centered blossoms of our many Roses of Sharon are still flowering. A few brugmansia flourish pastel trumpets. A few 'Nikko Blue' hydrangeas brandish one or two unlikely fresh, bright, springlike inflorescences. Some hostas still bear pluming white flowers. The ceanothus clings to its lavender-blue flowers. The sedum's ugly autumn flowers will be transformed again to the color of reddish tobacco before winter. There are still a few nasturtiums flowering and a few Oriental lilies. Some white phlox in the vista, a little lavender left in the cutting garden, and of course, geraniums/pelargoniums pink, white, and red, cleomes, cosmos, and zinnias. The daylily seedpods are like vases, flaring open at their ends, filled with shiny black seeds. The clematis vine growing over the trellised concrete walls by the swimming pool area has fuzzy seedheads. The butterfly milkweed on the bluff has long pointed pods on its stalks, and the swamp milkweed is flinging out shiny, white down-tipped seedlings from its wrinkled brown pods. The sea holly (*Eryngium x tripartitum*) next to other plants of sea holly has no flowers, no leaves, but its spiky blue-gray bracts look decorative along the steps down to the beach. I sit down on the wooden bench at the landing, next to the ground-based birdbath dripped into by a pipe. José has turned its water off in one of the many, many steps to closing the house for the winter. The birds can get water elsewhere. I've already asked Austin to get out the water heaters for certain birdbaths so that the birds will be guaranteed plenty of warm water, or at least unfrozen water, during the winter cold.

Now, upward and onward, José and I have chores to do. He will do all the heavy work. I will enjoy all the pleasures of watching him work and checking out details in the garden.

Generally, the best time to divide perennials is in the spring, except for peonies (*Paeonia*), Oriental poppies (*Papavar oriental*), Siberian iris (*Iris sibirica*), and Japanese ensata iris (*Iris ensata*). Siberian irises require division as infrequently as every six to ten years; shade-loving perennials, like hosta and aruncus, also prefer infrequent division. Signs that a plant needs to be divided are that its flowers become spare and smaller, or that it develops a hole in the center of its cluster, or that it has outgrown the space originally given to it. José and I walk about, looking at everything, and see only a few Siberian irises in the swimming pool area that should be divided and some daylilies in the daylily bed.

José begins to dig with a spading fork about 10" from the crown of the iris plant, pushing the fork under and prying up the iris, working his way around the cluster. He pries apart an iris clump with two spading forks back to back, then with a clean, sharp knife, cuts a clump apart. He cuts the leaves back to where they will stand up straight. He has already brought out a large plastic garage pail filled with compost and now amends the bottom of the holes he digs to replant the divisions with compost.

He backfills with soil and then pulls out the hose, which I turn on, so he can water in the divisions thoroughly. When about a dozen irises have been divided, we go through the same process in the daylily bed. It's good to know that the plants will keep on rooting and growing until the ground freezes solid.

Now what about sunscald? Do we have any trees that we have to protect by coating them with latex paint on the southside of their trunks to protect the bark by reflect-

The *Aruncus*, or Goat's Beard, around this birdhouse allows birds to feel they are in their natural habitat.

ing the sun's rays so the bark doesn't heat up during the day, only to cool rapidly at sunset? Painting keeps the trunks from heating unevenly on bright, sunny winter days. The bark tends to split if it cools rapidly after the sun has warmed it. José and I check the trunks of young peach and pear trees. Their bark is in good condition on their south and west sides. I was looking forward to painting a group of young fruit trees, from the ground level to the level of their lowest branches with water-based latex paint, using a half-and-half water and paint solution, with some bone meal mixed in to repel vegetarian rabbits and mice from gnawing on the bark.

José says there's no need to do this as the trees are planted in places that minimize sun damage on their trunks. To prevent damage from rabbits, rats, and mice that love to gnaw on tender, young bark, José wraps young trees with hardware cloth 12" larger than the trunk's diameter and 18" higher than the anticipated snow level. From September through October, he will put up burlap screens around tender bushes and trees to protect them from biting north winds. Since winds are drying, he sprays bushes

pleasure. To me, Jerry Baker is a common-sense pleasure; a source of information José and I share.

Our native summersweet (*Cletha*) clings to a few white flowers, while the burning bush (*Euonymus alatus*) shows no sign of turning scarlet. I don't see how the birds could possibly have eaten all the bright-red berries off the cotoneaster, but they have, while they have eschewed the holly berries. Our so-called horse chestnut trees with chestnuts that are toxic to eat, even when boiled—I tried them once—are laden with what Austin calls conkers. He tells me how, as a boy in Scotland, he played conkers, rapping his conkers against other boys' conkers. The one who

August-flowering Roses of Sharon (*Hibiscus syriacus* 'Diana') in luxuriant bloom.

with antidesiccants that have no chemicals, all natural, organic. José feeds acid-loving hydrangeas, rhododendrons, azaleas, blueberry bushes with weak, warm coffee water plus a teaspoon of corn syrup for each quart of coffee water as a fortifying pure-winter snack. "Jerry Baker said to do it on his radio program," José says. I read Jerry Baker's books and newsletters. José listens to Jerry Baker on the radio. Like reading *Star* or *The Enquirer*, I realize that, to some, Jerry Baker is an intellectual sin, a guilty

managed to split the other's conkers was the winner. He made it sound like an exciting game.

~ ~ ~

José and I take root cuttings from the scented pelargoniums to pot up in soil in the garage, and then get to work to plant a shipment of spring bulbs that augments the bulb plants we already have—daylilies (*Hemerocallis*), blue and white scilla, narcissus, grape hyacinths (*Muscari*), hyacinths, iris, tulips. I really dislike the way hyacinths look, yet delight in the way they smell. I've never found a way to plant them where they look attractive. To me, they look like frumpy dowagers in summer pastels, over-frilled, over-fussy, and they look that way as flowers, overly fussy and frilly. Yet, oddly enough, they look all right as cut flowers, or, at least, I'm able to put up with them because their scent is so fresh and sweet and original. José and I check out all the bulbs, keeping only those that are free of mold, large, plump, not dried out or mushy. The dried-out, mushy bulbs we toss into the nearest compost pile. The beauty of next spring's blossoms depends more on the quality of the bulbs than on a green thumb.

We fill the allotted holes with special bulb booster fertilizer I've ordered from White Flower Farm. Always plant flower bulbs clockwise, I tell José, a task accomplished by a firm rightward twist of the bulb before filling in with soil. My mother always told our gardeners to do this, and my grandmother's and my uncle's Scottish gardeners did this. I'm told Gertrude Jekyll also recommended doing this. I've no idea why you should do this, yet it feels right to do. I wonder if it has something to do with the way the water runs out a drain above the equator in a clockwise direction. In Australia and South Africa, would you then twist bulbs into the ground in an counterclockwise direction? I make a note to myself to ask the next omniscient horticulturalist I meet. We plant bulbs in the order of their appearance in the spring, saving the Japanese ensata irises and tulips for last, although they must be in the ground, of course, before it freezes.

During September, we plant and plant and weed and weed. José takes off time to rake up the leaves as they fall. If we have any diseased leaves, like mildew or black spot we will bag them and chuck them into the garbage to be taken away as garbage, and not be added to the island's store of compost to which all are welcome. Happily, our leaves, as usual, are healthy and José rakes them to use as mulch.

As we go about the garden, José cuts off perennial stalks, checks out the raspberry bed to be sure that odd bits and pieces there get pruned and tidied up, scrapes off weedlings just below the surface with a hoe, because any weeds that are only half-buried will regrow later. We concentrate on weeding in the autumn because the spring is not the time to weed—there's always so much else to do in the spring, and weeding is a waste of time in the spring.

We organize mulches to start putting out now and later. A few inches of organic mulch cuts down on watering, insulates roots from extreme temperatures, minimizes the soil's heaving up from alternate freezing and thawing, and prevents erosion. Good mulch improves the quality of the

The compost heap.

soil and also cuts down on weeds. The best mulches for flower beds and shrubs are those that decay quickly and are replenished annually. Others, of partially composted bark and wood chips, which break down slowly, are good around trees and to keep paths weed-free and looking attractive. **Around any plant, fully decayed mature compost is the best mulch.** If you mulch shrubs and perennials with composted bark and wood chips, which are only about half decayed, the decaying bark and wood chips may take nitrogen from the earth that will cause the plant's lower leaves to turn yellow. You never use half-decayed composted bark or composted wood chips on flower beds that are periodically dug for annuals or vegetables, as the half-decayed mulches rob the earth of nitrogen. José and I check everything and see no tell-tale yellow leaves, as we have in the past when we had what I now call our "garden non-helpers" at work. We use weed-free pine needles as mulch for our strawberry bed, and around all our acid-loving trees and shrubs. We use wood chips, shredded bark, partially composted, slow to break-down, to keep our nature paths weed-free. For underneath some trees and bushes, we use shredded leaves, excellent soil builders, weed-free, quick to decay, and providers of shelter for butterflies and their larvae. We never mulch right up to the trunk of a tree in order to discourage rabbits, rats, and mice from sheltering under the mulch and gnawing the bark while hidden from the hungry eyes of owls and hawks.

For large areas, like the beds of *Lycoris squamigera* on the bluff, we use salt hay, which José removes in the spring. Grass clippings, if kept to no more than 2", are a good mulch that breaks down quickly and are an excellent soil builder, but generally we just add our grass clippings to our compost piles and use our fully decayed mature compost as a mulch for our plants. Some gardeners also use weed-free, easy-to-apply cocoa and rice hulls, somewhat slow to decay, for mulch. I never have at Brillig. Not indigenous, cocoa hulls and rice hulls seem ectopic, not natural, not right in this island setting. Fine for the Caribbean or Central America, or somewhere south, but not here in the American northeast.

September's late-seasonal splendors flow into October when the hawthorn trees fruit with berries called haws, another childhood memory revivified. My uncle had hawthorns near his walled Scottish garden. They are beautiful trees in flower and generous in their fruiting. In October, the weather is like March, without the damp. Crisp, nippy. There is a flush of new color in the leaves of trees. As the green goes, it is replaced with browns, reds, yellows, purples.

The air is clear, and the frost arrives. All the hibiscus, the agapanthus, the perennial herbs, the evolvulus, the scented pelargoniums and the red pelargoniums, pink pelargoniums and white pelargoniums, have been brought indoors to the safe shelter of our living room cum greenhouse.

José has taken time to attend to cleaning and sharpening, storing, and repairing gardening tools. I am appreciative of this anticipation and forethought of being ready for spring. He thinks ahead. He plans. He cares about the garden. Both he and I always want the gardens at Brillig to be more beautiful.

November ushers in the month of the Dead, the trick and treat of Hallowe'en, the promise of Thanksgiving, harvests of fruit, and the feeling of the ebb of the year.

The living room as a winter greenhouse.

Chapter 19

The Winter Scene

Leaves and flowers have given way to the sovereignty of shape, form, texture, pattern, symmetry, and the colors of evergreens, branches, tree trunks, snow, seedpods, and berries. As summer days grew shorter, plants began hardening off by producing hormones that slow growth and induce dormancy. By the first hard frost, they are ready for freezing—or close to it—temperatures. In the autumn, José pruned any weak branches that might be vulnerable under the pressure of a heavy snowfall. Snow and ice can still accumulate on cedars, pines, spruce trees, and other

conifers, and he is always ready to brush off snow with a broom from tree branches while snow is falling before the branches get overly weighed down. It's easier to sweep off the snow earlier than later when the snow melts in the sun, refreezes, and clings to the branches.

We're lucky we live as close as we do to the beach. We always have access to sand. Sand mixed with baking soda melts ice from steps, patios, decks, the garage area pavement, helps us from slipping and sliding, and is far gentler on outdoor plants and indoor carpeting than rock salt or deicing chemicals.

If you are floundering in snow and ice, **please don't use salt on your steps, driveways, paths.** Salt is a disaster for all things you hope to see green and growing, and it's a champion stain maker when tracked indoors. Sand or wood ash (not ashes from burned coal) from your fireplace work just as well and harm nothing except plants that enjoy acidic soils. I hope you and I have learned not to put ashes on acid-loving plants! (The alkalinity of ash will turn 'Nikko Blue' acid-loving hydrangeas to the color of tea-stained lace or a buckskin moccasin. (See Chapter 10: "Coping with Mistakes")

The living room is denuded of furniture and is now a sunny-windowed greenhouse, as our hibiscus, pelargoniums, agapanthus, evolvulus, brugmansia, perennial herbs are brought in to overwinter. The living room windows are thermal windows. No cold leaks inside. No need to pad the windows with newspapers.

Needled and broad-leaved evergreens can suffer winter damage from sun and wind that can rob evergreens' leaves of moisture, and from dry or frozen soil that can prevent their roots from taking up water. To prevent

A light snow turns gold in the sun, smoky
blue in the shadows, and intensifies the
greens and blues of the conifers, the browns
and blacks of trunks and branches...

Left: Living room as winter greenhouse. Center: Burlap screens protect the lacecap hydrangeas. Right: Sun sparkles on the snow.

desiccation injury, which virtually affects all evergreens in late autumn and early winter, José has sedulously mulched and watered our evergreens in late autumn and early winter to provide and conserve crucial soil moisture. He coated leaves and foliage at the same time with an organic antidesiccant spray.

Outdoors, young trees are protected with cylinders of hardware cloth circling them, secured a foot from their trunks, and mulched around the outer edges of the hardware cloth cylinders. Shrubs are shielded with burlap screens squared about them. Everything has been watered well in the autumn, mulched, covered with salt hay, and, in some cases, covered with evergreen branches, ours and whatever is available from the community brush pile.

A light snow turns gold in the sun, smoky blue in the shadows, and intensifies the greens and blues of the conifers, the browns and blacks of trunks and branches, and the orangey-bronze leaves of the Siberian iris with their dangling blue-gray seedpods. The butterfly bushes are silvered with little rosettes of crinkled, withered leaves along their stems and branches. The bare blue-purple

prickly bracts of the eryngium are spicily dramatic, and the seed heads on the anise hyssop (*Agastache*) look like flowering lavender.

The snow, "the poor man's fertilizer," spreads a protective cover over the crowns of the beloved plants and insulates their roots; if the roots survive, so will the plants. The snow clings to gnarled branches and curved limbs, frosts the evergreens, stencils railings, wooden arches and roof gutters, gates and fences, and accentuates the rhythmic spacing and linear patterns of the posts and beams of the grape arbor pergola. The sunlight plays on the peeling bark of the paper birch tree in the Pit in the wooded area by the vista. The light snowfall has caught on the twisted stems and tendrils of the polygonum vine that covers the swimming pool shed so that it looks like a lace tea cloth flung over a table. The snow enhances the sculptured form of seedheads, delicately delineating the fanned branches of the espaliered pear tree and the twistings and writhings of the cinnamon-colored branches of the climbing hydrangea now covering the outside brick wall behind the library's fireplace.

Left: Gnarled trees in the vista dance in the cold wind. Center: The winter-bared balconies of my bedroom and the guest room balcony below. Right: The massive bird feeder Austin built offers welcome seeds and cakes of suet to birds in winter.

By October, the birds had eaten all the ripe berries on the cotoneaster, but more ripened and now a few, very few, remain. The native winterberry (*Ilex verticillata*) and the female hollies (*Ilex spp.*) are bright with red berries. I am thrilled with our *Ilex verticillata*, the most widespread of North American hollies, although now endangered in some areas. 'Winter Red' is among the best cultivars, if not **the** best, and our lovely female shrub was pollinated by a male hybrid, 'Raritan Chief.' A male winterberry can pollinate several females within a few hundred feet as long as male and females, prince and princesses, all bloom at the same time. 'Winter Red' and 'Raritan Chief' bloom at the same time. The branches of our female 'Winter Red' are lavishly beaded with brilliant-red berries. The holly prince and his princesses look splendid where we've planted them in the moist, rich, acidic soil they favor at the top of the wooded area by the vista where they can enjoy full sun. The 'Winter Red' shrub, which can grow to 10', blooms and sets berries on new wood and so can be pruned only in winter. The *Ilex verticillata* is such a beautiful shrub I feel like hugging her. I'm glad that my elder son

named his daughter Holly, glad that I have a granddaughter named Holly.

The pyrecanthus has not yet been picked clean of its harvest of pumpkin-orange berries. The sumacs (*Rhus glabra*) in the grape arbor area turned yellow, red, lost their leaves and are now each lifting on their bare branches a candelabra of fuzzy, brownish-crimson torch-shaped holders of red sumac berries that provide long-term emergency rations for overwintering birds. The mountain ash is studded with orange berries, and the branches of the bayberry are jeweled with bracelets and necklaces, brooches and rings of gray-blue berries.

The wooded area of the Pit by the vista is filled with evergreen white-flowering rhododendron and white-flowering azaleas. In the summer, they are overshadowed by Joe-Pye weed, butterfly bushes, angelica gigas, marsh mallows, almost unnoticeable, but now in the winter, they stand out, domes of glossy leaves, as wide as they are tall, giving the wooded area a rather overly cultivated look, formal, mannered, set apart from the rest of the property. It's a look that either I'm getting used to or one that is

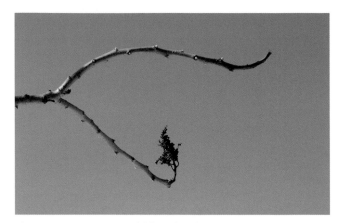

The sparse wintertime candelabra of a sumac.

improving as the rhododendrons and azaleas age and the winterberries have been added.

To remedy a garden's off-season appearance and jazz up it's back-to-the-basics look of form, shape, texture, pattern, symmetry, many gardeners plant specimens for "winter interest." Like red, yellow, and orange willow (*Salix alba 'virellina'*), or red osier dogwood, or red twig dogwood, or *Cornus alba 'siberica,'* a Westonbirt dogwood with deep red stems that can grow to 5' with a width of 7' or more; or they plant different kinds of evergreens, or trees with dramatically peeling bark, or fantastically gnarled and contorted stems or winter blooms, like helleborus (*Hellenorus niger*) or Chinese witch hazel (*Hammamelis mollis*).

It seems to me that we have more than enough for winter interest. We have archways where steps end or nature paths begin, a pergola or grape arbor, a fence around the cutting garden, teak and wrought-iron garden chairs, benches, tables, and two circular tree benches. We have stone, ceramic, and lightweight resin urns. We have a low stone wall. We have a fountain, many birdbaths, many birdhouses, quite a few nest pockets of sea grass, and many bird feeders.

To limit cold-weather damage, we have drained our fountain at the end of November and don't expect to refill it until the last expected frost in May. Whether splashing

or still, or even drained of water as ours now is, I think fountains, large or small, are as pleasing as passionflowers.

It's most important for birds to have water to drink during the cold weather when creeks and ponds may be locked in ice. Birds also take more baths in the winter, because they need to be able to fluff up their feathers for insulation against the cold. Dirty feathers don't fluff up as satisfactorily as clean ones. We have many birdbaths raised on pedestals and others for ground level use, with a couple of each equipped with water-warmers. Several manufacturers offer birdbaths with built-in, thermostatically controlled heaters. You can also use separate immersion heaters, available at most places bird feeders and bird food are sold. The latest models will turn off if the water in the bath dries up. For total safety, Austin puts our heaters on a ground-fault interrupted circuit (available from any hardware or electrical supply store) to eliminate the possibility, even the slimmest chance, of an electrical shock. I am told this is an ideal solution. I trust Austin to know the right, safe thing to do.

I have been asked to include the following cautionary advice. I thought it was an insult to the intelligence of my readers. "Please just include it," I was told. So I shall. Forgive me.

- **Never add antifreeze to a birdbath. It is poisonous to all animals, including birds.**

- **Never use glycerin as a makeshift antifreeze in birdbaths. Glycerin is a low-level toxin. If birds drink too much, it raises their blood sugar, often to fatal levels.**

- **When birds bathe in glycerin-laced water, their feathers can become matted. Matted plumage is poor insulation and renders birds unprotected and vulnerable to cold.**

We all know that one good way to attract many birds is to keep birdbaths full of fresh water at all times. We change the water every day to keep it fresh and free from algae. We scrub clean birdbaths once a week with vinegar, and rinse well afterwards, to get rid of any spoiled food, droppings, bacteria, algae, or other toxic organisms. NEVER USE CHEMICALS!

Another way to attract birds is to have plenty of food for them. There are berries on the evergreen native American holly (*Ilex opaca*) and other hollies (*Ilex spp.*), the females, for which we had to have a berry-less prince. Our winterberry vines (*Ilex verticillata*) are also dioecious, and the females keep their berries until almost spring if the birds don't eat them all. There are native red chokecherry bushes (*Aronia arbutifolia*) on the ridge. Although we have several cotoneaster bushes, cotoneaster berries are the first to go. We have bayberries, blueberries, elderberries, grapes, red haws from the hawthorn trees, mountain ash berries, raspberries, red rosehips from our rosa rugosas, and sumac berries. Only haws remain, winterberries, bayberries, mountain ash, many rose hips as we have rosa rugosas in abundance, and the sumac. The tiny red berries of the sumac are enfolded in an erect, nubbly, torch-shaped, brownish-crimson flame—flame is the only word that gives the right shape of this unique berry-holder—and each sumac has as many as six or seven seed-bearing "flames," which gives each bare-branched tree the look of upheld candelabra. The birds regard sumac berries as emergency rations, energizing fodder, welcome, necessary, but dull. They'll only go for sumac if there's little else around. Blue jays, cardinals, downy woodpeckers, tufted titmice, nuthatches, mockingbirds, kingbirds, mourning doves, resident birds, migrating birds all prefer the berries from our dogwoods, cotoneaster, junipers, mountain ash, cedars, hawthorns, bayberry, viburnums, shads, hollies. I am attentive to the needs of birds because I love to have birds around, to see them, to hear them. To my joy, birds flock to Brillig year-round.

Shad trees, cotoneaster, and holly add texture and color to the winter garden as well as providing food for birds.

Orange trees are wintered comfortably inside by the dining deck.

We have a dozen suet cages strung from tree branches, filled with a variety of processed suet featuring nuts, fruits, insects. In addition, we have put out cracked corn, peanut butter, raisins, birdseed, and halves of oranges in the bird feeders. This is the season of sacred and secular joy, of present giving and present receiving, of cooking, baking, shopping, decorating, writing notes, and Must Do lists. What else do I feel like doing? Making birdfood treats to put out for the birds on platform trays. I like to make air-dried popcorn for the birds and myself. Even the pheasants and ducks beak up popcorn.

For a favorite treat of blue jays and woodpeckers, I mix 1 cup of vegetable shortening (Crisco), 1 cup of all-purpose flour, 4 cups of cornmeal, and 1 cup of peanut butter. I cream the shortening and the peanut butter together, then slowly mix in the flour and cornmeal. This mix can be stored in the refrigerator and scooped out on a plastic plate secured to a platform feeder on a pedestal as well as a ground-based platform feeder. For other birds, I mix together 1 cup of Crisco, 1 cup of peanut butter, 2 cups of flour, 2 cups of regular oatmeal (not instant), 2 to 3 cups of cornmeal, 1 cup of raisins, the leavings of unsalted walnuts or pecans, and rehydrated dried cranberries, if we have any extra. I mix these ingredients together, put the mix in plastic containers and freeze until solid. Then I put portions on plastic plates secured to pedestal- and ground-based platform feeders. It's always astonishing to me how many different kinds of birds will wing in for a snack. So that the audacious herring gull won't barge in and hog everything, we distract him with fish heads Austin has saved and frozen from his many summer fishing trips.

If we celebrated Christmas at Brillig, which, alas, we don't, we would put out our Christmas tree near the bird feeders to shelter birds from the cold and biting wind, while letting them stay close to a delicious food source. As a substitute, José brings evergreen branches for the birds from the communal brushpile.

Pheasant footprints in the snow.

Epilogue:
A Thing of Beauty is a Job Forever

As a child, I thought "gardening" meant "Godning," playing God. I still think sprinkling seeds, no bigger than i-dots, on the ground, seeing them sprout, grow, leaf, bud, and flower is a miracle.

From the earliest days of our history, gardens have been with us as a source of food, medicinal plants, aromatic herbs and spices, plants to provide dyes, coloring agents and perfumes, plants to bring beauty into our lives, to offer serene retreats or a display of wealth, status, and horticultural artistry.

Gardens are an expression of ourselves, our creativity, and our connection with nature, the true beauty of life, and the mystery and wonder of all living things.

Here, in my garden by the sea, where the salt of both sharp, untempered winds and of cool, gentle breezes mix with the fragrance of leaves and flowers to give the air an exhilarating freshness, there is always a reminder of the intensity of elemental forces, of storms, hurricanes, crashing surf, as well as the benison of sun-sparkled waves, moon-polished water. Over the water from all directions came travelers, explorers, and pilgrims who brought seeds and plants in ships from Europe, Asia, Africa, South America, and Australia to America that have found their way to this garden where there are also many native plants.

I listen to the peevish grumbling of taut-winged herring gulls overhead, the squawk-awk-aawking of wild pheasant feeding on their daily spread of cracked corn, the diverse and diverting repertoires of mockingbirds and catbirds, the pinging chime of Latamer Reef Light in Fishers Island Sound, leaves rustling, myriad bees in the lavender.

Marigolds, like little shaggy suns, and nasturtiums, bright as stars, offer pungent whiffs of scent in savory contrast to the sweetness of roses, pinks, lilies, lilies of the valley, violets, verbena, nicotiana, and tuberoses I have coaxed to flower in pots placed to catch both the morning and the afternoon sunlight.

I pick dew-wet strawberries to eat as I meander, and later, sun-warmed raspberries, silvery blueberries, and perhaps a peach. Grapes and pears are inedible until they ripen in autumn.

I pick up an orangey-pink crab shell dropped by a gull, and am caressed by a velvety, furry lamb's ear, the leaf of a volunteer stachys growing in a bed of iris with pointed leaves as sharp as dagger tips.

An early morning, milky-pale skin of fog has peeled off and left the sky a smooth, enameled blue reflected in a variety of deeper tones by pole-climbing morning glories, bachelor's buttons, hydrangeas, campanulas, scabiosa, ceanothus, evolvulus, agapanthus. The classic cool of peaceful blue flowers in languid summer days, beside the sea, and beneath the sky's blue dome, is a tremendous delight.

If the air is fresher here than in inland gardens, flowers also seem to glow brighter, their tints and shades more distinct. Myth, magic, God, nature, the wellspring of a hymn to all things bright and beautiful—for me, all can be found in my garden that appeals to all my senses.

My grandmother learned much about gardening from her friend and icon, Gertrude Jekyll, one of Britain's most inspired gardeners, whose common-sense opinions Granny often quoted to me in conversations and letters. Born in 1843, a score of years before my grandmother, Gertrude Jekyll wrote 13 books and designed more than 300 gardens before she died at the age of 98. Her specialty was the English herbaceous or perennial border. She designed gardens as an artist, and was more interested in the over-all effect of color and texture than in individual plants. She usually selected popular, reliable plants and emphasized vistas in a garden. Although she integrated many different gardening styles, she almost always included places to sit, relax, take tea, or enjoy a cool drink where one would be charmed by both ambience and view.

Gardening at its best, she wrote, "is the ability to endow a place with all the beauty, delight and peace that comforts the travail of the human heart. To make such an enchanted place is a laborious process, but it is also a propitiation."

Or, as Milton Berle quipped, "A thing of beauty is a job forever."

Sources and Advice

Where to buy plants, seeds, garden furniture, pots and urns, both resin and clay, etc.

Chapter One
Heralds of Spring: Tulips and Daffodils

American Daffodil Society
www.daffodilsusa.org

Brent and Becky's Bulbs
7900 Daffodil Lane, Dept. FG03
Gloucester, Virginia 23061
Tel: 877-661-2852
www.brentandbeckysbulbs.com

Brent and Becky Heath are the authors of *Tulips for North American Gardens*, (Albany, Texas: Bright Sky Press, 2002), with a photographic reference of recommended varieties, information about tulip cultivation, festivals, and flower arranging.

Daffodils and More
P.O. Box 495
Dalton, Massachusetts 01227
Tel: 413-433-1581
www.daffodilsandmore.com

Dutch Gardens
U.S. Reservation Center
144 Intervale Road
Burlington, Vermont 05401
Tel: 800-944-2250
www.dutchgardens.com

John Scheepers, Inc.
23 Tulip Drive, Box 638
Bantam, Connecticut 06750
Tel: 860-567-0838
www.johnscheepers.com

Their specialty is tulips. There is even a yellow tulip named 'Mrs. John T. Scheepers.' The best yellow tulip ever produced, according to White Flower Farm's Amos Pettingill, whose word I trust.

Mitsch Novelty Daffodils
P.O. Box 218
Hubbard, Oregon 97032
Tel: 503-651-2742
Fax: 503-651-2792
www.web-ster.com/havensr/mitsch

Catalog $3 deductible on first order

Elise, the daughter of Grant Mitsch, and her husband, Richard Haven, are immensely helpful. They supply daffodil for horticulturists I know who enter flowers in flower shows.

The New York Botanical Garden
200th Street & Kazimiroff Boulevard
Bronx, New York 10458-5126
Tel: 718-817-8724
www.nybg.org

Old House Gardens
536 West Third Street
Ann Arbor, Michigan 48103
Tel: 734-995-1486
Fax: 734-995-1687
www.oldhousegardens.com
Catalogs $2

Owner-director Scott Kunst, landscape historian, offers bulbs whose provenance dates back to the seventeenth century. Besides his excellent catalog, Scott offers slides, digital images and expertise that is outstanding. He identified my *Angelica Gigas* before anyone else or any other horticultural organization did. He squared me away on the difference between *Lycoris squamigera* and *Amaryllis belladonna*. He has Mrs. R.O. Backhouse daffodils in stock, along with 'Willem van Oranje' tulips with coppery peach-colored flowers. He claims he is not an expert on bulbs for seaside gardening, but every bulb he has ever sent me is a star-quality performer.

White Flower Farm
P.O. Box 50
Litchfield, Connecticut 06759-0050
Tel: 860-567-8789 and 800-503-9624
Fax: 860-496-1418
E-mail: hort@whiteflowerfarm.com
www.whiteflowerfarm.com

For daffodils, their 100-bulb *The Works*, north or south versions, are the most reliable, dependable, wonderful mixture of spring daffodils I can imagine for gardeners at every level of expertise. Their tulips last longer than most. And, of course, their catalog, which induces a dreamlike trance of paradises to be created, are filled with offerings of other wonderful plants and flowers, potted plants, wreaths, gates and arbors, birdbaths, lanterns, bulb trowels, and other tools.

Information about tulips, daffodils, and other bulbs:

Netherlands Flower Bulb Information Center
246 Henry Street
Brooklyn, New York 11231
Tel: 718-693-7789

The International Bulb Society
P.O. Box 4928
Culver City, California 90230
Annual dues: $30

Chapter Two
Irises: Those Reliable Bearded, Dutch, Siberian, and Japanese Beauties

American Horticultural Society
7931 East Boulevard Drive
Alexandria, Virginia 22308-1300
Tel: 703-768-5700 or 800-777-7931
Fax: 703-768-8700
www.ahs.org

This is the contact to join the American Iris Society. I have friends who have joined the Society for Siberian Irises, a section of the American Iris Society. Membership is open to all members of the American Iris Society (AIS) in the United States and Canada, as well as to iris enthusiasts overseas. Single annual membership is $5. The Society publishes a semiannual journal, *The Siberian Iris*, as well as *The Check List of Siberian Irises*. An annual meeting is held in conjunction with the AIS national convention.

For more information:

Linda Doffek
5547 Jacqueline Drive
West Bend, Wisconsin 53095
E-mail: LDoffekSSI@aol.com
www.irises.org

Comanche Acres Iris Garden
12421 Southeast State Route #116
Gower, Missouri 64454
Tel: 816-424-6436
E-mail: commanche@ccp.com

Free 15-page sampler catalog, free catalog with first order, or $5.00 to buy. They only carry tall bearded and spuria (rhizome) irises. They introduced a tall bearded iris in a true, clear pink, cold hardy in Zones 4 to 11; heat tolerant in AHS Zones 8 to 1.

Ensata Gardens
9823 East Michigan Avenue
Galesburg, Michigan 49053
Tel: 269-665-7500
Fax: 269-665-7500
www.ensata.com
Free catalog

They carry the largest collection, as far as I know, of Japanese irises. Spectacular. For a fee of $75, you can arrange with them to become a life member of the Japanese Iris Society.

Schreiner's Iris Gardens
3625 Quinaby Road, Northeast
Salem, Oregon 97303
E-mail: iris@schreinersgardens.com
www.schreinersgardens.com

They carry tall bearded, dwarf, intermediate, Siberian, Louisiana irises. They introduced 'Abiqua Falls,' a tall bearded blue iris with twirled, ruffled petals "that give a sense of water in motion"; a vigorous grower, cold hardy Zones 3 to 8; heat tolerant in AHS Zones 9 to 1.

White Flower Farm
P.O. Box 50
Litchfield, Connecticut 06759-0050
Tel: 860-567-8789 and 800-503-9624
Fax: 860-496-1418
E-mail: hort@whiteflowerfarm.com
www.whiteflowerfarm.com

They carry Siberian, bearded, Dutch, and dwarf irises, also reblooming or remontant irises. A good selection, among many other choices of perennials, bulbs, gardening tools, shrubs and vines, trellises, watering supplies, garden tools, and accessories.

If you have a question about your irises, call their staff horticulturalist at 860-482-8915 from 9 a.m. to 4 p.m. (Eastern time), Monday–Friday.

Chapter Three
Hydrangeas

American Hydrangea Society
P.O. Box 11645
Atlanta, Georgia 30355
www.americanhydrangeasociety.org

Chapter Four
Geraniums and Pelargoniums

Ballek's Garden Center
90 Maple Avenue
East Haddam, Connecticut 06423
Tel: 860-873-8878
Contact: Nancy MacKinnon

Goodwin Creek Gardens
P.O. Box 83
Williams, Oregon 97544
Tel: 541-846-7357
Toll-free: 541-846-7359
E-mail: info@goodwincreekgardens.com
www.goodwincreekgardens.com

Logee's Greenhouse, Ltd.
141 North Street
Danielson, Connecticut 06239-1939
Tel: 888-330-8038 or 860-774-8038 (toll free)
Fax: 888-774-9932
E-mail: logee-info@logees.com
www.logees.com

Select Seeds
180 Stickney Hill Road
Union, Connecticut 06076
Tel: 800-684-0395 (toll free) and 860-684-9310
www.selectseeds.com

They offer plants as well as seeds. They also carry an excellent booklet, *Scented Geraniums: Knowing, Growing and Enjoying Scented Pelargoniums* by Jim Becker and Faye Brawner, a perfect companion for anyone who loves pelargoniums for flower arrangements, potpourri, and kitchen use.

Well-Sweep Herb Farm
205 Mt. Bethel Road
Port Murray, New Jersey 07865
Tel: 908-852-5390
Fax: 908-852-1649
www.wellsweep.com

Cyrus Hyde, founder of the nursery, tells me that over 100 varieties of scented pelargoniums are listed in his catalogue.

White Flower Farm
P.O. Box 50
Litchfield, Connecticut 06759-0050
Tel: 860-567-8789 and 800-503-9624
Fax: 860-496-1418
E-mail: hort@whiteflowerfarm.com
www.whiteflowerfarm.com

Chapter Five
Pinks

American Dianthus Society
P.O. Box 22232
Santa Fe, New Mexico 87502
Tel: 505-438-7038

Dues $15 year U.S., $18 Canada/Mexico; $20 elsewhere. A truly giving, brilliant, caring man, encyclopedically knowledgeable about every aspect of dianthus culture, Rand B. Lee, founder and president of the American Dianthus Society is the son of Manfred B. Lee, who wrote mystery novels under the pseudonym Ellery Queen. Membership in ADS will supply you with equally fascinating dianthus-gardening reading, access to plants and seeds, marvelous back issues, and information to assure you divinely fragrant dianthus displays.

The Thomas Jefferson Center for Historic Plants
Monticello
P.O. Box 316
Charlottesville, Virginia 22902.
Tel: 804-984-9821 (customer service)
Fax: 804-977-6140.

Chapter Six
Marsh Mallows: The Innocent Botanicals

Jackson Perkins
1 Rose Lane
Medford, Oregon 97501-0702
Tel: 800-292-4769
Fax: 800-242-0329
www.jacksonandperkins.com

Chapter Seven
When in Drought: Water Conservation, Flowers and Plants for Xeriscaping

The Brooklyn Botanic Garden
(Send a stamped self-addressed envelope to:)
Editors
Plants and Garden News
Brooklyn Botanic Gardens
1000 Washington Avenue
Brooklyn, New York 11225
www.bbg.org/gar2/topis/sustainable/
droughtresponse/plantlist.html

Drip Irrigation Online
www.dripirrigationonline.com

They will tell you all you want or need to know about drip/microirrigation components. Also check out their catalog.

Dripworks 2002
190 Sanhedrin Circle
Willits, California 95490-8753
Tel: 800-616-8321 (catalog request line)
800-522-3747 (order hotline)
707-759-6323 (technical assistance)
Fax: 707-459-9645
E-mail: dripworks@pacific.net
www.dripwork.com

Jerry Baker on the Garden Line
P.O. Box 1001
Wixom, Michigan 48393
Tel: 800-888-0010
Fax: 248-437-3884
www.jerrybaker.com

Chapter Eight
Garden Pests: Coping with Deer, Rabbits, Raccoons, Rodents, and Other Marauders

Frontgate
Tel: 800-626-6488
800-436-2100 (customer service)
800-537-8484 (product specialists)
www.frontgate.com

Gardens Alive
5100 Schenley Place
Lawrenceburg, Indiana 47025
Tel: 513-354-1482
Fax: 513-354-1483
www.gardensalive.com

Plant Pro-Tec, LLC.
P.O. Box 902
Palo Alto, California 93073
Tel: 800-572-0055
www.plantprotec.com

Walt Nicke's Garden Talk
36 McLeod Lane
P.O. Box 433
Topsfield, Massachusetts 01983
Tel: 508-887-3388
www.gardentalk.com

Weitech Company
Call for list of retailers
Tel: 800-343-2659
www.weitech.com

Chapter Nine
Increasing the Garden's Natural Charm with Bird- and Butterfly-Attracting Plants and Flowers

Audubon Workshop
5200 Schenley Place
Lawrenceburg, Indiana 47024
Tel: 513-354-1485
www.audubonworkshop.com

Cornell Laboratory of Ornithology
159 Sapsucker Woods Road
Ithaca, New York 14850
Tel: 800-843-2473
www.birds.cornell.edu

Offers superb information, as does the next source.

Duncraft
P.O. Box 9020
Peacock, New Hampshire 03303-9020
Tel: 800-593-5656
www.duncraft.com

Please just send for this catalog. For dedicated bird lovers who appreciate a variety of nesting boxes, bird food, bird feeders, gifts for bird lovers, and such items as an energy-saving solar sipper that keeps birds sipping water thawed even when temperatures sink as low as 20°F, this catalog is for you. I love it for browsing.

A multitude of other recommendations are contained in a comprehensive guide for attracting birds to your garden throughout the year; the National Audubon Society's *The Bird Garden*, by Stephen W. Kress, Dorling Kindersly Publishing, Inc., 95 Madison Avenue, New York, New York 10016

Howard Garrett
The Natural Way
Box 140650
Dallas, Texas 75214
www.dirtdoctor.com.

National Wildlife Federation
Backyard Wildlife Habitat
8925 Leesburg Pike
Vienna, Virginia 22184-0001
Tel: 703-790-4100

Peaceful Valley Farm Supply
P.O. Box 2209
Grass Valley, California 95945
Tel: 888-784-1722
www.groworganic.com

Stromberg's Birds
P. O. Box 4000
Pine River, Minnesota 56474
Tel: 800-720-1134
Fax: 218-587-4230
www.strombergschickens.com

Texas Plant and Soil Lab, Inc.
5115 West Monte Cristo Road
Edinburg, Texas 78541
Tel: 956-383-0739
www.txplant-soillab.com

Xerces Society
4828 S.E. Hawthorne Boulevard
Portland, Oregon 97215
Tel: 503-232-6639
www.xerces.org

Chapter Twelve
Passiflora (Passionflower) and Other Vines

The Cook's Garden
P.O. Box 535
Londonderry, Vermont 05148
Tel: 800-457-9703
Fax: 800-457-9705
www.cooksgarden.com

Chapter Thirteen
Volunteers

Ambergate Gardens
8730 Country Road 43
Chaska, Minnesota 55318
Tel: 312-443-2248.

Contact Michael Heger, the owner, a knowledgeable authority.

Old House Gardens
536 Third Street
Ann Arbor, Michigan 48103
Tel: 734-995-1486
Fax: 734-995-1687

Mr. Kunst has a trustworthy supply of *Lycoris squamigera*.

Chapter Fourteen
Annuals

Gardener's Supply Company
128 Intervale Road
Burlington, Vermont 05401
Tel: 800-427-3363
Fax: 800-551-6712
www.gardeners.com

Check out seed-starting soil-warmers such as waterproof cables for heating soil, heated grow mats with wire racks, and other interesting and convenient helpers.

Select Seeds
180 Stickey Hill Road
Union, Connecticut 06076
Tel: 800-684-0395
www.selectseeds.com

Chapter Fifteen
The Cutting Garden

Hawaiian Tropical Express
310 Copt Road
Kula, Maui, Hawaii 96790
Tel: 888-826-1444

Kihei-Wailea Flowers by Cora
Azeka-Place Shopping Plaza
1280 South Kihei Road, Suite 126
Kihei, Maui, Hawaii 96753
Tel: 808-879-7249 or 800-39-0419
(toll free)
Fax: 808-879-7184

They specialize in flower leis. The colors of Maui's flowers are mostly white, pink, yellow, red, and magenta.

Maui Floral
Tel: 888-826-1444 (toll-free)
Free catalog

They have an enticing variety of orchids, tropical flowers, proteas, and greenery. (Remember that Hawaii time is 6 hours earlier than Eastern seaboard time, 3 hours earlier than California time.)

Sunrise Protea Farm
Tel: 800-222-2797

They specialize in fresh and dried proteas.

Chapter Sixteen
Peaches, Pears, Grapes, and Berries

Edible Landscaping
P.O. Box 77
Afton, Virginia 22920
Tel: 800-524-4156
www.eat-it.com

Miller Nurseries
5060 West Lake Road
Canandaigna, New York 14424-8904
Tel: 800-836-9630
Fax: 585-396-2154
www.millernurseries.com

Stark Brothers Nurseries & Orchards Co.
P.O. Box 1800
Louisiana, Missouri 63353
Tel: 800-325-4180
www.starkbros.com

Chapter Seventeen
Houseplants

Ballek's Garden Center
90 Maple Avenue
East Haddam, Connecticut 06423
Tel: 860-873-8878
Contact: Nancy MacKinnon

Hilo Hattie's
Lahaina Center, Building D
900 Front Street
Lahaina, Maui, Hawaii 96761
Tel: 800-272-5282 or 808-667-7911
www.hilohattie.com

Logee's Greenhouse. Ltd.
141 North Street
Danielson, Connecticut 06239-1939
Tel: 888-330-8038 or 860-774-8038
(toll free)
Fax: 888-774-9932
E-mail: logee-info@logees.com
www.logees.com

Louisiana Nursery
The Durio Family
5853 Highway 182
Opelousas, Louisiana 70570
Tel: 331-948-3696
Fax: 331-942-6404
www.durionursery.com

Michigan Bulb Company
P. O. Box 4180
Lawrenceburg, Indiana 47025-4180
Tel: 513-354-1497
Fax: 513.354.1499
www.michiganbulb.com

Park Seed Company
1 Parkton Avenue
Greenwood, South Carolina 29647
Tel: 800-845-3369
Free catalog

White Flower Farm
P.O. Box 50
Litchfield, Connecticut 06759-0050
Tel: 860-567-8789 and 800-503-9624
Fax: 860-496-1418
E-mail: hort@whiteflowerfarm.com
www.whiteflowerfarm.com

Composting in the Kitchen and Outdoors

Rodale, Inc
773 Third Avenue, 15th floor
New York, New York 10017
Tel: 212-696-2040

They have launched a quality-assurance program for commercially produced compost, and will award an Organic Gardening® Seal of Approval to compost that meets its high standards.

The U.S. Composting Council
200 Parkway Drive South, Suite 310
Hauppage, New York 11788
Tel: 631-864-2567
www.compostingcouncil.org

This is a trade organization of commercial compost producers, has also initiated a labeling program. Called the Seal of Testing Assurance (STA) program, it is an effort by the industry to introduce standardized testing and to get compost producers in compliance with state and federal regulations. Participants in the program will have their compost tested on a periodic basis for pH, maturity, soluble salts, water, organic matter, nutrients, stability, particle size, pathogens, and trace metals. The test results for each product will also provide an ingredient list and instructions for use.

Additional Sources

Plants and Seeds

Digging Dog Nursery
P.O. Box 741
Albion, California 95410
Tel: 707-937-1130
Fax: 707-937-2480
www.diggingdog.com

Fairweather Gardens
P.O. Box 330
Greenwich, Connecticut 08323
Tel: 856-451-6261
Fax: 856-451-0303
www.fairweathergardens.com

Forest Farm
990 Tetherow Road
Williams, Oregon 97544-9599
Tel: 541-846-7269
Fax: 541-846-6963
www.forestfarm.com

Gardener's Eden
P.O. Box 7307
San Francisco, California 94120-7307
Tel: 800 822-9600

Heronswood Nursery, Ltd.
7530 NE 288th Street
Kingston, Washington 98376
Tel: 360-297-4172
Fax: 360-297-8321
www.heronswood.com

Oliver Nurseries
1159 Bronson Road
Fairfield, Connecticut 06430
Tel: 203-259-5609
Landscaping: 203-254-2303

Roslyn Nursery
211 Burrs Lane
Dix Hills, New York 11746
Tel: 631-643-9347
Fax: 631-427-0894
www.roslynnursery.com

Sheffield's Seed Company
269 Auburn Road, Route #34
Locke, New York 13092
Tel: 315-497-1058
Fax: 315-497-1059
www.sheffields.com

Shepherd's Garden Seeds
30 Irene Street
Torrington, Connecticut 06790
Tel: 860-482-3638
www.shepherdseeds.com

Spring Hill Nurseries
110 West Elm Street
Tipp City, Ohio 45371-1699
Tel: 513-341-1509
Fax: 513-354-1504
www.springhillnursery.com

Thompson & Morgan
P.O. Box 1308
Jackson, New Jersey 08524-0308
Tel: 800-274-7333
Fax: 888-466-4769
www.thompson-morgan.com

Wayside Gardens
One Garden Lane
Hodges, South Carolina 29695-0001
Tel: 800-845-1124
www.waysidegardens.com

Tools, Supplies, Furniture, Etc.

Charley's Greenhouse and Garden
17979 State Route 536
Mount Vernon, Washington 98273-3269
Tel: 800-322-4707
Fax: 800-233-3078
www.charleysgreenhouse.com

Garden Tools by Lee Valley
P.O. Box 1780
Ogdensburg, New York 13669-6780
Tel: 800-871-8158
www.leevalley.com

Smith & Hawken
P.O. Box 8690
Pueblo, Colorado 81008-9998
Tel: 800-776-3336
www.smithandhawken.com

Specialties

It's About Thyme (Herbs)
11726 Manchaca Road
Austin, Texas 78748
Tel: 800-598-8037
Fax: 512-280-6356

Lilypons Water Gardens (Water plants)
6800 Lilypons Road
P.O. Box 10
Buckystown, Maryland 21717-0010
Tel: 800-999-Lily
www.lilypons.com

Timber Press (Garden publisher)
133 S.W. Second Ave., Suite 450
Portland, Oregon 97204-3527
Tel: 800-327-5680
www.timberpress.com

Well-Sweep Herb Farm (Herbs)
205 Mt. Bethel Road
Port Murray, New Jersey 07865
Tel: 908-852-5390
Fax: 908-852-1649
www.wellsweep.com

Natural Products

Caswell-Massey, Co., Ltd.
100 Enterprise Place
Dover, Deleware 19904
Tel: 800-326-0500 (toll free)
www.caswellmassey.com

Earthmade Products
P.O. Box 609
Jasper, Indiana 47547-0609
Tel: 800-843-1819
Fax: 800-817-8251
www.earthmade.com

Composting in the Kitchen and Outdoors

A compost heap is a necessity to furnish black gold to enrich the garden.

When plants, insects, and animals die, their waste is returned to the soil, and as billions of microorganisms in the soil, including bacteria, fungi, and protozoa, as well as earthworms, spiders, and other creatures consume this organic matter, they break it down into carbon, nitrogen, phosphorus, and potassium, elements that many of them need to thrive and reproduce.

A compost heap must be at least a cubic yard, 3' by 3' by 3', to achieve the right size or critical mass. You can toss all the organic matter you accumulate into a shallow ravine, or heap it up somewhere out of sight, or buy metal cylinders with turning devices sold for composting at most garden centers, or available through garden catalogs. More satisfactory for us at Brillig is a compost bin, actually, four at the moment.

First you choose a site for a compost bin. The bin should rest on bare soil and have good drainage. The bin should be in a partially shaded area, and it should be

within reach of a water hose and a convenient distance from your kitchen or garden so that you don't have to traipse far to trundle kitchen scraps and plant trimmings. Since sunlight kills the bacteria needed to decompose organic material, it's important to keep sunlight out of the compost pile. You can use thick, black plastic, which absorbs heat and keeps sunlight out, as a bin cover, or use a lid to cover other sorts of bins.

You can make inexpensive compost bins out of cement blocks or bricks arranged in a three-sided square, with the fourth side left open, or construct a square picket fence bin with a gate. A bin should insulate your compost heap and keep it neat, but it must also allow good airflow and circulation. A compost pile needs adequate venting through its sides and bottom to allow air to penetrate the pile. Poor ventilation slows down the heating/cooking/oxidation process that heats the pile to 140°F, killing most weed seeds and disease organisms, caused when the billions of organic microorganisms digest the vegetable matter in the pile and break it down into nutrients your plants can readily absorb. The nutrient-rich material that resists breakdown provides bulk for the resulting humus. A gate or a removable panel easily lets you aerate and mix the pile by turning it with a pitchfork or aerating tool to let in the oxygen necessary for speedier decomposing. By stirring, fluffing, turning or moving the compost heap occasionally, you expose its insides to the air that is like fanning a fire. You are delivering oxygen to the microbial community within that they need to break down the materials quickly. Active decomposers congregate in the warm, moist center of the compost heap that can

reach temperatures of up to 160°F. When you move, fluff, turn, stir the pile, mix in the new material thoroughly, bringing fresh food to the center while redistributing the organisms and digging the new material into the middle of the pile.

Add water to keep the compost moist. Your compost pile should always be slightly damp, not wet, having the moisture level of a wrung-out sponge. People move, stir, turn, fluff their compost once a day, once a week, once a month, or when they think about it. The more you turn, the faster you get compost. You have to be careful not to overdo it and let in too much air. This will cool your compost and slow down the speed of its decay.

Chopping and shredding organic matter helps speed up the decay. The smaller the particles, the faster they will decompose. José often runs a lawn mover over leaves before he adds them, or puts dead, stalky plants into a shredder before piling them on the heap. If you turn your pile weekly, you should have finished compost in five to eight weeks. Friends of mine, a young girl and her grandmother, both disliked turning their compost, and came up with a clever idea of laying wooden stakes across their compost heap as they built it. To aerate and mix the pile, they just grasped the ends of the stakes and lifted a little. "Much easier than using a pitchfork," they said. Our compost piles are maintained in utilitarian slatted packing-case-like wooden containers with one side left permanently open, but I've been inspired by the way some people have turned their compost piles into structures of beauty, with roofed-over trellised arbors flanked by attractive high-gated fences enclosing their compost, and another fenced-in pile beneath an arbor trailed over with morning glories and nasturtiums.

Having constructed an ordinary or beautiful bin, your aim is to work out a specific balanced recipe for your compost pile. Organic matter is comprised of carbon and nitrogen in varying proportions. **Dry brown material, such as autumn leaves, straw, wood chips, small twigs, and cornstalks is high in carbon. Both manure (goat, sheep, cow, pig, poultry, horse) and fresh green material, such as grass clippings, vegetables, and kitchen scraps, weeds (always if possible, minus seeds) are high in nitrogen.**

Both **brown** and **green** material should be combined to create a balance of carbon to nitrogen, such as six parts of leaves to three parts of kitchen scraps (minus meat or cheese) and fresh grass clippings; or ten parts of dried brown debris, with two to four parts of grass clippings. The ideal compost pile has a thirty to one ratio of carbon to nitrogen. The importance of the ratio of carbon to nitrogen is that the organisms feeding on all those organic materials require a certain amount of nitrogen for their metabolism and growth. You know when everything is healthy and working properly when your compost actually steams, a sign that healthy microorganisms are hard at work munching, reproducing, and making more compost.

If a compost heap is too dry, it won't heat up and decompose. If it's too wet, or there's too much nitrogen, not enough oxygen, not enough carbon, or brown material, a compost heap will not have a sweet earthy smell. To remedy this, all you have to do is to add dry carbon material, even shredded black-and-white newspapers will do, and fluff up the pile to bring it back into balance.

If a compost heap is clumpy and gummy, it needs to be turned more often and needs more high-carbon matter like straw or sawdust.

Here's a list of what NOT to put into the compost:

• Grass clippings that have been treated with pesticides or herbicides.

• Plants, fruit, and vegetable peelings, weeds, flowers that have been treated with pesticides or herbicides. Anything that you can't be sure is free of chemical pesticides or herbicide residues.

• Diseased plants, although it's all right to burn them and add their ashes to the pile.

• Poison ivy.

• Colored newsprint from newspapers, magazines, catalogs. Colored paper is likely to contain toxic inks or non-biodegradable coatings; shredded black-and-white paper is all right.

• Kitty litter may contain pathogens harmful to children and pregnant women.

• Dog droppings and human excrement should not be composted either.

• Coal or charcoal ash. Coal contains excessive amounts of sulphur and iron.

• Charcoal can leach barbeque starter-fluid residuals and will resist decay even after thousands of years.

• Meat and dairy kitchen scraps. They rot, smell, and attract raccoons, feral cats, and rats.

• Fatty food wastes can be slow to break down because the fat can exclude the air the composting microbes need to do their work.

• Plastics and synthetics. They don't break down.

• Sawdust and wood scraps from pressure-treated wood, which contain arsenic, chromium, copper, and cyanide.

• Pernicious weeds. Ampelopsis, certain grasses, wild morning glories, kudzu, bindweed, pigweed can resprout from their roots and stems in the compost pile. Just when you hoped you had them all guillotined, you've actually helped them to multiply. Don't compost these weeds unless they are totally dead and dry. You may want to leave them in a sunny place

for a few weeks before composting. Bear in mind that composting weeds that have gone to seed will create weeds in next year's garden unless your compost pile is really hot and steaming.

What to compost:

• Grass/lawn clippings are rich in nitrogen, break down quickly, and provide moisture to your compost pile. Mix them well with dry ingredients to avoid clumping. It's easier to leave grass clippings on the lawn, where they will decompose and benefit the soil directly. However, they can also be composted. Be careful to add grass clippings in thin layers, or mix them in with other compost ingredients, or they can become matted down, cutting off air from the pile. Fresh grass clippings are high in nitrogen, making them a green compost component.

• Seaweed. Seaweed is a marvelous addition, rich in minerals and other valuable nutrients. However, **be sure to wash it thoroughly before you add it to your pile, as it is drenched in salt.**

• Manure from horses, cows, goats, pigs, rabbits, sheep, or chickens has been a staple of compost piles for generations. Be sure to compost it thoroughly in a steaming hot compost pile. Manure can burn plants if applied when fresh, so it's important that manure is composted. Manure contains quite a bit of nitrogen (the fresher the manure, the more nitrogen it contains) and is considered a green component of compost. Fresh manure can get a compost pile to heat up quickly, and will accelerate the decomposition of woody materials, autumn leaves, and other browns.

• Straw is a carbon-rich dry brown like autumn leaves and hay, and helps air circulate by creating passageways for air to get into the compost pile. Be sure to wet the straw before you add it as otherwise it is slow to decompose.

• Leaves. Living green leaves contain abundant nitrogen and are considered green components, but dead, dry leaves, rich in carbon, are in the brown category. Leaves are excellent compost material, except that they can mat down and exclude air. Be sure that any clumps are broken up and that leaves are only used in thin layers. Dead dry leaves help to dry out a too-wet compost heap. Save autumn leaves in plastic bags to use as needed. Shredding leaves reduces their volume and speeds up their decomposition.

• Weeds and other garden debris bring organic matter as well as soil on their roots to your compost pile. Remove any seed heads to avoid having more weeds later. Seeds may survive all but the hottest compost piles. Some pernicious weeds will resprout in the compost pile and should be avoided unless thoroughly dead and dry. (See the list of what not to compost). Green weeds are green material, and dead weeds are brown.

• Human and pet hair, which belongs in the green category.

• Wood ashes, though in moderation, as they are highly alkaline.

• Wood chips and sawdust, but never from chemically treated or pressure-treated wood that contains arsenic, chromium, copper, and cyanide. Wood chips and sawdust belong in the brown category, because they are fairly low in nitrogen. Some sawdust from broad-leaved/deciduous trees will break down quickly in the compost pile. Other sawdust, especially from coniferous trees, takes longer to decay. Stir sawdust thoroughly in the pile or use thin layers. Coarse wood chips will take a long time to decay, and are probably better used as mulch, unless time is no object.

• Shredded newspaper, black and white. Avoid newsprint with colored inks and colored magazine and catalog illustrations.

• Kitchen scraps. Fruit and vegetable peels and rinds and the fruit and vegetables themselves, eggshells mashed up into little pieces, tea leaves or tea bags, coffee grounds, bread crusts are all splendid stuff to add to the compost. They tend to be high in nitrogen, in the green category, and are usually soft and moist. Mix them with drier, bulkier material to allow for complete air penetration. Don't add fatty food wastes, meat scraps and bones, or dairy products as these attract raccoons, feral cats, and rats.

• Lobster shells and broken horseshoe crab shells from the beach. Shells should be broken in small pieces.

• Mussel shells broken up in small pieces.

• Fish skin and fish bones.

• Hay. Alfalfa hay will compost readily. Grass hay may contain a lot of seeds that can resprout in your garden unless your compost pile is steaming hot. Be sure any hay you compost is well moistened prior to adding it as otherwise it will decompose slowly.

The easiest way to begin a compost heap is to layer the carbon-rich browns with the nitrogen-rich greens. You can start with a base of carbon-rich dry leaves, add kitchen scraps, more leaves, and so on. Each layer should be about 5" to 8". Be sure to add thin layers of regular soil that transport necessary microorganisms into your pile. Continue to go along, adding material, remembering to cover new material with a layer of soil and to keep the pile moist.

If your pile isn't heating up, there probably isn't enough moisture for the organisms responsible for decomposition to thrive. Turn the pile, forking it up, and check the moisture level. If your compost pile seems dry, add water until the texture is like a damp sponge.

It's also possible that there isn't enough nitrogen in the compost. In that case, add nitrogen-rich material such as kitchen scraps, manure, grass clippings, or other green items.

If a compost heap should ever develop a less than pleasant smell—none of ours ever have, happily—it just means that bacteria living without oxygen are doing the decomposing rather than pleasant-smelling aerobic bacteria. The remedy is to turn the pile to aerate it and to add nitrogen-rich green items like grass clippings, manure, or green leaves, and then to shovel on a few spadefuls of earth.

Annual top-dressings of compost in the spring and autumn lightly worked into the top few inches of garden beds, conditions the soil, improves the soil's structure, texture, aeration, and introduces beneficial microbes that help break down existing nutrients, making them more available to plants. Compost aids root growth and plant vigor and encourages earthworm populations that further condition the soil. Compost increases the water-holding capacity of soil, improving drainage, thereby promoting soil fertility as well as protecting plants during drought.

Enhancing the soil's ability to hold water and air, both essential for plants, compost releases its nutrients slowly as plants need them. Over time, compost-amended soil darkens, becomes looser-textured, and warms up more quickly in the spring to extend the growing season of many flowers and plants, while arming them with a stamina that helps them ward off diseases.

Compost-amended soil, when tested at a soil-testing laboratory, has higher levels of nutrients than nonamended soil, as you would expect, but compost also helps to neutralize both alkaline and acid soils, making growing conditions more favorable for a wider range of plants.

Good quality compost is also available commercially, a man-made miracle. (See "Sources and Advice: Where to buy plants, seeds, garden furniture, pots and urns, both resin and clay, etc.")

List of Plants for Structuring a Garden

Spring

Perennials: Azaleas, bluebells, cherry, white-blooming crab apple, daffodils (*Narcissi*), grape hyacinth (*Muscari*), magnolia, poppies (*Papavar*), rhododendrons, white and blue scilla, tulips. Dianthus bloom by late spring, as do hyacinths, iris, peonies, and roses.

Summer

Perennials: Aruncus, astilbe, black-eyed Susans, bleeding hearts (*Dicentra*), buddleia, crocosmia, daylilies, hollyhocks, hostas, hydrangeas, Joe-Pye weed, Asiatic lilies, marsh mallows, passion flowers, tradescantia, orange trumpetvine. *Lycoris squamigera* bloom in August, as do Oriental lilies.

Annuals: Such as cosmos, cleome, impatiens, nicotiana, pelargoniums, petunias, and zinnias.

Autumn

Asters and chrysanthemums. Roses of Sharon in the early autumn. Many of the July and August flowers linger, including roses that go on often through November and into December.

Winter

Cotoneaster, holly, and winterberry all have red berries. Pyrecanthus has orange berries. Sumac has burnished brown flamelike seed holders. Boxwoods, evergreens, junipers, pines, spruces, and yews remain green, as does ivy.

It's important to try to combine plants in harmony and some in contrast like the lacy, feather gray-green foliage of bleeding hearts and the darker heart-shaped leaves of violets.

When a sense of theater rather than privacy is a main consideration, it's best to have a wall of windows with a garden view that also fills the room with light. The right windows can also make smaller rooms larger by visually borrowing the expansive space of your outdoor garden, which we do in our downstairs guestroom. You can also frame views in your garden by cutting a round hole in a hedge so that you can see a focal point, like a fountain or a statue, beyond in the next garden "room." You can draw attention to a particular object or area by screening out distractions and focusing concentration by using an arbor, or turning a path in a different direction. I like to have a distant view of the sea through a gap in the trees on the north side of the house, or a cove and a beach on the west side of the house. I like to feel a sense of space fanning out around me, never to feel closed in or closed off.

Just as it's a good idea to have a place where children can work inside on their craft projects, it's a good idea to have an area where children can play outside, as well as an entertainment area on a deck or patio for grown-ups outside. If you live in a cold area, but like tropical plants, you can surround yourself in the summer with plants native to heat-tolerant areas that differ from your own by setting them out on your dining deck or patio, as we have with our hibiscus and agapanthus.

You may want to train tomatoes or melons up bamboo tepees or more elaborate tuteurs in a kitchen garden, or plan a kitchen garden based on the utilitarian esthetic of an early American colonial garden or a World War II victory garden, or base your kitchen garden on the more formal geometric beds of European monastic gardens or elaborate French *potagers*. At Brillig, since we live in an area with easy access to organic vegetable produce, I skipped the idea of a vegetable garden and just concentrated on herbs, lettuce, parsley, and fresh berries.

Bibliographical References

Introduction

1. Deadheading is the removal of spent flowers to check the plant from forming seedpods, letting the plant channel its energy instead into growing more flowers. You purposely don't deadhead if you want to save seed for creating new plants, would like the seed to scatter and naturalize the growth of new plants, or want to provide goodies for the birds to eat.

2. With the cooperation of the U.S. Department of Agriculture and the American Horticultural Society, guidelines for the range of planting zones recommended for all 50 U.S. states for growing particular plants are coded by 15 cold-hardiness zones, identifying the winter range from the coldest to the least-cold zone in which the plant can thrive. The A.H.S. and U.S.D.A. have also recently developed United States' mapping for 12 heat-tolerance zones identifying the range of summer tolerance of plants, from the most "heat" days when temperatures rise above 86°F to the zone with the least-heat days. As of this writing, the listing of heat-tolerance figures is a work in progress and not yet in common usage.

Chapter One

1. Ted Hughes, "Daffodils," in Ted Hughes, *Flowers and Insects, Some Birds and a Pair of Spiders* (New York: Alfred A. Knopf, 1986).

2. William Shakespeare, *The Winter's Tale*, Act IV, Scene III, Line 118.

3. S.A. Etnier and Steven Vogel, "Reorientation of Daffodil (Narcissus: Amaryllidacaeae). Flowers in Wind: Drag Reduction and Torsional Flexiblilty," *American Journal of Botany* (January 2000), as reported in the Brooklyn Botanic Garden's Newsletter 15 (Fall 2000).

4. *Ibid.*, p.29–32

5. Graham Rust, *Some Flowers* (New York: Harry N. Abrams, Inc/London: Pavilion Books, Ltd, 1993), with watercolors.

6. Scott D. Appell, *Tulips* (New York: Metrobooks, 2002), with an introduction by Scott D. Appell, director of Education for the Horticultural Society of New York.

7. *Ibid.*

8. Mike Dash, *Tulipomania*, 2nd ed. (New York, Crown Publishers, 2000).

Chapter Two

1. Gerard Manley Hopkins, *Selected Poetry* (Oxford University Press, 1998).

2. There are many flowers and plants associated in legend, song, and folklore with the Virgin Mary.
   The Virgin's sewing needle—*Artemisia pontica*
   The Virgin's bower—*Clematis vitalba*
   The Virgin's shoes—Columbine
   (*Aquilegia vulgaris*)
   The Virgin's mantle—*Alchemilla pratensis*
   The Virgin's earrings—*Impatiens capensis* and Fuchsia
   The Virgin's adornments—Marigold
   (*Calendula officinalis*)
   The Virgin's candles—Mullein (*verbascum thapsus*)

Chapter Three

1. Alan Bewell, *Jacobin Plants: Botany as Social Theory in the 1790's* (New York: New York University Press, 1989).

2. Patricia Tara, *Sex, Botany and Empire: The Story of Carl Linneaus and Joseph Banks* (Cambridge: Icon Books, 2003).

3. Page Dickey, *Inside Out: Relating House to Garden* (New York: Stewart, Tabori, and Chang, 2000).

4. Diana Wells, *100 Flowers and How They Got Their Names* (Chapel Hill: Algonquin Books, 2000).

Chapter Six

1. Steve Brill, *Identifying and Harvesting Edible and Medicinal Plants in Wild (and Not so Wild) Places* (New York: Hearst Books, 1994).

Chapter Eight

1. Rhonda Massingham Hart, *Bugs, Slugs and Other Thugs* (Pownal, Vermont: Storey Communications, Inc., 1991).

2. Jeff and Marilyn Cox, *The Perennial Garden, Color Harmonies Through the Seasons* (Emmaus, Pennsylvania: Rodale Press, 1985).

3. Anne Raver, "Nature: A Fence to Deny a Deer its Dinner," *The New York Times* (April 17, 2003).

4. John Waite, *The Maine Organic Farmer & Gardener* (September-November, 1999).

5. Janet Marinelli, ed., *Brooklyn Botanic Garden's Gardener's Desk Reference*, (New York: Henry Holt, 1998).

Chapter Nine

1. Howard Garrett, *Texas Organic Gardening* (Houston, Texas: Gulf Publishing, 1998).

2. Howard Garret, *The Organic Manual* (Irving, Texas: Tapestry Press, 2001).

3. Susan H. Munge, *Common to this Country: Botanical Discoveries of Lewis and Clark*, illustrations by Charlotte Staub Thomas (New York: Artisan, 2003).

4. *Gardener* (Spring 2004).

5. *Horticulture* (Boston, Massachusetts)

Chapter Eleven

1. Beverly Nichols, *A Thatched Roof* (London: Jonathon Cape, 1933).

Chapter Thirteen

1. John Bryan, ed. *The New Royal Horticultural Society Encyclopedia of Garden Plants* (Portland, Oregon: Timer Press, 1995).

2. Francis Cabot, *The Greater Perfection: The Story of the Gardens at les Quatre Vents* (New York: W.W. Norton & Company, 2001).

3. Christopher Brickell, ed. *The American Horticultural Society A-Z Encyclopedia of Garden Plants* (New York: Dorling Kindersley Publishing, Inc., 1997).

4. John Gerard, *Herbal* (London: John Norton, 1597).

5. John Aubrey, *Brief Lives* (Boston: David R. Godine Publisher, 1999)

Chapter Fifteen

1. Charles Masson, *The Flowers of La Grenouille* (New York: Clarkson Potter Publishers, 1994).

Chapter Sixteen

1. Janet Martinelli, ed. *Brooklyn Botanic Garden's Gardener's Desk Reference* (New York: Henry Holt, 1998).

2. *Oxford English Dictionary* (1933 ed., reprinted 1970).

3. *Brooklyn Botanic Garden's Gardener's Desk Reference.*

Chapter Seventeen

1. Karyn Seigel-Meier, *The Naturally Clean Home: 101 Safe and Easy Herbal Formulas for Nontoxic Cleansers* (Vermont: Storey Books, 1999).

Recommended Reading List

10,000 Garden Questions Answered by 20 Experts (fourth edition), edited by Marjorie J. Dietz, Wings Books, New York, 1982

100 Flowers and How They Got Their Names by Diana Wells, Algonquin Books, Chapel Hill, 1997

100 Birds and How They Got Their Names by Diana Wells, Algonquin Books, Chapel Hill, 2002

The American Horticultural Society A-Z Encyclopedia of Garden Plants, edited by Christopher Bricknell & Judith D. Zuk, DK Publishing, New York, 1997

The Brooklyn Botanic Garden Gardener's Desk Reference, edited by Janet Marinelli, Henry Holt, New York, 1998

The Color Dictionary of Flowers and Plants for Home and Garden, 11th edition, ed. Roy Hay and Partick M. Synge, published in collaboration with the Royal Horticultural Society, Crown Publishers New York, 1992

Gardening by the Sea From Coast to Coast by Daniel J. Foley, Chilton Company, Philadelphia, 1965

Jerry Baker's Giant Book of Garden Solutions by Jerry Baker, American Master Products, Inc., Wixom, MI, 2003

Seaside Gardening by Theodore James, Jr., Harry N. Abrams, Inc., New York, 1994

Art Acknowledgments

Alamy Images: 65, 92, 126, 128, 146

Corbis: Back, 45

Cristina M. Russo: iv, 5, 7, 46, 49, 53, 74, 76, 89, 104, 105, 124, 157, 158, 161, 167, 177, 178, 179, 185, 190, 192, 193, 194, 195, 196, 197, 198, 199, 200, 201, 210, 217

Francine Whitney: vi, 39

Garden Picture Library: 64, 65, 67

Getty Images: 127, 129, 130, 131, 132, 133, 134, 136, 137, 150

JupiterImages: 24, 25, 26, 37, 52, 57, 58, 62, 66, 86, 88, 91, 93, 95, 101, 103, 105, 119, 129, 130, 154, 170, 174

Leila Hadley: Cover, iii, 2, 3, 7, 8, 10, 11, 14, 17, 18, 20, 21, 22, 29, 31, 32, 33, 35, 36, 38, 40, 42, 43, 47, 50, 51, 55, 56, 61, 63, 68, 70, 71, 72, 73, 75, 77, 81, 82, 83, 85, 91, 97, 99, 100, 107, 108, 111, 113, 118, 120, 121, 122, 123, 125, 131, 138, 139, 140, 143, 144, 145, 147, 149, 151, 152, 153, 155, 159, 160, 162, 163, 164, 165, 168, 169, 171, 172, 175, 180, 182, 183, 186, 188, 189, 191

Nedenia Rumbough: 26, 94, 106, 109, 112

Phillip Bauman: 12, 202

U.S. Department of Agriculture, U.S. National Arboretum: 4

Author's Acknowledgments

Appreciation to:

My husband, Henry Luce, for giving me Brillig's land to change to please us both;

Betty Ann Rubinow, editor and publisher of the *Fishers Island Gazette*, who encouraged me to write a column about gardening on Fishers Island in 1995 for the *Gazette*, and who then became a cherished friend;

Jade Zapotocky Barrett, without whom nothing would ever have been done or would ever be done, with love and gratitude always;

Milbry Catherine Polk, friend and mentor, executive director of Wings Worldquest, married to Phillip Bauman, M.D., who is also a photographer, fisherman, and birdwatcher, parents of Elisabeth, Bree, and Mary, my honorary god-daughters, for urging me to write this book and for introducing me to Manuela Dunn;

Book Laboratory and Manuela Dunn, beloved new friend and book creator who found me the best publisher for this book, and the best designer, Victoria Pohlmann;

Victoria Pohlmann, who is a superb book designer as readers can see as they look at the design of this book;

Sangeet Duchane for her copyediting;

Cristina Russo, who graced this book with a choice selection of her elegant photographs;

For Charles Miers, brilliant publisher of Rizzoli and Jane Newman, a marvelous editor;

For Kit and Tina Liu Luce, who found and gave me reference books of great value;

Andrew Harvey and Eryk Hanut, whose love, compassion and extraordinary help at all times have blessed my life immeasurably.

Index